MOUNTAIN
PARTISANS

MOUNTAIN PARTISANS

Guerrilla Warfare in the Southern Appalachians, 1861-1865

SEAN MICHAEL O'BRIEN

Westport, Connecticut
London

Library of Congress Cataloging-in-Publication Data

O'Brien, Sean Michael, 1944–
    Mountain partisans : guerrilla warfare in the southern
  Appalachians, 1861–1865 / Sean Michael O'Brien.
      p. cm.
  Includes bibliographical references and index.
  ISBN 0–275–96430–2 (alk. paper)
    1. United States—History—Civil War, 1861–1865—Underground
movements.   2. Guerrillas—Appalachian Region, Southern—
History—19th century.   3. Mountain whites (Southern States)—
History—19th century.   4. Appalachian Region, Southern—History,
Military—19th century.   I. Title.
E470.6.027   1999
973.7'45—dc21   98–56073

British Library Cataloguing in Publication Data is available.

Library of Congress Catalog Card Number: 98–56073
ISBN: 0–275–96430–2

First published in 1999

Praeger Publishers, 88 Post Road West, Westport, CT 06881
An imprint of Greenwood Publishing Group, Inc.
www.praeger.com

Printed in the United States of America

The paper used in this book complies with the
Permanent Paper Standard issued by the National
Information Standards Organization (Z39.48–1984).

10 9 8 7 6 5 4 3 2 1

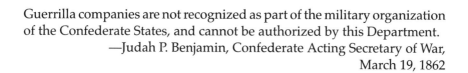
Guerrilla companies are not recognized as part of the military organization of the Confederate States, and cannot be authorized by this Department.
—Judah P. Benjamin, Confederate Acting Secretary of War,
March 19, 1862

Contents

An illustration essay follows page 124.

Prologue

Blood in the Snow

The dim rising sun of January 18, 1863, brought more bitter cold to the western North Carolina mountains. At a makeshift army camp in an isolated valley called Shelton Laurel, Confederate guards awakened thirteen captives suspected of being pro-Union raiders. The officer in charge, Lieutenant Colonel James Keith, told the prisoners that he was taking them to Knoxville, Tennessee, to face trial as guerrillas. Keith assembled them for what they thought would be a long, hard march in the snow, and the men moved out.

A few miles down the road, Keith suddenly halted the column. What happened next was described in contemporary newspaper accounts and by historian Phillip Paludan in his definitive study of the incident. Keith ordered his men to pull five prisoners out of line at random and to form a firing squad. Several soldiers refused to take part. Keith bullied them back into line. "Fire or you will take their place," he told them. The soldiers forced the five prisoners to kneel and face the firing squad. One of them, 60-year-old Joe Woods, cried, "For God's sake, men, you're not going to shoot us? At least give us time to pray!" Keith showed no sympathy. He drew his sword and prepared to give the command to fire.

"You said we'd get a trial!" another prisoner cried.

A volley from the firing squad tore into the kneeling men and thrust four of them backwards, killing them instantly. The fifth man's wound was not mortal, although a bullet had struck him in the stomach. He screamed and pleaded to be spared while he rolled in the bloody snow. A soldier stepped forward and shot him in the head.

The soldiers jerked five more prisoners from the column and pushed or beat them to their knees. Among them was 13-year-old David Shelton, who begged for his life. He pleaded with the soldiers, "You have killed my father and brothers. You have shot my father in the face; do not shoot me in the face." Again the muskets roared. The volley killed the other four prisoners but only wounded young Shelton in both arms. He was still alive, crawling toward them pitifully, wailing, "You have killed my old father and my three brothers; you have shot me in both arms—I forgive you all this—I can get well. Let me go home to my mother and sisters." Two of the soldiers dragged him back to the execution site and finished him off.

The soldiers disposed of the three remaining prisoners quickly, then prepared to bury the victims. The ground was frozen and hard, so they dug a shallow mass trench, tossed in the bodies, and covered them over hastily with dirt and snow. Sheer frenzy seized one man, who started dancing on the grave, clapping his hands to a minstrel tune, vowing to "dance the damned scoundrels down to and through hell." When they had buried the victims, the soldiers moved on and left the valley behind them.

The next morning the victims' families approached the mass grave. They discovered that during the night wild hogs had dug up the grave and eaten away part of one man's head (Paludan, 97–99).

In the mountains, people were waging a different sort of war from the one fought near Atlanta, Richmond, or Charleston. In the mountain war, one's loyalties often brought more personal, and sometimes tragic, consequences. The war in the mountains was not a war of armies marching with drums pounding and banners flying. It was a dirty, secret little war, where small groups of nameless bushwhackers struck at each other without warning, savagely. Where death often came suddenly from the silence of the wooded mountain slopes. Where the hangman's rope and the raider's torch were liberally applied. Where the real heroes were women and small children left at home, vulnerable to attack by marauders who struck without conscience or ethic. In the mountains, names like Kirk and Gatewood and Ferguson would be feared far more than names like Sherman and Hood and Forrest.

The Shelton Laurel incident received little attention at the time. It was only one event in a largely forgotten phase of the broader American Civil War, but to the people of the Southern Appalachians this was the reality of daily struggle and survival. The events of the war in the mountains would affect the lives of families there for decades.

Acknowledgments

Special thanks to Robert Scott Davis, Jr., for his assistance and encouragement on this project. Thanks also to Bill Kinsland and Jimmy Anderson of Dahlonega, Georgia; Ranee Pruitt, Huntsville–Madison County Public Library; and Marylin Bell Hughes, Tennessee State Library and Archives.

Civil War–era sources are used extensively. However, since many of these sources are relatively inaccessible in their original editions, I have cited secondary sources that quote from the originals wherever possible for the convenience of the readers.

Introduction

War in the Mountains

The wild and beautiful Southern Appalachians of western North Carolina, eastern Tennessee, northern Georgia, northern Alabama, and western Virginia formed part of America's first frontier. The Cherokees called this land home before white settlers displaced them. The whites—yeoman farmers with roots in Ireland, Scotland, England, or Germany—migrated from Pennsylvania, Virginia, or the Carolinas in search of a more abundant life and found it in the mountains.

Southern mountaineers were much the same as their brethren in the Piedmont and Black Belt regions of the South, but three characteristics set them apart: their isolation, their traditionalism, and their independence.

The mountain folk inhabited an area that was remote from the rest of the nation, with few roads or railroads to connect them with the outside world. Although small towns in the mountains enjoyed some commercial contact with the outside, the more rural mountaineers were much more isolated. They delighted in a closeness to the land, felt their destiny intertwined with it like blocks in a patchwork quilt. Family was the center of the mountaineer's life, and a sense of clan and tradition flourished. More than other Americans, mountaineers clung to the traditional roles of men as hunters and providers, and women as servers and homemakers. Mountain people learned self-reliance and independence and took care of their own without help from the outside world. Their own code of conduct regulated their lives. With little faith in local courts, they avenged wrongs through private retaliation.

Because of their poverty and rural isolation, the mountaineers were neglected, ridiculed, and stereotyped by the rest of American society. General Edmund Kirby Smith, while commander of the Confederate Department of East Tennessee, called them "an ignorant, primitive people" (Paludan, 29). They were a people who valued their independent lifestyle and their family ties, loved the remote beauty of their mountains, and cared for nothing better than to be left alone by the outside world. But the outside world was about to intrude on their peaceful land.

The political crisis that brought on the Civil War erupted with the wave of secession conventions that swept the Deep South in January 1861. Fundamental political differences separated the mountain regions of the South from the slaveholding Black Belt lands. Delegates from the mountain counties in Georgia, Alabama, Tennessee, North Carolina, and Virginia opposed secession from the Union.

In nearly all the northern counties of Georgia at least 50 percent of the delegates voted against secession, and in several—Walker, Gilmer, Pickens, Lumpkin, Union, and Towns—they enjoyed a huge majority (Sarris, "Anatomy," 686). The situation was similar in northern Alabama, where nine counties—Winston, Walker, Madison, DeKalb, Marshall, Limestone, Fayette, Marion, and Lauderdale—opposed secession by 70 percent or more (Dodd, *Historical Atlas*, 49). In western North Carolina eight counties—Cherokee, Macon, Madison, Watauga, Caldwell, Ashe, Alleghany, and Wilkes—opposed secession by 60 percent or more (Inscoe, *Mountain Masters*, 242). Eastern Tennessee, whose residents voted more than two to one against secession, was regarded as a hotbed of unionism throughout the war.

In February 1861, North Georgia resident James W. Aiken wrote a vehement letter to Governor Joseph E. Brown explaining the feelings of Unionists:

> We, the people of Walker County . . . do not intend to submit to . . . secession . . . which has been taken out of the hands of the people and has fallen into the hands of demagogues and office-seekers. . . . If southern Georgia want[s] to leave the Union, let her go. But, we, the people of Cherokee, want to stay in the Union. So I hope you will let us go in peace. . . . If not, we will try what virtue there is in flint and steel. (Lane, 20–21)

No single factor explains why Unionist sentiment was so strong in the mountains. Most white mountaineers owned no slaves and played no part in the South's plantation economy. Not all who owned slaves were Confederates, either. In Georgia's Fannin County, attorney William Clayton Fain, a slaveowner, was a staunch opponent of secession (Sarris, "Anatomy," 689).

And in West Virginia's Tug River Valley, Harmon McCoy, a slaveowner, was an outspoken Unionist despite his own family's Rebel ties (Waller, *Feud*, 30).

Mountain unionism was more a negative reaction to the Southern slave-holders than to slavery itself. Most white mountaineers disliked blacks and were not abolitionists, but they resented white slaveholders, who tended to be wealthier than themselves, distrusting the interests of what Knoxville publisher William G. Brownlow called "a hateful aristocracy . . . based on the ownership of a few ashy negroes" (Trotter, 76). A strong pro-Union heritage also existed among many mountain families whose ancestors had migrated from Northern states after the Revolutionary War.

There was still much support for secession in the mountains. Early in the war, the region furnished thousands of young volunteers ready to fight for the Confederacy, especially with Federal invasion a certainty. In some mountain counties like Logan County, West Virginia, and Pike County, Kentucky, secessionists formed a majority, and people generally supported the Confederacy as the best hope for preserving their region's autonomy (Waller, *Feud*, 30). The racial attitudes of white Appalachia were no different from those in the rest of the South. Many white yeoman farmers in the mountains—like their counterparts in the Black Belt and Piedmont—supported slavery out of fear of economic competition from free blacks and out of racial solidarity with the slaveowners (Ash, 39–62). White Unionists in the mountains shared these concerns. Although opposed to slavery as an economic system, they were in no way committed to racial equality.

Political choices in the mountains often reflected differences between families and neighbors rather than differing ideologies. The most trivial quarrel might cause one to embrace the opposing philosophy of an enemy and then become enmeshed in the violence of guerrilla warfare. Mountain feuds, like the famous Hatfield-McCoy conflict, did not necessarily have their origins in the Civil War, but the brutal guerrilla war in the mountains may have created a fertile climate in which such feuds could germinate. In his study of the war in the North Carolina mountains, Phillip Paludan concludes, "Although the feuding associated with the mountains was apparently a post–Civil War phenomenon, by the beginning of the conflict there seem to have been conditions out of which such antagonism might grow" (62).

Confederate nationalism, essential to the successful creation of a Southern nation, ran counter to the independence of the mountains, where people preferred to be left alone. The more the Confederate government intruded on their lives, the more the mountaineers resented it. Their opposition was more a negative reaction against the Confederacy than positive support for the Union.

Opposition to the Confederacy in the mountains became much more serious as the personal and economic impact of the war began to be felt. In April 1862 the Confederate Congress passed the first military conscription act, making men between the ages of 18 and 35 subject to the draft. A second conscription act in September 1862 raised the age limit to 45. By February 1864 the Confederacy was drafting men as young as 17 and as old as 50.

Conscription caused widespread hostile reaction in the mountain counties and produced a rash of draft evasions and desertions. Some men went to desperate lengths to avoid military service. A man in Murray County, Georgia, intentionally laid his right hand on the stump of a tree and cut off two fingers with an ax (Bryan, 142). Many secessionists opposed conscription as well. Georgia's Governor Joseph E. Brown, a champion of states' rights, condemned it as a usurpation of power by the Confederate central government (Sarris, "Anatomy," 690).

The mountaineers' poverty caused them to suffer most from conscription, and they soon regarded the war as a struggle fought by the poor for the enrichment of the wealthy. They were not able to take advantage of the provision in the law allowing the hiring of substitutes, and the loss of a farm family's males to the Rebel army placed an oppressive burden on the women and children left at home (Bryan, 143).

The law allowed exemptions for civil officials like tax collectors, county clerks and judges, mayors, sheriffs and their deputies, and officers in the state militia. These loopholes were of no comfort to the mountain folk. The hill farmers especially resented the so-called "twenty nigger law," part of the second conscription act, which exempted owners or overseers of plantations having twenty slaves or more. No provision was made for exempting heads of households with dependents. Although the conscription act of February 1864 attempted to provide greater social equity by ending the hiring of substitutes and plugging up many of the exemption loopholes, the hardships already caused to the poor farmers of the hills had generated too much ill will (Roland, 79, 87, 150).

The law also compelled Southern farmers to give a tenth of their farm produce as a tax-in-kind, a practice that caused bitter resentment in the mountains. Starving farm families hid food and livestock from prying eyes of Confederate officials (Davis, "Forgotten," 270). In 1863, Georgia's Brigadier General Robert Toombs prophetically warned, "The impressing agent has gone around, and, in many cases, robbed the families of their meagre support . . . the soldiers . . . have become discontented and desertions have taken place" (Bryan, 142).

The chief cause of desertion by Confederate troops was concern by the soldiers for the poverty of their families. In Alabama, 37 percent of families were receiving state aid by 1864, and most of these indigent families inhabited the mountains of north Alabama, the section with the highest rate of desertion (Martin, 127–129). Desertion became a serious problem for the Confederacy. Nearly 7,000 Georgia soldiers deserted; over half of northeastern Georgia's recruits had left their commands by 1862 (Sarris, "Anatomy," 690–691). By July 1863 there were 8,000–10,000 deserters hiding out in the north Alabama mountains (Fleming, 118). North Carolina led in number of desertions with an estimated 24,000, followed by Tennessee with 12,000, and mountain opposition to the Confederacy became epidemic in these regions by 1863 (Paludan, 70).

Deserters robbed the Confederacy of badly needed manpower on the battlefield. Additional time and personnel were required in trying to apprehend them. They also created a threat to civilians in the mountains. While some men left the army merely to return to their farms and provide for their families, others became "outliers" who either were unwilling to return home or were unwelcome in their communities. Soon there were bands of desperate men hiding out in the mountains trying to evade the law. They lived off the land and preyed on unprotected farm families.

By late 1862, deserters and their Unionist allies had formed at least one outlaw band in the mountains of northeastern Georgia, and soon there were thousands of deserters and draft evaders "laying out," intimidating civilians, and resisting state troops with force (Bryan, 144; Sarris, "Anatomy," 690). In Alabama, deserters gravitated to the mountain section of the state—"sparsely populated and difficult of communication," according to Governor John Gill Shorter—where there was strong Unionist sympathy and where, after April 1862, Federal military forces controlled the area north of the Tennessee River (McMillan, *Disintegration*, 128; Martin, 43). By early 1863, bands of deserters roamed the mountains of western North Carolina and virtually ran Cherokee and Henderson Counties (Paludan, 71). In the South Carolina mountains, deserters erected a log blockhouse twenty-five miles northeast of Greenville, prompting the local conscription officer to request a six-pounder to blast it apart (Otten, 102). Many deserters cooperated with Federal troops and even enlisted in the Union Army.

With husbands and sons away in the army, women left to manage the isolated mountain farms were easy prey for marauders, who would descend on the homesteads by day or night demanding food and stealing whatever they wanted. For the most part, it didn't seem to matter whether the victims were secessionists or Unionists.

Guerrilla bands were often well organized and well armed. Their effectiveness depended largely on the prowess and ruthlessness of the men who led them. Spies and lookouts posted on roads leading to their camps employed ingenious warning signals such as horns, bells, songs, and even hog calls to alert the guerrillas of an approaching enemy (Lonn, 73).

They devised clever methods of staying hidden. In Washington County, Tennessee, Confederate soldiers stumbled across a secret room—about four feet wide and long enough for a man to lie down in—built by deserters under the floor of an old stable and covered with a wooden plank topped by a pile of flax. Four dirty men were inside playing cards at an old box by the light of a dim candle. The sides of the shelter were lined with supplies of flour, bacon, butter, honey, tobacco, clothing, items stolen from families in the communities nearby. Chicken bones littered the room. An old tin coffee pot was smoking. The men admitted to having used the hole for about three months. Not far away in the woods, the soldiers found a basket hanging by a rope from a tree and filled with bread and cooked chicken. They surprised a young man sleeping behind a log and promised not to shoot him if he would lead them to the hiding places of other members of the gang. The frightened outlier complied, and the soldiers captured his brother and two other men (Moon, 57).

The rugged mountains played host to several types of military and paramilitary groups engaging in guerrilla activities, and their movements sometimes overlapped. Regular Union and Confederate army detachments prowled the mountains, although the bulk of the two armies was engaged in other areas of the South. Then there were the irregular outfits. On the Confederate side, Home Guards, Partisan Rangers, and independent units operated, sometimes aided by state troops.

Home Guards were local companies formed from men not already serving in the Confederate army or the state militia. By the end of 1863 the drain of manpower to the Rebel army left only old men and young boys to fill the Home Guard companies. Often they were no match for the guerrillas and had to be supplemented by detachments of state militia. Operating within a county—and sometimes in neighboring counties as well—Home Guards were charged both with catching deserters and outlaws and with protecting their communities from Federal invaders. They also were empowered to confiscate animals and supplies for the Confederacy. Many mountain families regarded the Home Guards as horse thieves and outlaws themselves. Unionists accused them of using torture, executions, and terrorism. Home Guards were often as much a source of concern to absent Confederate soldiers as was the Federal army or the guerrilla gangs. It was not unusual for Home Guards to be neighbors and personal enemies of the deserters they were hunting. They used their authority to conduct personal vendettas arising from feuds over land, property, and livestock and robbed and harassed the defenseless women and children left at home.

Deserters often took advantage of the loose discipline of the Home Guards to become members of these units and thus "hide out" with a kind of legal sanction. Sometimes bands of deserters and guerrillas successfully posed as Home Guards, militia, and even regular Confederate troops. In the mountain counties, remote from central state authority, there was little supervision and very little accountability.

The Confederate Congress authorized companies of Partisan Rangers in April 1862, and Colonel John S. Mosby's Rangers in Virginia became the archetype. Just a month earlier, Secretary of War Judah P. Benjamin had flatly rejected the use of guerrilla companies by the Confederacy. The act of April 1862 was an attempt by the Confederacy to control the guerrilla bands that already existed by recognizing them and by making them responsible to a central authority (Grimsley, 112; Howe, 8).

Home Guards and Partisan Rangers were often guilty of victimizing the mountain people. Some of their leaders were decent men trying to do an unpleasant job, but others were simply predators who used their authority to commit crimes and were little better than the outlaws that they sought.

Unionists in the mountains also organized Home Guard companies in their communities. In northern Alabama, the first documented Home Guard unit was formed by Unionists along the border of Walker and Winston Counties. In 1861 they organized for mutual protection from secessionist harassment and then as fighting intensified they became bolder. The secessionists responded with their own Home Guard companies. Many mountain Unionists also enlisted in the Federal army and returned to their old communities to make war on their Rebel neighbors (Thompson, 65).

Independent units, often called "bushwhackers," posed the most dangerous threat to civilians in the mountains, since they answered to no central authority. Although they sometimes cooperated with Rebel or Union military commands and professed an allegiance to one side or the other, bushwhackers made war on soldiers and civilians indiscriminately and by their own rules. They were difficult to apprehend, since they could disband and reform at will. Often they were little more than outlaws, who took advantage of the chaos of wartime to rob, pillage, and murder.

Probing the dynamics of partisan groups in East Tennessee, historian Noel C. Fisher identifies three spheres of operations undertaken by these commands: military, political, and criminal. Military operations targeted enemy soldiers and included raids on rail lines and communications, attacks on isolated patrols, and scouting and reconnaissance duties for regular army forces. Political activities were directed against enemy civilians and were designed to break their will or ability to aid the enemy army. Guerrillas shot suspected enemy sympathizers, terrorized their families, drove off their livestock, and burned their homes. Criminal acts were those that had no military or political objective. Theft, assaults, wanton mayhem, and random killing all took place during the war, often without discernible pattern. These spheres of operations sometimes overlapped, and many guerrilla commands participated in all three (62–63).

Fisher presents a profile of 100 Unionist and secessionist partisans in East Tennessee that reveals some common features of guerrilla bands. Most members of partisan units were family men in their late thirties with two or more children and a farm or small business. Unionist partisans tended to be slightly younger, and they almost always owned substantially less property than their Rebel antagonists. Guerrilla companies tended to be formed of men from the same local community. The leaders were well-to-do farmers, attorneys, or county officials. Some partisan chiefs, like Tennessee guerrilla Champ Ferguson, rose from more humble origins (64).

While fighting their own political revolution against the Union, Southern leaders faced a social revolution in the mountains where guerrilla warfare took on some of the ugliest aspects of class conflict. Though not always the case, members of Confederate guerrilla organizations tended to be slaveowners or wealthier property owners. Unionist guerrillas were most always nonslaveowners and poorer yeoman farmers (Fisher, 64; Paludan, 26–27; McKenzie, 202). Kenneth Noe, in his analysis of the war in southwestern Virginia, contends that class divisions existed before the war and were growing worse, especially as issues like conscription drove a greater wedge between rich and poor (Southwest, 5–6, 110, 120, 127). Peter Wallenstein, who studied east Tennessee Union recruits, asserts, "the lower their economic standing, the more likely men were to fight for the union" (16–18).

An added dimension to partisan class struggle was a noticeable division between towns and more rural communities. Poorer mountaineers in the more isolated areas harbored an acute distaste for what Tennessee Union spokesman Andrew Johnson called a "bobtailed aristocracy who infest all our little towns and villages" (Fisher, 31). Confederate leaders constituted a mountain elite, generally drawn from a planter-lawyer-merchant class with homes in the small towns, while Unionists more often were poorer independent farmers living in the more isolated rural areas (Groce, 48; Sarris, "Execution," 132, 143–144; McKinney, "Economy," 176–177). The mountain elite of the towns favored commercial expansion and greater contact with the outside world, while Union folk of the counties generally did not (Eller, 11–12, 58). While some independent bushwhackers raided from rural hideouts, Confederate partisans tended to be based in towns. Unionist partisans generally operated from rural enclaves in the counties and sought out wealthier Rebel targets in the towns or outlying plantations.

Other factors also determined partisan loyalties, including family, geographic origin, and heritage. Ralph Mann found that in the Sandy Basin area of southeastern Virginia, where a significant elite did not exist, partisans chose sides on the basis of family migration patterns (374–375, 387–389). John W. Shaffer concluded that in Barbour County, West Virginia, secessionists tended to come from families with Virginia roots, while Unionists had Northern heritages (114–115, 125). In his study of North Carolina mountain Unionists, Martin Crawford acknowledges, "The typical Unionist came from a poor, nonslaveholding tenant or small landowning household, located away from the county's main commercial and political centers" but suggests we should also weigh kinship, ideology, and changes in economic circumstances as important factors in determining loyalties (63–66).

The presence of large numbers of Union troops in West Virginia in 1861, in North Alabama in 1862, and in East Tennessee in 1863 acted as a catalyst in raising the level of guerrilla activity in these regions. Deserters and independent companies of Unionists took advantage of Federal occupation to raid and plunder (Fleming, 119). Federal troops treated the scattered groups of regular Confederate soldiers operating against them as guerrillas, and Confederate forces responded in kind (A. Moore, 430). Areas under Federal military occupation also became bases for Unionist raids against Confederate enclaves in nearby areas of North Georgia and Western North Carolina; and Union men in these neighboring states fled to towns like Cleveland, Tennessee, which became sanctuaries for refugees (Sarris, "Anatomy," 681). Many of them enlisted in Federal military units, welcoming the chance to settle scores with the Confederates. Union General William T. Sherman's invasion of Georgia in May 1864 triggered an increase in guerrilla activity in the mountains, and by 1865 there was a complete breakdown in law and order.

Confederate forces contributed to the problem. The Rebel army in East Tennessee from 1861 to 1863 adopted repressive tactics against loyalists. After Federal troops occupied East Tennessee in late 1863, Lieutenant General James Longstreet's soldiers invaded the war-ravaged region in an unsuccessful bid to reconquer it for the Confederacy. Again the Rebels foraged freely on local Unionist households. After General John B. Hood's defeat at Nashville in December 1864, remnants of his shattered army—without discipline or organization—were loosed in North Alabama and North Georgia. The commander of Confederate reserves in Alabama, Jones M. Withers, wrote in February 1865, "Deserters and stragglers by the hundreds are now scattered broadcast throughout this State and such is the state of public sentiment that in half the counties in the State they can remain with impunity" (McMillan, *Disintegration*, 130).

The Union and Confederate governments both were loath to sanction guerrilla warfare. Although military commanders on both sides publicly condemned guerrillas, they sometimes utilized them when it suited their purpose. Regular soldiers in the mountains often used guerrilla tactics and made war on civilians suspected of being enemy sympathizers, descending to the same level as the bushwhackers they hated (Fisher, 95). In his three-stage model in which Federal warfare escalated from "conciliation" or limited war, to "pragmatism" or intermediate war, to "hard war," historian Mark Grimsley argues that Federal troops were relatively restrained in their use of violence (2–4). But in the Unionist stronghold of East Tennessee, Federal soldiers showed little restraint in dealing with local civilians, even the loyalists, because they regarded the whole population as hostile (Fisher, 172–176). In the West Virginia mountains in late 1861, Federal troops already were adopting the tactics of the bushwhackers in a spiraling cycle of violence. It was a short step from hatred of bushwhackers to hatred of the mountain people in general. Historians Michael Fellman, Reid Mitchell, and Charles Royster accept that violence against civilians occurred practically from the start of the war and simply escalated (Noe, "Exterminating," 104–106).

"Hard war," at first a Federal military reaction to clashes with guerrillas in the mountains, rapidly spread to the general population. The "scorched earth" policy used by Sherman's troops in Georgia and by Philip Sheridan's army in the Shenandoah Valley of Virginia came to epitomize "modern" destructive war. Reid Mitchell contends, "making war on guerrillas required making war on civilians. Indeed, after 1863, when the Union realized it had to break the Southern people's will to fight, making war on the Confederacy required making war on civilians" (137).

Partisan warfare in the Civil War presents two extremes. In northern Virginia, Mosby's guerrillas operated relatively near the main armies and focused mainly on military targets. Supporters glamorized their adventures and treated them as patriots. In parts of the Trans-Mississippi West, where absence of regular armies lifted what little restraint existed, the guerrilla bands of both sides were the main contending forces. In Missouri, residents experienced what Michael Fellman calls "the worst guerrilla war in American history" (xv–xvi), and raiders like William Clarke Quantrill became notorious for their lawless actions against civilians.

The Southern Appalachians represent a middle ground. In parts of the mountain South where Union and Confederate forces were actively engaged, guerrilla warfare tended roughly to parallel the campaigns of the rival armies. As the armies contended, guerrilla bands hovered in the wings, and the line between regulars and guerrillas often was obscured. The further one ventured into the mountains themselves, away from battle lines, the more the conflict was defined by guerrilla chieftains who waged war by their own standards. By their tactics they more closely resembled the ruthless guerrillas of the West than the often romanticized Mosby's rangers.

   Guerrilla warfare was not an unprecedented phenomenon in the South. White Americans had practiced brutal warfare against Native Americans from the earliest days of settlement. During the Revolutionary War, Americans preferred to engage the British in European-style battle, but in the right circumstances guerrilla tactics were appropriate. The salient examples of guerrilla warfare that occurred during that conflict took place in the South, especially in South Carolina and Georgia, where vicious backcountry warfare between Patriots and Tories led to acts of unparalleled brutality. What shocked many Americans during the Civil War was that these same destructive tactics were being used once again on fellow white Americans (Mitchell, 138).

   The guerrilla conflict in the Appalachians raises questions for a larger society: Where is the fine line that separates conventional warfare from guerrilla warfare? When are the actions of a guerrilla excusable under the rules of war, and who is responsible when deaths of innocent persons occur during the haste and confusion of combat? The mountain war offers ample illustrations of these timeless dilemmas.

   The savage nature of partisan warfare exacerbated an already difficult situation for the mountain people. With so many armed groups—regular soldiers, Home Guards, deserters, bushwhackers—prowling the mountains, the risk of violence became much greater. By 1864, guerrilla warfare had escalated to an alarming level of brutality.

   Mountain people learned to live with uncertainty and the threat of violence. In Washington County, Tennessee, Adeline Deaderick described a night raid of Unionist guerrillas on her isolated farm. The household woke about one or two o'clock at night to the frightening sound of the front door being smashed open. A band of about forty armed men, yelling and cursing, stormed into the house. First they roused a black servant girl sleeping in the hallway and determined from her the number of men in the home. Then they went from room to room seizing guns and terrorizing the occupants. During the ordeal one of the women was overcome with fear and became hysterical. From the Deaderick house the raiders proceeded to the Westly Harris home less than a mile away. Knowing that the Harrises' young son Fisk was home from the Confederate army, they broke in the front door with a fence rail and began searching the house. Young Harris was dragged to the yard, where he was shot ten times. His four sisters were able to lift his bullet-ridden body into the house. He died before morning. The victims could only look in terror to the lights of the raiders' camp fires off in the distant mountains and dread the next encounter (Moon, 54–56).

   Continual exposure to brutality tended to desensitize the mountain people to killing. Union scout Daniel Ellis told of an occasion in August 1863 in East Tennessee when he went looking for water and found a tranquil mountain spring where he drank and filled his canteen. Suddenly aware of a terrible odor, Ellis discovered three rotting corpses hanging from a tree. Their clothes and flesh had wasted from their bones. The hipbones and legs of one of the skeletons lay on the ground beneath, leading Ellis to conclude that he had been shot through the backbone. Horrified, Ellis moved on, but soon he met a young woman walking down the road. Ellis questioned her about the skeletons, and the woman evidently knew about them. Bitterly and unemotionally she explained to Ellis that they were a "parcel of Lincolnites" killed by local Confederate soldiers and that they deserved hanging (185–186).

Violence begat more violence. A story circulated that early in the war a group of eleven men invaded the home of Tennessee mountaineer Champ Ferguson while he was away and terrorized his wife and 12-year-old daughter. They forced the women to strip naked, made them prepare a meal for them, then forced them to walk naked down the public road. The story did not reveal whether the women were raped, something not discussed openly by mountain folk. When asked about it later, Ferguson himself denied that the story was true. But he was so outraged, the tale goes, that he swore revenge against all Unionists (Sensing, 35–37).

Champ Ferguson became the most notorious guerrilla in Tennessee, killing viciously and without mercy. He murdered and mutilated over 100 Unionists in a four-year reign of terror that climaxed with the fatal shooting of a Union army lieutenant lying wounded in a hospital bed. Ferguson never expressed the slightest emotion or remorse for what he had done, denying to the end that he had done any wrong. He had, he insisted, only killed in self-defense and said that his victims would have killed him first if they had had the chance (Sensing, 32–33).

Like guerrilla wars throughout history, the war in the mountains bred intense cruelty. It was as if the code that defined moral behavior had been suspended and all boundaries lifted. As Fellman writes, "The normal routes by which people solved problems and channeled behavior had been destroyed" (xvi—xviii). Men and women quickly became desensitized to violence and committed acts that would have been inconceivable in peacetime or in conventional war. Unionists and Confederates alike brutalized and killed their neighbors in the name of their own cause. Ideologies no longer really mattered, only survival and revenge (Sarris, "Anatomy," 680).

PART I

Western North Carolina

Chapter 1

"The Best We Could"

The thirteen Unionists killed in Shelton Laurel were either patriots butchered by an unholy enemy or terrorists who deserved killing. "Thirteen men and boys," Unionist scout Daniel Ellis asserted, "recklessly and brutally murdered" by an "inhuman gang of rebel desperadoes" (Ellis, 411). "Thieves and robbers," a Confederate mountain resident retorted, lawless criminals who had murdered and brutalized and had been executed for their crimes (Paludan, 100). As in all civil wars, it depends on one's viewpoint. Such extremes of feeling reflect the bitterness of western North Carolina's schism between Unionists and secessionists, a civil war within a civil war.

In spite of considerable opposition in the western mountain counties, North Carolina seceded from the Union on May 20, 1861, more than a month after Confederate forces fired on Fort Sumter. Even in the mountains there was an initial flurry of patriotic support for the Confederacy, but this soon gave way to apathy as the war entered its second year. When the Confederacy began conscription in April 1862, Unionists in the Carolina mountains began to feel more pressure to take part in a war they did not want. On the distant battlefield, a string of Rebel victories that summer prompted Robert E. Lee's invasion of Union-occupied Maryland. The Rebel offensive failed after the bloody battle of Antietam on September 17, 1862. Five days later President Abraham Lincoln issued his Emancipation Proclamation and signed it into law on January 1, 1863.

The bloody road that led to the Shelton Laurel Massacre started in eastern Tennessee. In an attempt to sabotage the Confederacy's critical railroad line through East Tennessee, Unionist guerrillas burned several key bridges on the railroad in November 1861. Although the raid was only partially successful, it triggered isolated Unionist rebellions in eastern Tennessee that invited Rebel retaliation and had repercussions beyond. Former bridge burner David Fry escaped to the mountains of western North Carolina.

Fry led occasional forays into East Tennessee and preyed on Confederate homesteads. Through the winter of 1862, he and his band terrorized Confederates along the border, robbing them of their horses, weapons, money, and supplies. Since he held the rank of a captain in the Federal 2nd Regiment East Tennessee Volunteers, Fry also was an effective recruitment officer, enlisting volunteers from among Unionist sympathizers in the mountains (Paludan, 67; USWD, I, 7: 513–514).

Fry's favorite hideout was Shelton Laurel, an isolated valley in Madison County, nearly impenetrable from the outside. Only a few rugged paths led into the valley, and the rough terrain was covered with stubborn undergrowth. Unionist sympathies ran high in Shelton Laurel, a community of some twenty poor families. Confederate authorities regarded the valley as a Unionist guerrilla base. In early 1862, Confederate troops entered the mountains in an attempt to capture Fry. Alerted by sympathizers, Fry rode out with nineteen of his men, trying to break through to Kentucky. He had evaded pursuers before, but this time he was captured, shackled, and sent to prison in Atlanta (Trotter, 209–212).

Confederate forces next launched a punitive raid against the Shelton Laurel enclave. On April 7, 1862, troops of the 43rd Tennessee Infantry set out from Greeneville, Tennessee, with orders to "put down any illegal organization of men that might be found" in Shelton Laurel. During the following three days, the soldiers played hide-and-seek with unseen bushwhackers concealed in the dense thickets and rough terrain of Shelton Laurel. The Tennesseans managed to kill fifteen guerrillas and lose three of their own men before returning, exhausted, to Greeneville (Trotter, 212).

A week later, Confederate troops launched a more comprehensive operation against the tough mountain stronghold. Tennessee state militia troops under General Marcus Erwin blocked off all the mountain passes into Shelton Laurel, swept the valley, and arrested over thirty guerrillas. In spite of the best Confederate efforts, Shelton Laurel remained a determined refuge for Unionist partisans, with raids continuing from the valley against Tennessee Confederates (Paludan, 68).

Opposition to the government rose dramatically in Madison County after the Confederacy's first conscription act went into effect in April 1862. With fewer men to raise crops, families suffered from lack of food as winter approached. Throughout the mountains there was a severe shortage of salt, desperately needed as a preservative for what little meat was available. The staunchly Unionist Shelton Laurel families accused local Confederates of withholding salt from them. So, early in January 1863 about fifty men from the valley decided to raid the county seat at Marshall and take what they needed by force.

Marshall was a village of about nine homes nestled into the mountainside by the French Broad River. The Madison County courthouse, an aging brick structure, stood there, and a badly deteriorating wooden jail. The rest of the town consisted of a blacksmith, a shoemaker, three stores, and two hotels. Fifty raiders turned out to pillage Marshall on that bitterly cold January night, fifty miserable men, freezing, starving, and desperate for salt (Paludan, 84).

The raiders broke into the salt warehouse near the home of Captain John Peek, an officer in the 64th North Carolina Infantry Regiment. It happened that Peek was home on leave that night and was awakened by the noise. When Peek dressed and ran outside to check on the disturbance, a raider shot him in the right arm. After looting the warehouse, the raiders invaded the home of Colonel Lawrence Allen, commander of the 64th North Carolina. They found only Allen's wife and children with some servants. They looted the home, terrorized the occupants, and took clothing and valuables. The raiders even stole clothing belonging to Allen's small children, who were sick in bed with scarlet fever, severely traumatizing the children (Trotter, 222).

Confederates reacted to the Marshall raid quickly. North Carolina's Governor Zebulon Vance feared an impending Unionist uprising in the mountains. Although rumors estimated loyalist strength there at 500 armed men, the Marshall raid did not touch off a general rebellion. But Vance cautiously dispatched Brigadier General William G. Davis' militia and Colonel William Thomas' Legion to the mountains to search for marauders. Colonel Lawrence Allen's 64th North Carolina Infantry Regiment was on the way (Trotter, 225).

About 60 percent of the men in the 64th North Carolina came from Madison County. Raised in August 1862, the 64th was filled with conscripts, and desertion was a problem from the beginning. At one time 300 of its soldiers deserted en masse. Many of the Unionist guerrillas who had raided Marshall were deserters from the 64th. On the other hand, many loyal soldiers of the 64th were Marshall residents who disliked the Shelton Laurel folk. Many of the loyal soldiers did not care for their officers who came from the well-to-do class, but they hated deserters even more, perhaps envious of their having evaded armed service (Trotter, 216).

The 64th spent the war on the move chasing deserters and guerrillas in the mountains along the Tennessee–North Carolina border. It was a thankless, frustrating duty. Most of these soldiers wished they were in Virginia fighting pitched battles, instead of skirmishing with bushwhackers.

Soldiers of the 64th became all too familiar with guerrilla warfare. Ten of them, on patrol in Transylvania County, were ambushed on a mountain trail by bushwhackers firing from the top of a granite outcropping. One soldier was killed, and every other man in the patrol was wounded, one of them six times. When the soldiers returned fire, the guerrillas melted away into the forest. The soldiers never learned how many ambushers there were or if any had been hit (Trotter, 218).

Captain B. T. Morris, an officer in the 64th, wrote, "No one except those who have tried it can realize what those who do this kind of service have to endure. . . . Our enemies were at home—knew all the roads, byways and trails, and were much in heart over the success of their arms elsewhere. . . . [W]e slashed them every time we had a chance at them [but] [t]hey never gave us a fair fight, square-up, face-to-face, man-to-man" (Trotter, 217).

So in these dark and troubled mountains that many in the regiment called home, the men of the 64th North Carolina survived from day to day, lived with the fear of sudden death from an invisible enemy, and tried to get through the war. They saw comrades killed or maimed, felt the fear and hatred of embittered women and children, and tried to follow orders for a remote government that many of them did not even believe in.

Historians Phillip Paludan (xv, 92, 95–96) and William R. Trotter (217) compare the experiences of Confederate soldiers fighting guerrillas in the North Carolina mountains with those of U.S. soldiers fighting in Vietnam. Many members of the 64th were draftees, fighting in an environment where it was difficult to tell friend from foe, not really sure why they were there, and exposed to daily brutality with little accountability. The despair they felt mirrored that of Federal troops already engaged in a destructive war with Rebel guerrillas in West Virginia. Kenneth Noe, in his study of the guerrilla war in West Virginia, concludes that fear and anger, clouding the line between combatants and noncombatants, and the feeling that the bushwhackers were escaping punishment drove Federal regulars to discard the rule book and fight like guerrillas ("Exterminating," 109–112). It became easy to justify the most ruthless methods against such an uncivilized enemy. Of the Union soldiers waging guerrilla war in Missouri, Michael Fellman writes, "the frightening 'they' out there had become everyone but themselves. Under intense and continuous pressure, they gradually lost most of their ability to discriminate between guerrilla and civilian targets" (166–169). The 64th North Carolina felt the same way toward the Shelton Laurel folk, and they were ready to use whatever brutal methods it took to survive, not caring what civilians thought.

Colonel Lawrence M. Allen commanded the 64th North Carolina. Bright, ambitious, and anxious to succeed, Allen was a well-to-do land-owner with a home in Marshall and two live-in servants. Active in local Democratic Party politics, he served as clerk of superior court for Madison County and represented the county as a delegate at state party conventions. He and his wife, Mary, had two children, a 6-year-old daughter and a 4-year-old son (Paludan, 33).

No one epitomized the feelings of the 64th's officers like Lieutenant Colonel James Keith, Allen's second in command. The son of a Baptist preacher, Keith had started as a laborer but by hard work had become a doctor and a farmer, one of the wealthiest men in Madison County. Keith's family was prosperous; and his brother John was one of the few slaveowners in the county. Like Colonel Allen, Keith had a home in Marshall and two children, a daughter aged four and a son who was still a toddler (Paludan, 32).

Keith was 35 years old at the time of the Shelton Laurel troubles. His lanky hillbilly frame, pale face, and long coal-black hair and beard belied the fact that he was an educated, ambitious man. Like many Southern property owners, he had much invested in the outcome of this war. After months of the most wrenching antiterrorist warfare, in which his young nephew had been killed by the bushwhackers, Keith was hardened and could be a ruthless adversary. After the Marshall incident he was clearly in a vengeful mood (Trotter, 219).

News of the Marshall raid reached Allen and Keith a day or so after the event and filled them with rage. Allen was incensed by the treatment of his wife and children. The two men went to Knoxville to Brigadier General Henry Heth, the new commander of the Confederate Department of East Tennessee, to request permission to conduct a retaliatory raid on Shelton Laurel. Technically Keith would be in command because Allen was under suspension for an alleged incident of drunkenness.

Unlike Allen and Keith, who were self-made men, Henry Heth came from an aristocratic Virginia family. He was a close friend of Robert E. Lee. But his military career had not been distinguished. He graduated next to last in the class of 1847 at West Point, where he was remembered mainly as a hell-raiser. After fighting guerrillas with the U.S. Army in Mexico, Heth was already used to the kind of partisan warfare now being waged in the Southern Appalachians. As a Confederate officer, Heth had received a disappointing series of assignments before being transferred to General Edmund Kirby Smith's command at Chattanooga. In November 1862 Heth replaced Kirby Smith as commander of the Department of East Tennessee. He found the assignment frustrating and unrewarding. Heth yearned for a transfer and hoped his present duty would be a short one (Paludan, 36–37).

What happened at the meeting between Allen, Keith, and Heth is a matter of controversy. Heth approved a punitive raid on Shelton Laurel. Keith claimed Heth told him, "I want no reports from you about your course at Laurel. I do not want to be troubled with any prisoners, and the last one of them should be killed." Heth would deny issuing any such orders, although Keith later produced witnesses verifying the remarks. He did admit that he had told Keith that if there was any fighting with the men who had taken part in the Marshall raid, he did not need to take prisoners, since these men were guerrillas not entitled to be treated under the rules of war (Trotter, 223).

In any event, Keith felt sure he had a clear understanding of what he was expected to do in Shelton Laurel. As Captain Morris wrote, "When an officer finds himself and men bushwhacked from behind every shrub, tree, or projection on all sides of the road, only severe measures will stop it" (Trotter, 217).

Allen and Keith set out on the road to Madison County on or about January 14 in a snow storm. Each officer led a detachment of the 64th into Shelton Laurel, Allen's column coming through the mouth of the valley and Keith's crossing higher ground over the Bald Mountains to the north. The march to Shelton Laurel was an arduous one. Biting, cold winds howled through the valley blowing heavy snow at the column. Twenty-five of Keith's soldiers developed frostbite from the damp and the cold (Trotter, 226).

The faraway sound of horn calls put the soldiers entering the valley on their guard: guerrilla lookouts hidden on the ridges and in the tree clumps warned their fellow outliers that the enemy was near. As the soldiers came within range, snipers hiding behind trees and rocks opened up on them with their rifles. The soldiers could barely see the guerrillas but nonetheless returned fire. Some of them were wounded, but Allen's troops killed eight of the guerrillas. Near William Shelton's farm they confronted a band of about fifty bushwhackers and killed six of them in an exchange of gunfire. As night fell, Allen's troops pitched camp. Keith and his men were just arriving (Trotter, 226).

That night Allen was awakened by the news that a courier had arrived with word from Marshall. His 4-year-old son had just died of scarlet fever. His 6-year-old daughter was not expected to live. Devastated, Allen sprang into the saddle at dawn and, accompanied by four of his men, headed for Marshall. The party was fired on many times as it left Shelton Laurel. Allen arrived at Marshall and rushed into his house to find his daughter already dying. He was able to hold her for a short time before she died. He buried her the next morning.

On January 16, Allen returned to Shelton Laurel. He was in no mood to show mercy to the Unionists. Although most of his conscripts disliked him, they sympathized with his loss. They already were miserable, wet, cold, and fed up with being shot at (Trotter, 227).

The 64th began a general search of the valley. During the day they captured about a dozen renegades. Three more men came in and gave themselves up in Marshall. The rest of the outliers, particularly those who had taken part in the Marshall raid, were long gone. Some of the prisoners, the lucky ones, were turned over to Keith's adjutant, W. H. Bailey. Bailey sent them across the French Broad River to Warm Springs to the custody of General Davis, but Davis wanted them to be tried by civil authorities and sent them back. Bailey sent four of them to the jail in Asheville and one to the conscript collection center in Greeneville, Tennessee. He placed three more prisoners, who were just boys, on probation if they would work at the county jail in Marshall cutting firewood and fetching water. They were spared the terror to come (Trotter, 227).

Perhaps it was the intense strain of weeks of gut-wrenching warfare against an enemy that would not fight in the open but who struck from cover and then vanished into the hills. Perhaps it was the brutal cold and snow and unending dampness. Perhaps it was hatred for the deserters who had done what most of the reluctant conscripts in the 64th would like to have done. Perhaps these men had become so brutalized and so desensitized to the violence of guerrilla warfare that they no longer recognized the fineries of civilized behavior. In any event, things were about to go terribly wrong in Shelton Laurel.

The search for more guerrillas continued; soldiers interrogated suspects' families to learn their whereabouts. They resorted to torture to get the information they wanted. Allen's interrogators would hang a suspected Unionist by the neck until she nearly lost consciousness; they then lowered her to the ground before she strangled. The process went on repeatedly until the woman answered the soldiers' questions.

The soldiers beat several women, including an 85-year-old grandmother, to make them talk. They tied one woman to a tree in the snow, set her baby in the doorway of her cabin, and told her they would leave both of them that way, with the child crying and the mother unable to reach him, until she told where the men were. Mary Shelton, whose husband was suspected of taking part in the Marshall raid, was whipped and hanged over and over until her face turned blue. Sally Moore, a 70-year-old woman, was flogged so badly that the skin on her back was torn off. Martha White, a young mentally retarded girl married to one of the Sheltons, was whipped and was left tied by her neck to a tree all day (Paludan, 96). Sexual assaults probably occurred during these ordeals as well.

Allen and Keith's men arrested fifteen guerrilla suspects, some at their homes and some in the valley. Most were taken without resistance, but a few tried to run and were subdued. Five of them probably had participated in the Marshall raid; the others are believed not to have taken part, although they may have been guerrillas guilty of other activities. Keith told them they would be taken to Knoxville to stand trial (Paludan, 96–97).

The prisoners were tied up and kept in the valley overnight while the 64th searched for more suspects. Two captives managed to escape in the night. When the search yielded no more prisoners, Allen and Keith prepared to dispose of the remaining thirteen suspects. The two officers had already decided to shoot them. They had even picked out an open spot where the executions would take place and where any mountaineer nearby could see it (Trotter, 229).

Thirteen prisoners left the 64th's camp on the morning of January 18, under armed guard. By the day's end, all thirteen lay dead in a mass grave. The 64th North Carolina moved on to other valleys, other skirmishes (Paludan, 97–98).

How could it happen? It is difficult to determine how much of the soldiers' actions resulted from loss of control and how much was a calculated tactic of terror against guerrillas. Were they just following orders? Some of the soldiers at least had been reluctant to participate in the execution. Some of the soldiers apparently talked later to investigators and harbored deep feelings of guilt. According to Keith, he had been following orders; Heth had authorized him to take no prisoners, had wanted it done "off the record" (Paludan, 99–100). As in Missouri and in East Tennessee, Confederate commanders often issued contradictory orders. On the one hand, they ordered their troops not to make war on civilians; on the other, they told them to take whatever steps they deemed necessary to destroy the guerrilla threat. If some junior officers chose to interpret these orders very broadly—to sanction making war on women and children—they did not question them too closely (Fellman, xviii; Fisher, 78). Union troops in West Virginia were following a "no prisoners" policy as early as October 1861; the practice seems to have been initiated by the enlisted men themselves, with their officers either privately encouraging it or conveniently looking the other way. As one Yankee soldier wrote from West Virginia, "if we ant [sic] out here to kill Bushwhackers what are we for?" (Noe, "Exterminating," 115–117).

With killings this public, news was bound to spread. Governor Zebulon Vance first learned about the massacre in a letter dated January 31, 1863, from his friend, Judge Augustus S. Merrimon. He was stunned to hear of the atrocity, not only because of the overt brutality of the act but because he feared the negative impact it would have in western North Carolina, an already Unionist region that the Confederacy desperately needed to win over. Vance's own birthplace lay just ten miles southeast of Marshall, and he knew how mountaineers would react to the Shelton Laurel killings. He authorized Merrimon to conduct an investigation of the incident.

Merrimon returned preliminary and detailed reports to Vance and listed the names and ages of the victims at Shelton Laurel. Vance was appalled to learn that two of the victims were 13 and 14 years old. He wrote to Confederate Secretary of War James A. Seddon and pressed the army to take action against James Keith. "I desire you to have proceedings instituted at once against this officer," he wrote, "who, if the half be true, is a disgrace to the service and to North Carolina" (Blackmun, 346).

By the end of February 1863, an army investigation of the 64th North Carolina and its conduct at Shelton Laurel had begun. By the middle of April, four junior officers either had resigned or been relieved of command. Although Keith was the officer who had been present and had given the actual orders to execute the prisoners, the army hesitated to press the case against him. Keith would doubtless have tried to implicate Brigadier General Henry Heth, and because of Heth's close friendship with Robert E. Lee, the army feared a scandal. Vance was furious. He promised to pursue Keith "to the gates of Hell" to bring him to justice (Trotter, 231).

Allen was never punished for his part in the massacre. He stayed in the army, but in August 1863 he was court-martialed for extorting over $20,000 from draft evaders. He was found guilty and was suspended for six months without pay. Allen remained with his regiment, though, staging antiguerrilla operations in the mountains until he resigned from the army on June 3, 1864 (Paludan, 106–107).

Brigadier General Henry Heth may bear the ultimate blame for the massacre at Shelton Laurel, but he was never charged with any wrongdoing. Within a month after the killings, he received what he had hoped for—a transfer to the Army of Northern Virginia. He was wounded at Chancellorsville and promoted to major general, but neither his service at Gettysburg nor at the Wilderness brought him glory, and real distinction continued to elude him for the rest of the war (Paludan, 106–107).

James A. Keith was left to be the scapegoat. He was court-martialed and allowed to resign from the army. But the army was not aggressive in prosecuting him and did not hold him for trial by a civilian court. Instead, Keith rode out of Knoxville and disappeared into the Carolina mountains. Vance marshalled the resources of the state to bring him to justice, and soon civil authorities were on his trail. Keith was now a fugitive himself; the hunter was now the hunted. He stayed on the run for two years, hiding in caves or in secluded mountain cabins, aided by friends. Sometimes he slept in the open at night. Occasionally he might be spotted, but he never stayed long enough in one place to be captured. There was little serious effort to apprehend him, even though civil authorities in Marshall were making plans to try him for the Shelton Laurel murders. Finally, Keith's luck ran out. Near the end of the war, in 1865, he was taken captive by Union soldiers. He spent eight months as a prisoner in Castle Pinckney, Charleston, was transferred to Raleigh, and finally was returned to Marshall for his long-awaited trial (Paludan, 107–108).

Keith had already spent twenty-six months in prison when his trial began in December 1868. His case generated considerable interest, and emotions ran high. On the one hand, families of the Shelton Laurel victims had waited a long time to see justice done. But there were many people in North Carolina who felt that Keith was justified in what he had done. The Keith case was enmeshed in the ambiguities of wartime conduct, the influence of mountain feuds, and the politics of postwar Reconstruction in North Carolina; a laborious legal system dragged the case out interminably. Keith's lawyers managed to obtain a change of venue, moving the case from Madison County to neighboring Buncombe County.

Prosecutors in the Keith trial issued indictments against him for thirteen separate acts of murder. He would be tried on each indictment, each murder, separately. At his first trial for murder an Asheville jury acquitted him on December 9, 1868. The next day he was charged with a second murder. He remained in jail, and no one with any political clout was willing to try to free him.

The North Carolina legislature in December 1866 had passed a law granting full pardon and amnesty to all officers, both Union and Confederate, who had committed "any homicides, felonies, or misdemeanors," while acting under orders of a superior. Keith's defense attorneys argued that the amnesty law gave the former officer immunity from prosecution in the Shelton Laurel incident. The prosecutors countered by citing a provision of the North Carolina Constitution of 1868 that nullified the amnesty. The district court judge agreed with the prosecution's interpretation and ordered Keith to remain in custody (Paludan, 111).

Keith's lawyers appealed the judge's decision, and the North Carolina Supreme Court finally heard the case of *State v. Keith*. The court ruled in favor of the defense, saying that the provision of the 1868 Constitution that nullified the amnesty was an ex post facto law. "We think," the court said, "the Judge should have discharged the prisoner" (Paludan, 113).

Still Keith was not freed, because technically the Supreme Court decision only applied to his first single murder indictment. The prosecutors could still indict and try him for eleven more murder cases, and Keith's lawyers could still argue the applicability of the amnesty law on each separate indictment. It appeared that the case might drag on for years. Meanwhile the prosecution filed five more indictments against Keith for murder (Paludan, 113).

Keith believed he was a good soldier obeying orders and doing what had to be done to deal with a ruthless enemy. Shelton Laurel was a haven for marauders. The men he executed were guerrillas who preyed on helpless civilians and who murdered soldiers from ambush. They had stolen, terrorized, and tortured and would do so again unless they were stopped. He felt, as did many in the 64th, that the harsh measures used at Shelton Laurel were necessary. And now he was to be judged by a civilian court and jury that could not possibly understand what it was like to fight an enemy like that. So far removed in time and distance from the cruel war in Madison County, they could never see things the way he saw them.

Disgusted with the legal system, Keith gave up on the hope of ever being cleared and took matters into his own hands. He escaped from the Buncombe County Jail on the night of February 21, 1869, and fled the state. Authorities sought his arrest for two more years but could not find him. The prosecution finally gave up looking for him in June 1871. Keith never returned to North Carolina (Paludan, 113, 120).

The Shelton Laurel Massacre failed to make front-page news at the time it occurred. A few newspapers picked up the report after the Memphis *Bulletin* first broke the story in July 1863. But there was very little public uproar, and the incident was never considered a major event of the Civil War. To Americans outside the Appalachians, the obscure deaths of a few poor mountain whites were insignificant compared with the horrendous combat deaths at Gettysburg, Vicksburg, and Chickamauga.

The Shelton Laurel executions failed to end the Unionist threat from that region. The valley remained a guerrilla base, raids continued, and in the summer of 1863 Governor Vance was receiving numerous letters from people in the region asking for more protection. By April 1864 Shelton Laurel sheltered an even greater menace, George W. Kirk and his feared Unionist raiders (Paludan, 101–102).

The 64th North Carolina Regiment's luck failed to improve as the war continued. Barely a year after it was formed, most of the regiment was captured at Cumberland Gap in September 1863. However, some of its soldiers managed to escape and continued to serve in East Tennessee and the North Carolina mountains, chasing deserters and fighting bushwhackers. The regiment was disbanded in May 1865. In his history of the regiment, Captain B. T. Morris wrote what is probably a fitting legacy for the 64th, "we did the best we could" (Trotter, 216).

Chapter 2

"Nothing More than Mounted Robbers"

In 1863, partisan warfare intensified in the western North Carolina mountains. Federal victories at Gettysburg and Vicksburg in July gave the loyalists hope. Unionist guerrillas stepped up their raids on unprotected communities, and Confederate authorities responded by increasing their patrols in the area. Union troops under Major General Ambrose Burnside captured Knoxville in September 1863, and Tennessee became a base for Unionist raids into the vulnerable western Carolina region.

Burnside authorized Unionists in eastern Tennessee to form their own military companies for Federal service in the National Guard of East Tennessee. North Carolina native Goldman Bryson was commissioned a captain in the 1st Tennessee National Guard. He recruited men in Cherokee County, North Carolina, Fannin County, Georgia, and Monroe County, Tennessee. Bryson became a menace to Confederates in the tri-state region and carried out at least a dozen border raids before Rebel forces brought his destructive rampage to a bloody end.

Bryson hailed from the Great Smoky Mountains, where he gained a reputation as a troublemaker. Besides being a refuge for mountain whites, this area was home to the Cherokees, dispossessed in the Indian Removal of 1838. In northern Georgia and in western North Carolina whole Cherokee families had been forced from their homeland and marched westward to Oklahoma. A small portion, the Eastern Band of Cherokees, remained in the western North Carolina mountains. When the Civil War broke out, the Eastern Cherokees chose to support the Confederacy and served in Thomas' Legion, a major Rebel military unit in the mountains.

In August 1856 the Indian community at Valleytown was shocked by the murder of John Timson, a respected local Cherokee. On the night of August 31, a gang of thugs surrounded Timson's home and set it ablaze, then shot and killed the luckless victim as he attempted to flee. Although a witness swore that Goldman Bryson was a ringleader in the brutal attack, his sister and brother gave him an alibi, and an all-white jury acquitted him. Many local residents felt Bryson had cheated justice, and the incident earned him the Cherokees' undying hatred (Trotter, 91).

Now Bryson commanded a Federal military company, 150 strong, and his activities spread fear as far as North Georgia. The Confederacy's theater commander, General Braxton Bragg, described Bryson and his men as "nothing more than mounted robbers" (Trotter, 91).

The ambiguities of warfare in the mountains, compounded by conscription and family divisions, are sharply illustrated by the case of Bryson's brother James. According to James, the Confederates prevented him from joining his brother's command in July 1862 by conscripting him into Thomas' Legion, which in fact fought against Bryson in the mountains. James deserted the legion a year later and joined the 7th Tennessee Mounted Infantry, a Union command (Barker Papers, Vol. 1).

In July 1863 Bryson's guerrillas captured the village of Murphy, the Cherokee County seat, seized the jail, and looted the town. The raiders captured 400 guns and a considerable amount of supplies and ammunition which they turned over to the Federals in Knoxville (Crow, 50; Jones, 33; Barker Papers, Vol. 9).

Confederate guerrillas struck back at Bryson that same month. They raided the Cherokee County home of Jonothan McDonald, Bryson's acting commissary. The raiders entered the home, clubbed McDonald with their rifle butts and knocked him unconscious. McDonald's wife, Catherine, snatched an iron frying pan from the stove and brained one attacker, who fell senseless to the floor. McDonald's daughters tried to bar the door of the cabin to the Rebels outside while Mrs. McDonald took on the assailants inside with her skillet. Another attacker pulled out his knife and stabbed Jonothan McDonald, still lying on the floor, in the right eye. As a result, McDonald was blinded. The Rebels finally fled, thinking that McDonald was dead. Later he was taken to the Union lines in Tennessee. McDonald was unable to rejoin Bryson because of his injuries, but after recovering from his wounds, he joined the Union 3rd Tennessee Mounted Infantry in October 1864 (Barker Papers, Vol. 9).

Bryson's activities began to generate alarm across the border in Fannin County, Georgia. Two Home Guard commanders at the little village of Morganton, William A. Campbell and Elijah W. Chastain, heard of Bryson's recent looting of Murphy, just twenty miles away. Both men were concerned about Unionist raiders crossing the state line to rob local citizens of their firearms. Campbell wrote to Governor Joseph E. Brown on August 4, 1863, that Bryson's guerrillas had "robbed our people of every single gun and all the ammunition in two whole districts," shot horses, and destroyed property, and that no one was able to stop them. He described Bryson as "shrewd and cunning and with all bold and defiant." As a Home Guard officer, Campbell was preparing to confiscate weapons and ammunition from the remaining citizens of the county before they could be stolen by the guerrillas (Lane, 129)!

Chastain reported that Bryson's guerrillas were operating in squads of fifteen to twenty men, intimidating local residents, seizing their guns, and threatening to hang them "to the first limb of a tree they can find" if they tried to have them arrested. Chastain noted, "These rascals say openly that no secessionist shall keep a gun or any other kind of arms." He went on to say that the company of cavalry he was organizing to defend the county would have no arms, because the guerrillas would have them all (Lane, 130). On August 11, he wrote Brown that 125 guerrillas were five miles from Morganton threatening to burn the town, but that the county sheriff had talked them into leaving. The sheriff had several Georgia deserters who had agreed to join the local Home Guard company, but they swore they would die before they would go back into the army. "I am not skeard," Chastain concluded, "But I confess that the times are any thing but pleasant to contemplate. I intend to hold this place if I can, but how it is to be done without arms or ammunition I must confess looks doubtful" (Jones, 33).

On August 10, Captain D. C. Pearson, a Confederate enrolling agent at Asheville, wrote that he could no longer carry out his conscription duties in the western North Carolina counties because of Unionist guerrilla activity there. Pearson said he had reliable information that 300 to 500 deserters and loyalists virtually controlled the counties of Cherokee and Henderson. "They are killing stock," he said, "disarming the citizens, and the militia, if they were even disposed, I don't think would be sufficient to capture or entirely disperse them. . . . The militia is worth nothing, now that they are to be conscripted." Pearson asked for cavalry or mounted infantry to be stationed in the mountains to deal with the problem (USWD, I, 30, iv: 734).

As the summer of 1863 ended, Rebel commanders speculated on Bryson's next move. On October 14, Colonel M. H. Wright in Atlanta reported the guerrilla chief at Murphy planning a raid on the branch mint at Athens, Georgia. In fact, Bryson was preparing for another foray into the Carolina mountains. He received orders from Burnside on October 22 ordering him back into the state to recruit men (USWD, I, 30, iv: 748; 31, i: 235). After replacing their worn-out horses with fresh ones, Bryson's troops crossed into western North Carolina armed with 100 new rifled muskets and forty rounds of ammunition per man (Barker Papers, Vol. 8).

Bryson's activities had annoyed the Confederates to action. At the head of 100 Rebel horsemen, Brigadier General John C. Vaughn, the former sheriff of Monroe County, Tennessee, closed in on Bryson's command on October 27, 1863. The Rebels surprised the guerrillas camped at Beaver Dam in Cherokee County. Vaughn's surprise attack spelled the end for Bryson's company. After a furious gun battle on horseback, two of the guerrillas lay dead, half a dozen were wounded, and seventeen were captured along with thirty horses. The rest of the guerrillas disbanded and fled to Tennessee. Bryson escaped during the engagement and remained at large (USWD, I, 31, i: 9, 235).

Apparently Vaughn's men killed all seventeen prisoners, since they were never seen again. Among them were Jonothan McDonald's son, William Marcus McDonald, and his cousin, William Marion McDonald, just turned 18, taken prisoner eight miles from his home. According to one source, the seventeen prisoners were taken across the border into East Tennessee to a place on the Tellico River near the foot of the mountains, and there all of them were shot (Barker Papers, Vol. 9).

When news reached Murphy that Bryson had escaped, Lieutenant Cameron H. (Cam) Taylor set out in pursuit with a detachment of nineteen Cherokee soldiers from Thomas' Legion. Taylor was part Cherokee. His men remembered Bryson from the John Timson affair and welcomed the opportunity for revenge. Taylor's Indians were excellent scouts and knew the country. Soon they were able to pick up Bryson's trail.

The Cherokees tracked the elusive guerrilla for twenty-five miles across the mountains into Tennessee without even stopping to eat. Taylor found the tracks of two horses leaving the main trail and heading toward Bryson's home on Coker Creek in Monroe County. On October 28, they caught up with Bryson and one of his men near Bryson's house. Taylor ordered the guerrilla chief to halt, but when he tried to run, he gunned the fugitive down. The Cherokees were later spotted riding into Murphy proudly wearing Bryson's bloody bullet-ridden uniform. John Ledford, captured with Bryson, was hanged from a tree on the courthouse square. When Cam Taylor searched Bryson's body, he found the recruiting orders from Burnside. He also found the guerrilla chief's muster roll, which the Cherokees probably used to identify members of the Unionist company (Crow, 51).

The Rebels had eliminated Bryson, but a more formidable raider rose up to take his place. Any remaining doubts that the Carolina mountains were dangerously susceptible to Federal attack should have been laid to rest in late October 1863 when Union partisan George W. Kirk gave the mountain people a grim foretaste of his ruthlessness. With 600 to 800 mounted men

Kirk swept into Madison County and boldly occupied the little village of Warm Springs only a few miles from the Shelton Laurel community, site of the bloody massacre of Union men ten months earlier.

When news of the raid reached Major John Woodfin, Confederate commander at nearby Marshall, he mustered 150 mounted men and rode recklessly toward Warm Springs to challenge the Unionists. A respected Asheville attorney and a former instructor to Governor Zebulon Vance, Woodfin rode ahead of his column with a party of his staff officers in order to reconnoiter the enemy's position and approached Warm Springs' hotel across the French Broad River bridge. Kirk's men were waiting for him, lying in ambush. As enemy snipers opened fire from a building only yards away, Woodfin toppled from his handsome black warhorse. The Rebel major lay dead in the road, and two of his staff officers were hit as well. Woodfin's death demoralized the Rebels, and his outgunned soldiers withdrew to Marshall. The following day a party of civilians from Asheville arrived to retrieve the major's body. They found Woodfin's corpse lying in the road. Kirk was long gone. An enraged Governor Zebulon Vance, hearing of the raid and vowing to meet the enemy head on, caught the train from Raleigh to Morganton and rode overland to Marshall, only to arrive too late to attend his friend's funeral. Vance was just as stunned as the community at the swiftness of Kirk's raid (Trotter, 98–99).

Colonel George W. Kirk carved out a reputation as the most effective and most feared Unionist partisan in the mountains. From his base at Greeneville, Tennessee, Kirk led his forces on raids into western North Carolina spreading terror far and wide. Although he mainly hit military targets, Confederate civilians suffered from his raids as well and termed him a marauding outlaw (Blackmun, 349–350).

Although North Carolina Confederates regarded him as a "Home Yankee," the 26-year-old Kirk actually hailed from Greene County, Tennessee. A former carpenter, he had enlisted in the Confederate army in 1861. He deserted to become an officer in Colonel William C. Bartlett's 2nd North Carolina Mounted Infantry Regiment, a command formed from mountain Unionists. Kirk first worked as a scout helping Unionists escape to Federal lines. Like fellow Tennessean Daniel Ellis, he utilized an underground network of Union sympathizers in the mountains and enlisted volunteers from among the hill people (Current, 71).

Kirk favored a loosely organized, flexible military command. Sometimes his operations required small raiding parties for intelligence gathering or scouting, sometimes larger forces for a broader campaign. One thing was sure: Kirk's command was one of the best armed Southern Union regiments. Kirk provided his men with the highly efficient Spencer repeating rifle, giving them much greater firepower than their Rebel adversaries. Although bitterly condemned by Carolina Rebels, Kirk did not go out of his way to kill and torture, but he did not hesitate to destroy enemy property and had no qualms about killing if he had to. Kirk led numerous forays into western North Carolina in 1863 stealing horses and burning homes. He even raided a Baptist Church meeting near Mars Hill, killing two men and wounding another (Trotter, 114–115).

Kirk's aggressiveness was rewarded. On February 13, 1864, General John M. Schofield, who had replaced Burnside as commander at Knoxville, authorized Kirk to raise a new regiment, the 3rd North Carolina Mounted Infantry, from Unionists and deserters along the North Carolina–Tennessee border. Kirk's men would have to provide their own mounts from "private or captured horses." The partisan chief recruited selectively in nearly every mountain county in western North Carolina, and sixty of his men were from bloody Madison County. Kirk formed one of the Union's best armed and best equipped guerrilla forces (Trotter, 114–115).

Schofield assigned Kirk a mission even as the new regiment was being organized: to disrupt the supply line of Confederate Lieutenant General James Longstreet, withdrawing to the Tennessee-Virginia border after his failure to capture Knoxville. The raiders would hit the rail line near Jonesborough, Tennessee, and follow the railroad into Virginia, all the while burning bridges, destroying depots, and tearing up track. By April 1864, Kirk was back in the North Carolina mountains operating from the safe haven of Shelton Laurel (USWD, I, 32, iii: 386).

Kirk stands out among the partisan chiefs in the high regard in which he was held by his superiors. When the guerrilla leader was arrested in Knoxville on an unspecified charge, Union Brigadier General J. D. Cox had the complaint dropped. Cox wrote on April 16, "I think it important that he should rally his command as soon as possible" (USWD, I, 32, iii: 377).

By June 1864 Kirk was ready for a major strike deep into western North Carolina. His destination was the little hamlet of Morganton in Burke County at the terminus of the railroad line seventy-five miles inside North Carolina. Morganton had seen more development than most settlements in the mountains. Summer terms of the North Carolina Supreme Court had been held there since the 1840s. The little town was a thriving banking and commercial center and was regarded by state bureaucrats in Raleigh as a cultural and social hub in the mountains (Phifer, 294).

Schofield ordered Kirk to damage the rail center at Morganton and then move on to his main objective at Salisbury about eighty-five miles further east, where the Confederates had a prison. There he was to destroy the railroad bridge over the Yadkin River. But Kirk intended to add his own dramatic twist to the mission. He planned to commandeer a locomotive at the Morganton depot. He even had an engineer with him. His troops would board the railroad cars for a run eastward to Salisbury where they would raid the Confederate prison and free the Federal soldiers being held there. Kirk then planned to escape the same way he had come and return to Tennessee (Trotter, 116).

Kirk's raiding force of 130 men, which included two dozen or so Cherokee defectors from Thomas' Legion, crossed into North Carolina's Mitchell County on June 27 without being spotted by Rebel patrols. Riding under cover of night, they reached Camp Vance, a Confederate conscript center six miles east of Morganton. Camp Vance, actually a few log cabins in a woodland clearing, offered only the crudest living conditions for the unenthusiastic conscripts billeted there (Trotter, 116–117).

On the morning of June 28 Kirk and a party of his men rode straight into the camp under a flag of truce and boldly demanded the surrender of the post from Lieutenant William Bullock. Bullock stalled for time, scrambling to issue muskets to as many of his unarmed draftees as he felt he could trust, and sent another officer out to discuss the surrender terms with Kirk. Kirk offered to parole the Rebel officers and soldiers and agreed not to destroy the camp. But Bullock and some of his men apparently did offer resistance. In the struggle Kirk's men killed ten Rebel soldiers and one officer (Trotter, 117).

The raiders burned the camp but spared the hospital. They captured 1,200 guns and considerable ammunition, and they destroyed 3,000 bushels of grain. A Confederate officer who arrived the following morning wrote that Camp Vance was "a heap of ruins." The guerrillas paroled the camp's surgeons, but they took the Rebel officers and soldiers with them as prisoners, minus seventy men who managed to get on the "sick" list in the hospital (USWD, I, 39, i: 236–237).

A Rebel army surgeon at Camp Vance reported that Kirk "carried a U.S. flag, and his men were all in Federal uniforms." Not only were they well armed and equipped, they carried extra weapons with them as well. When forty of the conscripts at Camp Vance decided to join Kirk rather than stay and be forced into the Rebel army, Kirk's soldiers handed each new volunteer a Spencer repeater and told them to mount up (Current, 72).

Kirk canceled his planned strike on Salisbury when he learned that the Home Guards there had received word of his approach. Instead he turned westward to Morganton and struck the railroad depot. The raiders destroyed a locomotive and three cars, as well as a few buildings. Kirk captured 132 Rebels and 48 horses and mules, taking them with him as he withdrew from Morganton. That night he camped on the opposite side of the Catawba River (Crow, 105–106).

On the morning of June 29 the raiding party mounted up again and moved on westward, but about sixty-five old men and boys from Colonel

George Love's Rebel Home Guard caught up with them at Brown Mountain, fourteen miles from Morganton. Kirk used his Rebel prisoners as human shields, placing twenty of them in front of his troops as he deployed them for battle. Some of the mounted Home Guards opened fire anyway. One of the captives was killed and another wounded. One Rebel reported that Kirk cried out, "Look at the damned fools, shooting their own men." Fearful of hitting more of the captives, the Home Guards broke off the engagement, and Kirk withdrew. In the gunfire Kirk was slightly wounded in the arm, the only time in the war that he sustained an injury (Trotter, 118).

The Unionist raiders had ridden about seven miles further when they were again attacked. Morganton Home Guards led by Colonel William Waightstill Avery, reinforced by prison guards from Salisbury, overtook Kirk at Winding Stairs Road along Jonas' Ridge. Once again the superior firepower of his Spencers, as well as his mastery of the mountainous terrain, gave Kirk the decided edge. In the thick mountain fog Kirk needed only twenty-five troopers, including a dozen Cherokees, to hold off the pursuing Rebels on the narrow, winding road. Colonel Avery, a promising North Carolina politician, was killed, and Kirk's men melted away in the mist (Phifer, 326).

Kirk had accomplished one of the most successful raids yet seen in the mountains. As a final insult he burned the Mitchell County home of Colonel John B. Palmer, commander of the Western North Carolina District, and then he crossed the mountains into Tennessee. The entire operation had cost him two men killed and five wounded. Palmer was left chagrined at the raider's boldness. He had not even known that Kirk was in the area until it was too late (Trotter, 119).

Kirk's raid underscored the vulnerability of the western Carolina mountains. Although the raiders had failed to reach their primary target at Salisbury, they had destroyed the Morganton depot and captured a considerable number of enemy troops, weapons, and supplies. Many mountain Unionists were encouraged to become more aggressive in their struggle against the Confederates (Crow, 106). Schofield regarded the operation as a success and congratulated Kirk "for the gallant and successful manner in which you have conducted the expedition," although he added, "Such daring and hazardous expeditions should be undertaken but rarely." He felt Kirk would be more useful for recruiting, scouting, and occasional raids against enemy supply depots (USWD, I, 39, i: 234).

Schofield sent his report of Kirk's raid to a delighted General William T. Sherman in the field near Atlanta. On July 21, Sherman responded:

> Please convey to Col. G. W. Kirk the assurances of my appreciation of the services rendered by him in his late expedition. You may encourage him all you can more in organizing the element in North Carolina

hostile to Jeff. Davis rather than in undertaking those hazardous expeditions. If he could form a series of companies in North Carolina that could protect each other, and give us the information needed, he would fully earn his compensation and our thanks. (USWD, I, 39, i: 233)

Confederate reaction was predictably bitter. An outraged Governor Vance wrote that the war in the mountains was being "conducted on both sides without any regard whatever to the rules of civilized war or the dictates of humanity. The murder of prisoners and non-combatants in cold blood has, I learn, become quite common" (Crow, 108). He received no comfort at all from the hard-pressed Confederate commanders to whom he appealed for help. Colonel John B. Palmer wrote on July 4, "I fear this is but the prelude to something more serious" (USWD, I, 39, i: 235). Palmer did not have enough manpower to guard a 250-mile-long frontier from Virginia to Georgia. What troops he did have were stretched too thin.

Kirk was not the only raider that Carolina Rebels feared. An associate of Kirk was 28-year-old Keith Blalock, a bold Unionist renegade from Grandfather Mountain in Watauga County. Reluctantly, Blalock had joined the Confederate 26th North Carolina Infantry, but he had not left home alone. With him was his teenage wife, Malinda, who had disguised herself as a man and was using the name Sam Blalock. "Sam" actually served with her husband and kept her true identity a secret until April 1862, when Keith gave himself an infectious case of poison oak to obtain a discharge. The plucky young bride confessed her secret, and the army discharged her. Once more secure in the haunts of Grandfather Mountain, the young couple took up the way of the guerrilla.

Riding together with other Unionists, Keith and Malinda engaged in bloody shoot-outs with Confederate sympathizers. In one gunfight Malinda was wounded in the shoulder, and Keith lost an eye on another occasion. A wave of violent feuds and revenge killings engulfed Watauga County as Keith Blalock acquired a reputation as a ruthless desperado. The violence reached a peak in February 1865, when a neighbor betrayed Keith's Unionist stepfather, Austin Coffey, into the hands of Rebel guerrillas. The old man was missing for a week. Then a wandering dog was spotted on the road with one of Coffey's hands in his mouth. Keith Blalock swore to avenge his stepfather's murder no matter how long it took. One year later he made good his promise, ambushing his target, a man named John Boyd, and blasting him with a Sharps rifle at close range (Trotter, 147–154).

As the dreary winter of 1864–1865 unfolded, the mountain people yearned for an end to the long, violent ordeal that had shattered their peaceful lives. In western North Carolina the "Red Strings," secret Unionist societies whose members wore red strings in their coat lapels, conspired to create a separate breakaway state in eastern Tennessee and western Carolina. In spite of such efforts the war continued, and the guerrilla violence remained unchecked. The stage was set for the last military campaign of the war in the mountains in the early months of 1865.

On February 1, 1865, Kirk struck out across the mountains into Haywood County at the head of a formidable force of 400 cavalry and 200 infantry. On February 4 he reached the undefended village of Waynesville, where his raiders burned the jail after freeing the prisoners. As in Kirk's raid on Morganton six months earlier, a number of the prisoners joined him on the spot. As a defiant gesture Kirk burned the home of Revolutionary War hero and town founder Robert Love (Crow, 121).

As the raiders withdrew from Waynesville, Rebel troops from Thomas' Legion gave pursuit. A handful of legion sharpshooters took up positions on the mountainsides overlooking strategic Soco Gap and held Kirk's men at bay. Kirk was forced to withdraw and exit through the mountain pass at Balsam Gap on February 6. He continued westward to Webster, then turned north along the Tuckasegee River heading for Quallatown. But 150 Cherokees and 150 whites from Thomas' Legion waited for him in ambush at Soco Creek. Kirk was approaching a sacred place to the Cherokees, the site of the famed Tecumseh's meeting with local chiefs prior to the War of 1812, and the Cherokee Confederates were more than ready to exact vengeance for his transgression. Kirk stumbled into a perfect ambush. His men were hemmed in on three sides, and the Cherokees poured on a deadly fire. Kirk should have finally met defeat, but the Rebels ran out of ammunition (Crow, 123).

Kirk was able to disengage and escape across the mountains into Tennessee. Their failure to capture Kirk was a bitter pill for the Cherokees to swallow and was a sign that the war was reaching a climax in the mountains. Kirk's raid was just a preliminary to a major Union operation in western North Carolina, George Stoneman's great cavalry raid. Legion officer Lieutenant Colonel William W. Stringfield wrote, "the enemy everywhere became more active and aggressive. The end was now rapidly approaching" (Trotter, 238–239).

Chapter 3

"Where Yankees Never Come"

The Carolina mountains were home to many men and women who embraced the cause of the Confederacy. William H. Thomas, one of the most influential men in western North Carolina, owned more than 100,000 acres of land. More important, he had lived in the Cherokees' country since the age of 15 and was their trusted friend. Thomas had operated a store, traded with the Indians, and learned to speak their language. He became a spokesman, lawyer, and business agent for the Cherokees and represented their interests with the government. A Cherokee neighbor, Yonaguska, had adopted Thomas as a son and called him Wil-Usdi' or "Little Will." Though only five feet eight and slightly built, Thomas was a handsome young man and was considered an eligible bachelor, but not until 1858 did he marry. His bride, just half his age, was Sarah Jane Burney Love, 26-year-old daughter of Thomas' business partner, James R. Love of Waynesville (Frome, 113–115).

Thomas had an ambitious vision for the mountains of western Carolina, which he saw as potentially the industrial and commercial center of the new Southern nation. Always a promoter, Thomas encouraged the development of the region and hoped to see a road built across the mountains to connect western Carolina with East Tennessee. Like Lawrence Allen and James Keith, who lacked both his political influence and his humane nature, Thomas perceived a Southern victory as essential for the future growth of the mountain region. During the war he formulated strategic plans for the defense of the mountains that unfortunately were overlooked by his superiors.

When war broke out and Thomas sought to raise a regiment in the mountains, it was only natural that the Cherokees should follow his lead and enlist to fight for the Confederacy. Thomas' Legion of Indians and Highlanders became one of the most effective anti-guerrilla units in Confederate service and one of the unique commands of the war. Organized at Knoxville in September 1862, the legion contained a battalion of cavalry under Lieutenant Colonels James A. McKamy and William C. Walker and a regiment of infantry under Thomas, with Lieutenant Colonel James R. Love, Jr., and Major William Stringfield as his staff officers. The men of the legion, a mixture of mountain whites and Cherokees, came from Cherokee, Jackson, and Haywood Counties. Four whole companies were Cherokee.

Thomas never intended his legion to be used for fighting guerrillas, but that was their fate for most of the war. Stationed in East Tennessee during the bridge-burning incident of November 1861, the legion guarded railroad crossings, particularly the Holston River bridge at Strawberry Plains, for the rest of the winter. They also went out searching for deserters in the mountains.

The Cherokees' knowledge of the terrain of the mountains made them invaluable as scouts. They hated the deserters and marauders and were highly effective in rooting them out. But they frightened the local Unionists, especially after an incident at Baptist Gap in the Cumberland Mountains on September 15, 1862, when the Cherokees, angered by the killing of one of their officers, scalped several wounded Federal prisoners. William Stringfield denied that scalping took place after this incident. But former Indian agent and trader James W. Terrell, a friend of Thomas and an officer of one of the Indian companies, said, "Throughout the war they did scalp every man they killed, if they could get to him, which they generally managed to do. . . . [A]t the end of the war, they had at least as many scalps as there were survivors among them." Thomas was always uncomfortable with the scalping controversy, and he sought to ignore the issue whenever it arose. He once asked that the subject not be brought up in the presence of his Indians (Crow, 16).

The Cherokees earned a fearsome reputation among mountain Unionists. Daniel Ellis wrote that every Indian taken captive should be executed on the spot for the cruelty done to the Union men, but he conceded that the Cherokees still treated the Unionists more humanely than the white Rebel soldiers did (Trotter, 97).

When Union forces under Burnside captured Knoxville in September 1863, Thomas and two of his Indian companies fell back to the unguarded mountain passes into North Carolina to prevent them from being blocked by Union sympathizers. Troopers of the 5th Indiana Cavalry chased Little

Will and nearly caught up with him but finally turned back in frustration as the Cherokees disappeared into the mountains. The Union commander, Colonel Felix W. Graham, reported, "I pursued the Indians as far as their encampment. The citizens failing to blockade the road in their rear, I was able to capture but one. They won't fight and the country is so mountainous it is almost impossible to catch them" (Trotter, 89).

Thomas constructed a base camp at Gatlinburg on the Tennessee side of the border and set to work building a military road from Quallatown in the Cherokee country to his forward post fifteen or twenty miles east of Sevierville, Tennessee. In December 1863, after a Unionist raiding party captured one of his Cherokee patrols, Thomas conducted a daring raid on Sevierville and rescued his Indians from the county jail. A quantity of new rifles also fell into his hands (Trotter, 99).

The Federals soon struck back. On December 10, Colonel William J. Palmer's 15th Pennsylvania Cavalry attacked Thomas' camp at Gatlinburg. Raised a Quaker, the 27-year-old Palmer would see many skirmishes with Rebel guerrilla bands in the mountains. After a fire fight that lasted about an hour, Thomas and his men fell back into the mountains, leaving their camp to be destroyed. Thomas also left without his hat, which the Federals found in his headquarters (Frome, 125–126).

In January 1864, the war struck close to home for Thomas when his cavalry commander, Lieutenant Colonel William Walker, was gunned down in Cherokee County. Walker had returned home to recuperate from a lingering illness. On the night of January 3, an unidentified group of men approached the Walker house and asked to see the colonel. When his wife summoned the ailing Walker to the door, one of the men shot him dead. The murderers were never caught (Trotter, 93).

As the frigid winter of 1864 unfolded, Little Will and his Cherokees waged a stubborn war of resistance against the Yankees in the mountains. Unionists accused him of being "a terror to the Union people of East Tennessee and borders of North Carolina," and Federal forces continued to hammer at him. On February 2, 1864, troopers of the 14th Illinois Cavalry attacked him near the junction of the Tuckasegee and Little Tennessee rivers. Thomas lost between twenty and thirty men captured and five killed. Later in the month a detachment of the 1st Wisconsin Cavalry raided into the Cherokee country reaching within twenty miles of Franklin (Frome, 127).

The Legion was not immune to the difficulties and hardships that frustrated most of the Confederate forces fighting in the mountains. Desertion was a serious problem, even among the Cherokees. Thomas also had to contend with petty jealousies and apathy among his superiors. By the winter of 1864 the families of Thomas' Indians were starving. Women and children at home were eating tree bark and weeds to stay alive. Thomas requested aid for them from his superiors but got no sympathy. He then intervened on the Cherokees' behalf by appealing to the governor of South Carolina, reminding him that his troops in the western Carolina mountains were the only barrier against Union invasion of that state. South Carolina finally agreed and provided 100 bushels of corn to feed the Indian families (Crow, 59).

The Cherokees were fanatically loyal to Thomas. According to a report published in the Raleigh *Daily Confederate* on May 17, 1864, some of Thomas' Cherokees captured by the Federals were offered their freedom and $5,000 in gold if they would kill Thomas and bring in his scalp. The Indians accepted the offer and were set free to return to the mountains. Once back home, they revealed the whole account to Thomas and continued fighting Unionists (Frome, 127).

By May 1864, Little Will and a portion of his command remained on duty in the mountains, trying to hold the passes, although their insufficient numbers made this a hopeless task. Meanwhile Colonel James R. Love, Jr. took the bulk of the legion, about 400 men, to Virginia where it joined General Jubal Early's Confederate forces in the Shenandoah Valley. The legion fought bravely and raided with Early to the outskirts of a startled Washington, D.C. When they returned home in December 1864, fewer than one man in four had survived the fighting in Virginia.

There were other Rebel diehards in the mountains. From his camp near Boone, Major Harvey Bingham and his Watauga County Home Guard prowled the nearby mountains in search of deserters and Union men making for Federal-occupied Tennessee. He soon gained a reputation as formidable, no-nonsense partisan. After a Union raiding party from Kirk's command pillaged Watauga County in the spring of 1864, Bingham launched a punitive raid into Tennessee. The operation netted him some cattle and three enemy prisoners. When the returning Rebels camped for the night near Beech Mountain in western Watauga County, they were unaware that they were being watched by Union scout Jim Hartley and fifteen of his men (Trotter, 161–162).

Hartley planned to ambush Bingham's column the next morning at Bowers Gap, where the Rebels would have to work their way between two precipitous cliffs with many good sites for hidden snipers. The Unionists took up positions on both sides of the narrow trail and waited for morning. That same night Hartley slipped away and called on Polly Aldridge, a Unionist woman with a cabin near the Home Guards' camp. Hartley told Polly about what he planned for Bingham in the morning (Trotter, 161–162).

Bingham was cautious. As if anticipating an ambush, he and his men took a different path over Beech Mountain early the next morning. The Rebels wound their way up a less obvious, more rugged path that would avoid the Unionist trap. When Polly Aldridge noticed what Bingham's men were doing, she ran to warn Hartley, who hustled his men after the Rebels by yet another overland trail (Trotter, 162–163).

The Unionists opened fire on the rear of Bingham's column when they overtook him, killing one Home Guard and one horse. The two sides skirmished on the run as they made their way across the mountain. During the fighting, Hartley spotted his own brother, Cal Hartley, among Bingham's troops and taunted him: "Ha, Cal! Come here and shake hands with your brother!" Cal replied with a musket shot that ripped through Jim's coat sleeve. When 17-year-old Elliot Bingham recklessly tried to charge Hartley, the Unionist scout fired several shots into the boy with his Spencer repeater. The Bingham lad died the next day, cradled in his mother's arms. Harvey Bingham now confined his activities to defensive operations (Trotter, 163–164).

State and central authorities were aware of the sad conditions in the mountains, but there was very little they could do about it. Governor Vance told the North Carolina General Assembly in 1864, "The western border is, however, subject to constant raids and the situation of the inhabitants is distressing in the extreme. Bands of lawless men, many of them our own citizens, acting or pretending to act under commission from the enemy, swarm into the mountain frontier, murdering, burning, and destroying. Totally regardless of the laws of civilized warfare, they have inaugurated a system of cruelty at which humanity shudders" (Blackmun, 347). Confederate Assistant Secretary of War J. A. Campbell had already written in September 1863, "The condition of things in the mountain districts of North Carolina, South Carolina, Georgia, and Alabama menaces the existence of the Confederacy as fatally as either of the armies of the United States" (USWD, IV, 2: 786).

The Rebels simply lacked the manpower to defend the mountain passes. Thomas' Legion still guarded the Smoky Mountains of the Cherokee country. John Woodfin's old battalion, now led by one-eyed Lieutenant Colonel James L. Henry, patrolled the French Broad River valley north of Asheville. The battalion was known as the "One-Eyed Battalion." One cavalry company in Madison County, Bingham's Home Guard in Watauga County, and a company in Ashe County near the Virginia border were the only other forces available (Van Noppen and Van Noppen, 7–8).

Both sides recognized the strategic value of the Carolina mountains. General Ulysses S. Grant had toyed with the idea of a mountain offensive after his victory at Chattanooga in November 1863. The proposed plan called for 50,000 Federal troops to occupy western North Carolina and southwestern Virginia, but the appalling lack of decent mountain roads caused Grant to drop consideration of the plan. Little Will Thomas felt General Robert E. Lee might consider using the mountains as a last ditch Rebel stronghold. He also feared Grant might occupy the mountains and use the area as a springboard for an invasion of Georgia or South Carolina or Virginia (Van Noppen and Van Noppen, 7).

The Confederacy's embarrassment over Kirk's raid on Morganton in June 1864 only highlighted its growing impotency in the Carolina mountains. Three different commanders had wrestled with the difficult task of defending the mountains in 1864. Brigadier General Robert B. Vance, the first commander of the Western Carolina district, had been captured on January 14, 1864, along with fifty of his soldiers when his troops were surprised by the ever-cunning and relentless Colonel William J. Palmer and his 15th Pennsylvania Cavalry. Vance spent the rest of the war in a Northern prison. His replacement, Colonel John B. Palmer of the 58th North Carolina Infantry, showed no more ability than Vance. After his failure to deal with Kirk's raiders in July, Palmer was replaced by Brigadier General James G. Martin (Crow, 56–57, 108).

Known as "Old One Wing," the 45-year-old Martin was a West Point graduate who had lost his right arm in combat in the Mexican War. He had served as North Carolina's adjutant general and had won distinction at Petersburg in Virginia. On August 16, 1864, Martin took command of the Western North Carolina District. He energetically set about to beef up Rebel defenses in the mountains (Crow, 108–109).

Thomas' Legion remained Martin's most effective force although weakened by sickness and desertions in 1864. The legion was divided, with most of the command serving in Virginia. Back in the mountains, where the Cherokee companies remained, there was friction between Thomas and his superior, Colonel John B. Palmer.

Thomas never could mold his legion into the type of guerrilla force that the Confederacy needed. The courage and indomitable spirit of the Cherokees were without equal. A Rebel officer wrote of seeing a Cherokee soldier standing sentry duty for fourteen uninterrupted hours in the open in a mountain snowstorm. But the vast numerical superiority of the Federals was an awesome obstacle. Thomas faced on a small scale the same manpower problem that the Confederacy as a whole faced: every soldier lost became irreplaceable. Thomas had a high regard for his Indians and hesitated to expose them to needless danger. The Cherokees by nature favored defensive rather than offensive warfare. So the legion, in spite of its potential, never became the Confederate equal of Kirk's raiders (Trotter, 96–97).

Little Will adopted a more defensive stance as 1864 wore on. The murder of his cavalry commander, William Walker, in January had affected him deeply, and he seemed to care less for the prosecution of the war as a whole and more for the defense of the mountains against renegades. Concerned about threats against his own life, he formed a bodyguard of twenty Cherokees for his own protection. Soon he gave up trying to apprehend deserters. Thomas felt the best he could hope to do was to provide some protection for local communities against the more active bands of marauders, so he sought to recruit deserters into the legion to fill his depleted ranks. Such activity was contrary to Confederate army policies and brought him into conflict with Colonel Palmer. The stage was set for Little Will's court-martial (Crow, 56).

Thomas was wearied by the war in the mountains. He had not seen his wife, Sarah, for more than nine months when he wrote her in January 1863, "if I live through the war I shall have done enough to be satisfied to spend the remainder of my life in retirement surrounded by my family and friends" (Crow, 29). In 1864 Thomas was suffering signs of manic depression, and those around him began commenting on his unpredictable mood swings. His brother-in-law, Dr. W. L. Hilliard, recorded that at times Little Will seemed to be "laboring under some peculiar mental excitement—that his mind was a little out of balance" (Frome, 128).

In September 1864, Thomas was charged with insubordination, with harboring deserters, with conduct unbecoming an officer, and with incompetency. Governor Vance did not support him and wrote, "Colonel Thomas is worse than useless, he is a positive injury to that country. His command is a favorite resort for deserters, numbers of them I learn are on his rolls, who do no service, he is disobedient of orders, and invariably avoids the enemy when he advances" (Frome, 128).

Details of his court-martial at Greensboro are unknown, but Little Will apparently entered the proceedings on the attack. He argued that he was doing what he had to do to operate in the mountains and that winning the Unionists over was a better strategy than trying to fight them. The court found him guilty, but he immediately appealed the decision to his old friend Jefferson Davis and traveled to Richmond to meet with the president, who overturned the court's decision and reinstated Thomas in November 1864. The legion's Major William Stringfield was not surprised that Little Will had prevailed. "As he is a very shifty and polite man," Stringfield wrote, "he is likely to come out OK in the end" (Trotter, 123–124).

Thomas remained in Richmond, probably cultivating his political connections, while Stringfield assumed command of legion operations in the mountains. The portion of the legion that had been serving in Virginia was due to return home, but in the mountains Stringfield had only four Cherokee companies, two of which contained a large number of mountain whites, with which to patrol four counties—Cherokee, Clay, Macon, and Jackson. From his headquarters in Franklin in Macon County, Stringfield tried to coordinate his scattered detachments, often riding twenty or thirty miles a day. He faced a hopeless task (Trotter, 124–125).

Willie Stringfield grew up in Strawberry Plains, Tennessee, and attended the local college that his father, a well-known Methodist minister, had helped establish. He was a Union man at first and ran for the state legislature in March 1861 as a pro-Union candidate. But when Tennessee seceded, he withdrew from the political race and enlisted as a private in the 3rd Tennessee Cavalry Battalion in July 1861. In November he raised his own company in the 31st Tennessee Infantry. Stringfield became acquainted with Thomas in the spring of 1862 at the home of his stepmother in Strawberry Plains, and after two months of frustrating and unrewarding duty chasing down draft dodgers as a deputy provost-marshal in staunchly pro-Union East Tennessee, he was relieved to be assigned to the legion (Crow, 9–10).

Earnest, ramrod straight, and handsome—with a boyish face, blue eyes, and sandy hair—Willie had always been popular with the women. During the war he began actively courting the beautiful Maria M. Love, the youngest sister of Sarah Thomas, Colonel Thomas' wife. Stringfield was 27 years old in 1864 (Crow, 9–10, 142).

When he reached Quallatown to take command of the legion on October 31, 1864, Stringfield naively wrote in his diary, "After a long and tiresome journey of one month, I arrived at this haven of rest—this long heard of place of security where Yankees never come and conscripts find shelter" (Crow, 99). He soon learned how wrong he was. Stringfield termed the mountains "a wild section . . . almost a pathless wilderness . . . lonely, perilous and desolate." Contending with Unionist guerrillas as well as Rebel marauders who preyed on civilians, he wrote, "I gave protection to such as deserved it and ordered the others to leave the State" (Trotter, 125).

Stringfield came to admire the Cherokees as much as Thomas had. Union and Confederate residents alike seemed to welcome his attempts to restore order and fairness to the mountains. Once he faced down members of his own legion, men from Love's regiment who were returning from Virginia. The Rebel soldiers were about to shoot two Unionist prisoners when Stringfield rode up and ordered the men to untie the captives. When they made no move to obey, Stringfield jumped off his horse and untied them himself. A lieutenant with the Rebels pulled out his pistol, Stringfield drew his sword, and bloodshed was avoided only when several enlisted men stepped in and separated the officers (Crow, 120).

Late in December 1864, the beleaguered Rebel mountain defenders got another chance at George W. Kirk. Palmer's scouts spotted the Unionist partisan at Paint Mountain Gap with about 400 men moving off in the direction of Tennessee. Palmer concluded he must be returning to Greeneville and decided to cut him off. He ordered Stringfield to rendezvous with him at Warm Springs, and the legion commander arrived there the day after Christmas with 300 men. On December 27, Stringfield's troops set out in pursuit of Kirk, winding their way along the Nolichucky River in miserable freezing weather and slogging through snow eighteen inches deep. When a fresh snowstorm left ten more inches of snow on the ground and reduced visibility to zero, Stringfield and his officers wisely decided they could go no further. They turned back and returned to Warm Springs, where Palmer accused Stringfield of disobeying orders. The legion would have to wait for yet another chance to fight Kirk (Trotter, 130–131).

The Confederacy's hold on western North Carolina was now pitifully tenuous. Martin had only 1,500 soldiers to defend the district from Yankee invasion. To minimize discord between his two feuding commanders, Martin made Palmer responsible for defending the counties east of Waynesville, while Thomas and his legion would guard the area from Waynesville westward. Thomas made his headquarters at Quallatown, with Stringfield further west at Valleytown. Stringfield's men were desperately short of shoes and knapsacks, and they were now down to five or six rounds of ammunition per man. The legion was larger now, since the return of troops from Virginia led by charismatic Colonel James R. Love, Jr.; and Thomas, back in the mountains since late November 1864, seemed more confident and aggressive (Trotter, 236).

After their failure to defeat Kirk following his Waynesville raid in February 1865, the Rebel forces in the mountains braced for the last major Union offensive in western North Carolina. On March 21, 1865, 6,000 Federal horsemen led by Major General George Stoneman thundered out of Tennessee. On March 28, they arrived at Boone, and after a short action with the surprised Home Guard—the rest of Bingham's command—they occupied the town. Stoneman's men burned the county courthouse, the jail, and several other public buildings. Stoneman moved on northward across the mountains into Virginia, and Kirk arrived in Boone on April 6. He fortified the town and built a log blockhouse at Watauga Gap to block the mountain pass and protect Stoneman's route back into Tennessee (Van Noppen, 36–42).

Stoneman turned south from Virginia and marched on Salisbury, where he burned the military prison along with cotton mills and supply depots. By April 17 he was back in Tennessee, leaving Brigadier General Alvan C. Gillem, a bitter foe of Confederates, to deal with Martin's troops in Asheville, the main Rebel stronghold in western Carolina.

Gillem's troops overran and plundered Morganton, and on April 25 they were on the outskirts of Asheville. A little mountain town with several dirt streets, Asheville boasted no railroad, water supply, or municipal building. Yet it was still the main town of western Carolina, and because of its central location in the mountains many felt it might well become the Confederacy's last capital should Jeff Davis and Robert E. Lee decide to make their final stand in the Appalachians. The mountain people did not yet know that Lee's army had laid down its arms in Virginia on April 9 (Sondley, 691–692).

Gillem hoped to avoid a costly engagement with Martin's soldiers defending Asheville. He offered Martin a truce if he would agree to provide his troops with three days' rations. To avoid further bloodshed, Old One Wing accepted, and the community managed to scrape together enough rations for Gillem's men. Gillem withdrew on April 25, but at sundown the next day part of his cavalry returned, surprised the Rebel garrison, and took Martin and his men prisoner. The raiders burned Martin's home and several others, and looted the community. When recently promoted Brigadier General William J. Palmer, a more honorable Union commander, learned of the breach of the truce, he apologized to Martin and released him and his men (Crow, 128).

With more Federal troops moving on Asheville and the partisans of Kirk and William C. Bartlett close behind, Martin decided to pull his remaining men westward to Waynesville and dig in for a final stand with Thomas' Legion, the last Confederate troops in western Carolina. The legion, down to about 500 men, held Soco Gap and Balsam Gap, the two strategic mountain passes west of Waynesville (Trotter, 295–296).

Rumors were flying, and Martin had heard that Lee and Joseph E. Johnston had surrendered their armies in Virginia and in North Carolina. He sent Stringfield, with a twenty-three–man escort and a flag of truce, to Knoxville with a sealed dispatch to George Stoneman, the new Federal commander there, asking for verification and for terms of surrender for his own troops. Stringfield set out from Franklin on April 28.

Stringfield and his mounted party made their way across the Smokies. The trip was uneventful until the Rebels approached Maryville, Tennessee, where they were halted by a force of eighty Yankee cavalrymen. Stringfield explained his mission to the Federal commander, and tempers were kept under control until a Union lieutenant whom Stringfield described as "a large fine looking East Tennessee loyalist" recognized one of Stringfield's officers, Captain Eppa Everett. The Union officer pointed a finger at Everett and blurted, "There is the man that killed my daddy" (Crow, 131–132).

Angry men on both sides drew pistols and braced for a fight. With a Rebel yell, Stringfield and his men prepared to defend themselves. But another Yankee officer rode up and intervened. He told Stringfield that he had known his father and allowed him to continue on his way. On May 1, Stringfield's party, exhausted and hungry, rode into Knoxville only to be disarmed by blue-coated troops and thrown in jail. Stoneman dismissed

Martin's letter and told a fuming Stringfield he didn't need to respond, because he already controlled all of western North Carolina (Crow, 133–134).

Federal troops occupied Asheville, and the partisan regiments under Kirk and Bartlett were dispatched westward to Waynesville with orders to disarm Rebel guerrillas. Bartlett occupied Waynesville with no resistance while Kirk raided elsewhere, and Martin fell back to the mountain passes. Bartlett seemed to feel that Martin and the legion posed no great threat and turned his cavalrymen loose to pillage.

But the legion was far from finished. Scorning the rumors of Lee's surrender at Appomattox and hoping to catch Bartlett off guard, Jim Love's Cherokees advanced out of Soco Gap toward Waynesville. On May 6 at White Sulphur Springs the last engagement of the war in the Carolinas took place. Twenty-three-year-old Lieutenant Robert T. Conley, the most decorated man in the legion, led his sharpshooter company—probably fifty men—in a skirmish with Bartlett's troops in which the Federals lost one soldier. The Federal casualty, a man named Arwood, was the last regular soldier east of the Mississippi to die in the war (Trotter, 298).

Suddenly Thomas and Love had Bartlett hemmed in at Waynesville. Although he knew that more Yankee troops were on the way, Bartlett was concerned because Kirk had not arrived. His confidence was shaken that night as he and his men listened to the sounds of Thomas' 300 Cherokees dancing the war dance around their campfires in the surrounding mountains (Crow, 138).

On the morning of May 7, Martin, Love, and Thomas, with twenty of his fierce painted warriors at his side, met Bartlett under a flag of truce at the Battle House, Waynesville's resort hotel. In one last defiant gesture of saber rattling, the usually composed Thomas threatened to turn his warriors loose to scalp Bartlett and his men if they did not surrender. But emotions soon cooled, and talk became more realistic. Bartlett conceded that Martin and Thomas had him at a disadvantage in Waynesville, but he reminded them that more Federal troops were due to arrive. He also confirmed that both Lee and Johnston had surrendered and for all practical purposes the war was over. Martin decided that any further fighting would be useless (Crow, 138).

On May 9, 1865, the Cherokees and white mountaineers of Thomas' Legion laid down their arms, bringing formal warfare to an end in the mountains of North Carolina. Officers and enlisted men of the legion were paroled and could return to their homes on their promise to fight no more against the United States (Crow, 139).

While mountain Unionists gleefully celebrated their long-awaited victory over the hated Rebels, cooler heads advised restraint. William J. Palmer cautioned against giving troops unlimited freedom to plunder. He recommended that Kirk "be recalled to East Tennessee to prevent his men from pillaging and committing excesses, now that hostilities have ceased." He also suggested stationing troops in the mountains to intercept small parties of armed Rebels who might be tempted to continue their own private warfare as they returned home from Virginia. There was still the potential for violence in the mountains; and conditions remained unsettled for years (USWD, I, 49, i: 550).

Chapter 4

"Power Unrestrained"

George Stoneman's stunning raid across western North Carolina was not the first such operation he had conducted. The dress rehearsal for this campaign took place three months earlier in southwestern Virginia, which the Federals had long targeted for a strike on the Virginia-Tennessee Railroad, a vital link between the two major Confederate armies in the east and west. They also wanted to destroy the lead mines at Wytheville and the salt works at Saltville. The region's abysmal transportation system retarded serious military operations until December 1864.

Stoneman, a 42-year-old West Pointer, was pleased to lead the raid into southwestern Virginia. A capable cavalry commander, he had been captured during an abortive attempt to liberate the Union captives at Andersonville prison camp in July 1864. Remembering his brief confinement in a Rebel military prison, Stoneman wrote, "I owe the Southern confederacy a debt I am anxious to liquidate, and this appears a propitious occasion" (Walker, 128).

Stoneman swept out of East Tennessee with about 4,000 cavalry headed into Virginia. Opposing him was a paltry 1,000-man Rebel force under General John C. Breckinridge, whose main priority had to be the defense of the indispensable salt works. Realizing this, Stoneman bypassed Saltville and concentrated on tearing up the railroad and destroying the lead mines at Wytheville. When Breckinridge moved out of Saltville to intercept him, leaving the town unguarded, Stoneman divided his command and sent part of his force to destroy the salt works. On a miserable December 21, 1864, as freezing rain turned to snow, Stoneman's raiders destroyed the salt works while he fought an inconclusive battle with Breckinridge (Walker, 152).

In an operation lasting just twenty days, Stoneman had ridden 870 miles, brushed Confederate opposition aside, destroyed railroad bridges, burned thirteen depots, wrecked foundries and mills, and destroyed the lead works and the salt works, as well as the Virginia towns of Bristol, Abingdon, Wytheville, and Saltville. Stoneman's raid dealt a crushing blow to the region and to the Confederate war effort. Lee's army under siege at Petersburg would have a harder time linking with Rebel forces across the mountains. The raid left Rebel civilians in Southwestern Virginia cold and hungry after Yankee cavalrymen looted and burned their way across the region. Stoneman admitted, "I regretted the necessity of giving orders that may cause suffering to noncombatants" (Walker, 153).

Stoneman's more ambitious March–April 1865 raid into western North Carolina and Virginia was one phase of the final grand campaign of the Civil War. Stoneman's hard riding cavalrymen lived off the land and burned public buildings, cotton mills, and supply depots. They smashed the Virginia and Tennessee Railroad and did significant damage to the Confederacy's ability to wage war. At Salisbury, Stoneman's men destroyed 10,000 stands of arms, a million rounds of ammunition, 10,000 rounds of artillery ammunition, 6,000 pounds of gunpowder, 75,000 uniforms, 250,000 blankets, 10,000 bushels of corn, 6,000 pounds of bacon, 50,000 bushels of wheat, 27,000 pounds of rice, and 100,000 pounds of salt (Trotter, 275–276).

While Stoneman limited his destruction to military and industrial targets, his Unionist subordinates did not. George W. Kirk's partisan cavalry helped in the operation by barricading roads, blocking mountain passes, and securing Stoneman's route back into Tennessee. They also wreaked havoc in occupied Boone, where Stoneman had warned his troops that destruction of private property was off limits. When Kirk's men rode in, they sacked the town. Kirk appropriated the J. D. Councill home in Boone as his headquarters, as Stoneman had done a few days before. When Stoneman returned there three weeks later, he found Kirk's men had left it in shambles: "the fencing gone—the flowers and shrubbery trampled bare, the yard covered with beef hides, and sheep skins, chicken feathers, and pieces of putrid meat" (Van Noppen, 41–42).

Likewise, Unionist recruits in Stoneman's cavalry, which he left behind under Brigadier General Alvan Gillem to neutralize the Rebel forces in western North Carolina, seemed to go out of their way to make life miserable for Confederates. While local residents commented on the good discipline of the 15th Pennsylvania Cavalry, they bitterly denounced Gillem's troops, especially the 13th Tennessee Cavalry, a Unionist outfit made up of many men from the Carolina and Tennessee mountains. Rebels had burned their homes and driven out their families, and now these Union men were out for blood. Stoneman dubbed them his "Cossacks" (Trotter, 251–252, 258–259). Troops from General Simon B. Brown's brigade broke the truce between Gillem and Martin at Asheville on April 26. Brown's soldiers looted private homes, beat local citizens, terrorized women and children. Martin contended, "I have heard of no worse plundering any where than was permitted in and near Asheville by General Brown" (Van Noppen, 521–522).

Stoneman's raid illustrates the strategy adopted by the North in the last phase of the Civil War. The Federal war machine now targeted both the Rebel military and the South's ability to wage war. This was part of the evolution, with General Ulysses Grant's promotion to command of Union armies in March 1864, of "hard war" as the primary Federal military policy. Thus far, Federal forces had neither destroyed Rebel armies on the battlefield; nor had they troops enough to occupy and subjugate Southern territory. Historian Mark Grimsley sees the "strategy of raids" as an alternative to conquering territory. Yankee armies, in lieu of seizing and occupying large tracts of territory, would strike from key secure bases—Knoxville, in Stoneman's case—into the Southern countryside to destroy railroads, military goods, and crops (Grimsley, 162–163).

"Hard war" was at first a reaction to Rebel guerrilla tactics. By embracing a "no prisoners" policy toward Rebel bushwhackers and by its increasing cruelty toward noncombatants, the Union military raised the level of violence because it invited retaliation by the guerrillas. This created a spiraling escalation of brutality. Federal war policy in the southern Appalachians evolved through three stages: First, a negative perception of the native population in occupied areas, based partly on the conduct of local guerrilla bands and partly on preconceived prejudices. Second, an increasing willingness to adopt guerrilla tactics, to mistreat civilians and their property, and to take no prisoners, either as encouraged by commanders or as practiced by many soldiers with commanders giving a wink and a nod. Third, the absorbing of this experience into a military policy that generalized toward the treatment of the South as a whole in the "total war" tactics of Sherman and Grant.

In West Virginia, guerrilla warfare became a way of life as conventional warfare faded out after 1861. Federal occupation troops loathed the Rebel guerrillas as much as the 64th North Carolina Confederate soldiers detested the bushwhacking Union men of Shelton Laurel. An officer of the 14th Pennsylvania Cavalry called the guerrillas "cowardly assassins, and cruel freebooters who hid in mountain passes and sent murderous shots into our ranks from positions where pursuit was impossible" (Noe, " 'Appalachia's,' " 103). Many Northern soldiers painted the guerrillas as less than human. In Braxton County, Major Rutherford B. Hayes, who one day would become president of the United States, described a "wild man of the mountains" taken by Federal soldiers for bushwhacking: "He wore neither hat nor shoes, was of gigantic size—weighing two hundred and thirty pounds; had long hooked toes to climb, a very monster" (Howe, 9).

Northern troops in West Virginia considered the mountaineers an inferior people. Since it was difficult to distinguish guerrillas from civilians, soldiers quickly generalized their hatred of the bushwhackers to the entire population, even including mountain loyalists. Although struck by the beauty of the mountains, Hayes called the poor mountaineers "unenterprising, lazy, narrow, listless, and ignorant . . . serfs." "The height of their ambition," he commented, "is to shoot a Yankee from some place of safety." Soldiers' remarks about mountain women were especially harsh. One man wrote, "The women are worse than the men one old bitch said she wished all the union army were in hell." By thinking of them as savages, as inferiors, it was easier for soldiers to rationalize treating the mountain folk as whites had treated Indians (Noe, "Exterminating," 106, 110–111).

Confederate hatred of Unionists in East Tennessee was equally intense, so much so that the Confederate government declared East Tennessee as enemy territory in April 1862 (Noe and Wilson, xvii). Even before the war, many Southerners considered the mountain people backward, ignorant, and lazy. Rebel soldiers came into the region with these prejudices, and their experiences with the Unionist population only reinforced their hatred. One Rebel officer declared, "the people of this country are almost all of them at heart against us." Another soldier remarked, "What I have seen of East Tennessee, the Yankees are perfectly welcome to it." Bushwhackers were backstabbing, dirty cowards who were unworthy of any degree of respect. Rebel soldiers thought of them as little more than animals and described anti-guerrilla activities in terms of "hunting," as if they were chasing wild game. One Rebel officer wrote that the mountain women "by their conduct, lose all claim to be respected and regarded as ladies" (Fisher, 71, 77, 116–117).

Soldiers quickly adopted the tactics of the bushwhackers they hated. Federal troops in West Virginia confronted the guerrilla menace almost immediately. Major General George B. McClellan's army entered the region in May 1861 and defeated Rebel forces at Phillipi and Rich Mountain that summer, leaving the Union army in control of two-thirds of the state. McClellan promised a limited war, "to confine effects to those who constitute the organized armies and meet in battle," to "cause the persons and property of private citizens to be respected." But the war degenerated into partisan warfare when secessionist guerrillas burned two bridges on the Baltimore and Ohio Railroad near Farmington. McClellan modified his position. While still promising to respect the homes and property of civilians, he declared that he would arrest all persons in arms, "unless of known loyalty," and that bushwhackers would be "dealt with in their persons and property according to the severest rules of military law." Arrests of suspected guerrillas and their sympathizers quickly began (Noe, "Exterminating," 104–107).

McClellan's successor in July 1861, Brigadier General William S. Rosecrans, continued the policy of conciliation, promising to respect private property and to protect "unarmed and peaceful civilians." He continued to order the arrest of guerrillas and their supporters and appealed to the people of the area to support him. Although he forbade his soldiers from pillaging private homes, many of his troops did so anyway, stealing food, livestock, and fence rails, which they burned for fires after uncommonly early snows began in mid-September. Rosecrans acknowledged that his Ohio soldiers pilfered and committed vandalism, but he felt Unionist troops from the region were responsible for most of the offenses. However, by the end of 1861 Rosecrans' Ohio troops were adopting the way of the guerrilla, escalating the level of violence in the West Virginia mountains (Noe, "Exterminating," 108–109).

Colonel George Crook, West Pointer and veteran of frontier Indian fighting, took command of the 36th Ohio Infantry, a regiment that became legendary in its brutality toward guerrillas, in September 1861. The 36th Ohio had already clashed with guerrillas on several occasions. Cold, hungry, and demoralized, the Ohioans were as fed up with the bushwhackers as were the 64th North Carolina at Shelton Laurel; and they longed to strike back at them. They expected Crook to introduce the tactics he had used against the Plains Indians, and he did not disappoint them. In October 1861, the 36th Ohio launched a vindictive war of extermination against the guerrillas, looting and burning homes, seizing food and livestock, taking hostages, and killing suspected partisans. Crook conceded that in rooting out the bushwhackers, his troops "spread terror" among the general civilian population in the mountains (Noe, " 'Appalachia's,' " 103–104).

The most controversial tactic adopted by the Ohio soldiers was the practice of shooting prisoners. Crook encouraged the policy. "When an officer returned from a scout," he wrote, "he would report that they had caught so-and-so, but in bringing him in he slipped off a log while crossing a stream and broke his neck, or that he was killed by an accidental discharge of one of the men's guns, and many like reports. But they never brought back any more prisoners." (Noe, "Exterminating," 115).

Not all soldiers approved of the "no prisoners" policy. Captain William H. Dunham wrote, "Our fellows shoot them down wherever they find them with arms in their hands. . . . [I]t is the most disgraceful outrageous mode of warfare imaginable" (Noe, "Exterminating," 115–117). In January 1862 Crook's soldiers burned several towns between Summersville and Sutton in retaliation for guerrilla attacks. They also killed twenty Rebels, including an unarmed civilian. Dunham wrote that the soldiers captured a young man who had been casting bullets—"evidence incontestable that he was a bushwhacker"— but that a few miles from Summersville, they "in cold blood, barbariously shot him. . . . [T]old the fellow now was his time to escape and for him to run for his life . . . fired upon him and brought him to the ground. . . . [T]hey left him unburied. My God: has it come to this?" (Mitchell, 134–135).

Other soldiers were comfortable with the practice. One wrote home, "We never take any of their class prisoners. They have murdered our men and we have retaliated." Another commented, "they may have shot a poor bushwhacking cuss, & I am one of the kind that believes in them doing so every chance they get,—If I did not, I would not have been here" (Noe, "Exterminating," 117).

In March 1862, Major General John C. Fremont replaced Rosecrans as commander in West Virginia. Fremont, who had fought Rebel guerrillas in Missouri, took an even tougher position against the bushwhackers. He encouraged his soldiers "to fight them in their own style, and by rapid marches, vigorous attacks and severe measures, annihilate them." In just nine months Union military policy in West Virginia had gone from conciliation to hard war. To the soldiers' approval, Fremont clamped down hard, declaring martial law and ordering quick trials and executions for captured guerrillas (Noe, "Exterminating," 104, 118–119).

Fremont ordered Crook to destroy the Rebel enclave in rugged Webster County, base for Duncan McLaughlin's Webster Dare Devils. On April 23, 1862, Crook's soldiers fought skirmishes with the guerrillas and burned the town of Addison, the county seat. The operation in Webster County was a temporary setback for the guerrillas. They lay low for several months, but by the fall of 1862 they were again raiding Unionist homes. In fact, the Federals never were able to contain the guerrillas, much less destroy them. Their tactics of destructive war failed. The war in West Virginia bogged down into a stalemate until the final months of the conflict (Noe, "Exterminating," 119–121).

The Federals could have learned from Missouri, where Union commanders had already discarded "conciliation" in 1861. Their treatment of the area as enemy country—in spite of the large numbers of Unionists—triggered the savage guerrilla warfare that afflicted Missouri until the end of the war. In December 1861, Major General Henry Halleck, who replaced Fremont as Union commander in Missouri, pronounced all guerrillas "outlaws" to be "immediately shot" as soon as they were captured.

Rebel guerrilla chief William C. Quantrill, who initially shot only prisoners believed to be rival Jayhawkers, reacted to Halleck's "no prisoners" policy by raising the black flag; henceforth, he would give no quarter (Castel, 8–9, 14). Although it was not official Union military policy, Federal soldiers routinely shot, hanged, and tortured prisoners, as did the Rebel guerrillas in Missouri. "The only way to get the country rid of these sneaking devils who are laying around in the brush and killing men as they pass along the road," an Iowa soldier wrote in December 1861, "is to play their own game. Just shoot them down wherever we find them" (Fellman, 166–168).

The Confederate army showed no greater restraint in dealing with Unionist guerrillas. Brigadier General Felix Zollicoffer, the Confederacy's first commander of the Department of East Tennessee, attempted conciliation there, hoping to win over the area's loyalists. Like McClellan in West Virginia, he ordered his soldiers to respect civilians and their property, maintained discipline, and tried to restrict soldiers to their camps so as to forestall clashes with loyalists. Zollicoffer abandoned conciliation after the bridge raid and Unionist uprisings in November 1861. These events, coupled with fear of a Federal military invasion, led him to declare martial law and to arrest hundreds of suspected guerrillas (Fisher, 45–46, 50–54).

General Edmund Kirby Smith, who succeeded Zollicoffer, stepped up arrests in East Tennessee and threatened loyalist troublemakers with deportation to the Deep South. Early in 1862, Kirby Smith dispatched 1,000 troops under Brigadier General Danville Leadbetter to break the Unionist guerrillas' hold on Scott and Morgan Counties. "I give you carte blanche," he told Leadbetter, "and will sustain you in any course you find necessary to adopt." The guerrillas resisted with force, sniped at Rebel troops, and fought a skirmish with them. As in West Virginia, the guerrillas broke up temporarily but resurfaced as soon as the Rebel troops left (Fisher, 68–70).

Although Zollicoffer and Kirby Smith ordered troops to respect civilians and to refrain from pillaging, many Rebel soldiers disregarded their orders, with the unofficial approval or indifference of their officers. Unauthorized foraging, theft, and vandalism were common. One soldier conceded in November 1861, "We will cause a famine in a county where we stay long." Confederate troops also committed atrocities. In 1862 they put twenty houses to the torch in the town of Tazewell. Rebel cavalrymen reportedly tortured and killed Unionists, raped women, and burned and looted homes in Cocke County in early 1864. They burned thirty-seven homes in Johnson County in July 1864 and killed several loyalists (Fisher, 117–118).

Confederate troops faced the same frustrations in East Tennessee as Federals in West Virginia. They adopted guerrilla tactics, including the shooting of prisoners, as the 64th North Carolina did at Shelton Laurel. One soldier reported, "Here is said to be 60 out Lyers in this country. The boys killed 4 or 5 since I came out. I did not see either I saw them put the rope around one fellows neck." A Unionist near Bull's Gap in October 1863 accused Rebel troops of hanging several women to force them to disclose their husbands' hiding places and of shooting another woman for "making a too free use of her tongue" (Fisher, 74–78).

Occupation of East Tennessee by the Federals in late 1863 brought the mountaineers no relief. Union troops displayed the same hatred and contempt for the local people as the Rebels had, alienating many Unionists. The Federals regarded the region as occupied territory. One loyalist wrote, "The Union Army is more destructive to Union men than the rebel army ever was." He accused Federal soldiers of stealing livestock and food, burning fences, and verbally abusing the people. The Federal occupation forces showed less restraint toward Rebel civilians than the Confederates had shown toward loyalists (McKenzie, 204–205).

Even "Mosby's Confederacy" in northern Virginia was not immune to destructive violence as standards of warfare deteriorated. Grant ordered in August 1864 that any of Mosby's men who were captured should be hanged and that members of their families should be taken and held as hostages. Federals burned portions of Fauquier and Loudoun Counties, where the guerrillas were based. In September 1864, Federal troopers executed six of Mosby's rangers in Front Royal, Virginia. Mosby retaliated by executing seven Union prisoners in November. None of these measures ended the Rebel guerrilla activities (Wert, 197–198, 214–219, 245–250).

Federal adoption of hard war as a policy was at least in part a reaction to the reality of guerrilla warfare. The deterioration of warfare to the level of guerrilla tactics early in the war in Missouri, West Virginia, and East Tennessee helped set the stage for its acceptance as a Federal military policy. From 1862 to 1864, the policy evolved in North Alabama and North Georgia. Finally it influenced Grant's and Sherman's final concept of destructive war in 1864–1865 (Noe, "Exterminating," 104–106).

Ironically, northern Alabama, the section of the state with the strongest Union sentiments, was the region that suffered most from the war and Federal invasion. Northern Alabama's long agony began shortly after the Federal victory at Shiloh in April 1862, when Union forces under Major General Ormsby M. Mitchel invaded the Tennessee River Valley. Three long years of bitter warfare followed.

Mitchel occupied Huntsville on April 11 and made it his headquarters. From then until the end of the fighting the region was torn by violence. Federal detachments pillaged the relatively unguarded Tennessee Valley, while Confederate troops were busy in more strategically important areas. The valley was not a major military theater of operations, but the Yankees wanted to prevent it from supplying men and food to the Confederacy. Guerrilla actions became common in the valley. Rebel bushwhackers fired into troop trains, cut telegraph lines, and tore up railroad tracks. Union commanders retaliated by burning towns, seizing civilian hostages, and imprisoning suspected secessionists.

Union soldiers waged a ruthless war of attrition up and down the valley. Federal troops sacked the undefended town of Athens, twenty-five miles west of Huntsville, on May 2, 1862. Soldiers looted stores and homes, burned the courthouse and other buildings, and raped several young women. The Union officer responsible was Russian-born Colonel John B. Turchin—Ivan V. Turchinov—who reportedly told his soldiers that he would turn his back for two hours to allow them to plunder the town (Grimsley, 81–82). Even Mitchel, no stranger to charges of brutal occupation tactics, conceded that "the most terrible outrages—robberies, rapes, arson, and plundering—are being committed by lawless brigands and vagabonds connected with the army. I hear the most deplorable accounts of excesses committed by soldiers" (A. Moore, 432–433).

Major General Don Carlos Buell, Mitchel's superior who removed him from command in June 1862, described the Athens incident as "a case of undisputed atrocity" (A. Moore, 432). He held Mitchel responsible for the conduct of Turchin and his men and pointed out that the episode alienated even many of the strong Unionists in Athens. The treatment of Athens also stiffened Confederate resistance in the area and helped to create a climate of bitter partisan warfare. Turchin was court-martialed, but charges later were dropped, and he was promoted to brigadier general. Historian Mark Grimsley believes the court's lenient treatment of Turchin was an indication that Northerners, shocked by news of McClellan's defeat near Richmond that summer, were ready to abandon the conciliation policy altogether (Grimsley, 83–85).

The violence in northern Alabama intensified. On June 21 Confederate guerrillas fired on a troop train in Jackson County, in the northeastern corner of the state, killing ten men and wounding several others. One of their leaders said they were retaliating against Mitchel for his policy of burning private homes, and they threatened to hang Federal prisoners if the practice continued. Federal forces punished local civilians for actions of the Rebel guerrillas. Hostage taking was not uncommon. After Christopher C. Sheats, a prominent Unionist from Winston County, was captured and held at Montgomery, Union troops in Huntsville arrested local secessionist William McDowell in December 1863 to hold until Sheats was released.

General William T. Sherman seemed to endorse the policies of Mitchel and Turchin when he wrote the following in January 1864:

The Government of the United States has in North Alabama any and all rights which they choose to enforce in war, to take their lives, their homes, their lands, their everything, because they cannot deny that war exists there, and war is simply power unrestrained by constitution or compact. If they want eternal warfare, well and good. We will accept the issue and dispossess them and put our friends in possession. To those who submit to the rightful law and authority all gentleness and forbearance, but to the petulant and persistent secessionists why, death is mercy, and the quicker he or she is disposed of the better. (A. Moore, 433)

Sherman's "hard war" philosophy was evident as early as the summer of 1862, when his troops in western Tennessee encountered the same type of guerrilla warfare that Mitchel and Buell had encountered in northern Alabama. In September 1862, Sherman ordered his soldiers to burn the town of Randolph, twenty-five miles above Memphis, in retaliation for Rebel guerrilla attacks on Union troop transports on the Mississippi. Sherman's directions were precise: The troops were to conduct the operation in good order, were to let residents know the reason for the action, were to burn the town but leave one house standing as a reminder. Although Sherman was aware that no one in the town had taken part in the attack, he felt it would be a lesson to the secessionist population. Sherman also threatened to remove ten families in Memphis for each further attack. The attacks continued, and Sherman ordered more retaliatory raids and deportations. Sherman wrote Grant in October 1862, "They cannot be made to love us, but they can be made to fear us, and dread the passage of our troops through their country." Sherman's measures failed to end guerrilla activity (Grimsley, 114–118).

Grimsley points out that Sherman's and Grant's policies in the summer of 1862, unlike their hard war policies later in the war, served merely to "curb civilians" so that the army could go about its business of fighting Rebel soldiers, not to destroy the Confederacy's economy and political will. "Yet by accustoming soldiers to regard Southern civilians as enemies," Grimsley writes, "and by making the destruction of private property a normal practice, the antiguerrilla campaign helped lay the groundwork for the greater hard war measures still to come" (119).

Sherman's policy had clearly evolved by the Atlanta campaign in 1864. Throughout the summer of 1864, Confederate raiders disrupted Federal communications in North Georgia with persistent attacks on the vital Western and Atlantic Railroad line. The railroad was attacked and sabotaged more often than any other rail line in the occupied South. Guerrillas derailed one train on June 11 by planting a land mine on the track. They derailed another train on June 18 and then burned sixteen of the cars. On June

19, a Union patrol caught partisans tearing up track, and the Rebels opened fire, killing two of the soldiers. The raiders were constantly cutting telegraph wires (Kennett, 96–98).

A frustrated Sherman increasingly blamed the civilian population who aided the raiders, and he urged stern countermeasures. He wrote to Major General Stephen Burbridge on June 21, 1864, that guerrilla activity constituted "nothing but simple murder, horse stealing, arson and other well defined crimes, which do not sound so well under their real names." Burbridge was to direct his subordinates that guerrillas were "wild beasts . . . to be treated accordingly." He ordered "all males and females who have encouraged or harbored Guerillas and Robbers" to be arrested and to be deported from the area. In a letter to Secretary of War Edwin M. Stanton on that same day, Sherman wrote, "there is a class of people who must be killed or banished, men, women and children, before you can hope for peace and order." He suggested they be deported to places as far away as Haiti, Honduras, Baja California, or Madagascar (Kennett, 99).

Sherman's wishes were translated into General Order No. 2, issued by Major General James Steedman for the District of the Etowah on June 28, 1864: "All citizens except government employees found within three miles of the Railroad from Bridgeport to the Federal Army in Georgia, outside of any post or station of troops after the 7th day of July, 1864, will be arrested and forwarded to these headquarters to be tried before a military commission as spies 'found lurking' within the lines of the United States." Under these guidelines several hundred Georgians were deported north of the Ohio River. Despite these harsh measures, the Federals still were unable to protect the railroad from sporadic Rebel guerrilla attacks (Kennett, 100–104).

In November 1864 Sherman's troops burned the Georgia towns of Canton, Cassville, Kingston, Rome, and Cartersville in retaliation for depredations by the guerrillas. Sherman now was committed to the use of "hard war" to break the will of the South, and destruction of these towns served as a springboard for the Federal burning of Atlanta, destroying much of the South's industrial base. Commenting on his plans to lay waste Georgia in his "march to the sea," Sherman wrote, "I want to make a raid that will make the South feel the terrible character of our people" (Kennett, 226).

The influence of Sherman's thinking went far beyond the Civil War. His concepts of warfare had a pronounced effect on military thought. Historian Charles Royster contends that our concept of destructive warfare in the twentieth century "all went back, along 'a straight line of logic,' to Sherman" (357). War follows its own law, Royster writes. "For Sherman that law consisted of the use of force until one side submitted to the other" (353).

Wherever guerrilla tactics were used against regular troops, warfare quickly degenerated to that level of fighting. By the beginning of 1865, it was the level of fighting applied to the South as a whole. The road to "hard war" began in the mountains. Guerrilla warfare in the Appalachians helped mold Federal military policy, setting the stage for the way the war ultimately was fought. It also contributed to violence and influenced Federal treatment of civilians elsewhere in the South along the paths of the Union armies. For the mountain people such strategic concepts were beyond their knowing or caring. All they knew was that outsiders, enemies, men in uniform, were destroying their way of life.

PART II

East Tennessee

Chapter 5

"Bleeding at Every Pore"

The outbreak of the Civil War brought sectional differences to the boiling point in Tennessee. Despite strong Confederate support in the rest of the state, East Tennessee voters rejected secession by more than two to one in June 1861. The mountain Unionists firmly believed that the state's secession vote had been rigged by wealthy slaveholders, a class they hated and distrusted, and that a planter-dominated Confederacy would make non-slaveholders second-class citizens. East Tennessee Unionists held their own convention at Greeneville, where they declared secession unconstitutional and petitioned for separate statehood (Fisher, 31–33).

Autonomy was not a new idea. From 1784 to 1788, early settlers had created the short-lived state of Franklin, never recognized by Congress and ceded to the new state of Tennessee in 1796. A new state in 1861 could have included portions of western North Carolina, northern Georgia, and even northern Alabama. The Confederate-dominated state government at Nashville rejected the idea. Realization of independence for East Tennessee was unlikely without Federal military intervention, and this did not occur until September 1863. Still, Lincoln recognized the strategic importance of the region, through which ran the main railroad line connecting Virginia with Tennessee and Georgia (Current, 29).

As the summer of 1861 unfolded, East Tennessee Unionists became more militant. Although alarmed by the Rebel victory at Manassas, Virginia, they remained firm as they formed military companies, stockpiled weapons and supplies, and prepared for confrontation with secessionists. In July, 700 Bradley County loyalists openly challenged Confederate troops, and in

August Rebel soldiers hastened to Roane County, where 300 armed men were said to be mobilizing. There were outbreaks of violence all across the region. Loyalists in Johnson and Carter Counties killed two secessionists, wounded several more, and forced many to seek refuge in North Carolina. Rebel soldiers assaulted Union men in Fentress County and in Knoxville, and attempted to kill Unionist leaders in Greeneville and Tazewell (Fisher, 41–50).

As opposition to the Confederacy began to mount in East Tennessee, the Rebel government came to regard it as a disloyal region. Duty for Confederate troops stationed there was like that of an army of occupation. Confederate commander Felix Zollicoffer, hoping eventually to win over Unionists, tried to follow a lenient policy toward local civilians, but there was to be no peace between the two factions.

In November 1861, the descent into open warfare began. William B. Carter, a Unionist and Presbyterian minister, devised an ambitious plan to cripple the Confederacy's important railroad line running through eastern Tennessee. Carter planned a surprise strike against the entire 225-mile length of the line from Bristol, Virginia, to Stevenson, Alabama. His raiders planned to capture and burn nine bridges on the railroad. Carter hoped that the raid could be coordinated with a Union army offensive from Kentucky through Cumberland Gap. Unionist uprisings in East Tennessee would keep the Rebels occupied. With the railroad bridges destroyed, Confederate forces would be unable to bring in reinforcements to stop the Yankees, and eastern Tennessee would fall into Union hands.

Carter's raiders, if successful, would knock out a vital enemy transportation link. The scheme was brought to the attention of Brigadier General George H. Thomas, passed on to Major General George B. McClellan, and ultimately reached the desk of President Lincoln, who endorsed the plan and provided $2,500 in government funds to finance the raiders (Fisher, 52–53).

The night of November 8, 1861, was set for Carter's raid. But things did not go according to plan. Fearful that Zollicoffer might launch an unexpected incursion into Kentucky, Federal commanders aborted the planned offensive into Tennessee, leaving the bridge raiders without support. Carter did not learn of this in time to cancel the operation, which went forward as scheduled on the night of November 8. The raiders burned five of the nine bridges, but four escaped damage entirely (Fisher, 53–54).

The most violent encounter took place at the Lick Creek bridge in Greene County. A raiding party led by David Fry surprised the guards and set fire to the bridge. Fry and his men abused their captives, cursing and beating them unmercifully, but the guards survived the brutal attack. Fry continued on a path of destruction further south along the railroad line between

Chattanooga and Marietta, Georgia, tearing up tracks, stealing locomotives, and cutting telegraph lines (Trotter, 211).

The attack on the Holston River bridge at Strawberry Plains had a different outcome. There ten raiders scaled a steep embankment in the dark to confront one of the two bridge sentries, mountaineer James Keelan of Thomas' North Carolina Legion. Keelan discharged his single-shot pistol into William Pickens, leader of the raiders, then took on the other nine guerrillas with his Bowie knife. The raiders fired on Keelan, who received wounds in his hip and right arm but still managed to slash away at his attackers until he either fell or jumped off the embankment. The raiders then tried to burn the bridge, but their matches were wet. With more guards on the way, the guerrillas withdrew, carrying their wounded with them (Trotter, 78–79).

Carter's bridge raid triggered isolated Unionist rebellions in eastern Tennessee, but without the anticipated Federal military invasion from Kentucky, the uncoordinated uprisings were easily quashed by Confederate troops. Carter escaped to Kentucky where he reached the camp of his brother, Union Colonel Samuel P. Carter. The most active of the raiders, David Fry, fled into the North Carolina mountains. Others, like A. M. Cate, who had burned the Hiwassee River bridge at Calhoun, managed to travel 300 miles on foot to reach sanctuary in Kentucky.

The bridge raid led to a Confederate military crackdown in eastern Tennessee. Zollicoffer declared martial law, and there were hundreds of arrests. Confederate Secretary of War Judah P. Benjamin directed, "All such as can be identified as having been engaged in bridge burning are to be tried summarily by drum-head court martial, and, if found guilty, executed on the spot by hanging. It would be well to leave their bodies hanging in the vicinity of the burned bridges" (Horn, 34).

The military arrested and hanged five men suspected of taking part in the bridge raid. The bodies of Jacob Hensie and Henry Fry—whom the Rebels may have thought to be David Fry—were left swaying from an oak tree by the side of the railroad track near Greeneville, Tennessee. Trains were instructed to slow down when passing so that riders could view the corpses. Some passengers entertained themselves by whacking the lifeless bodies with sticks or firing their guns at them. After two days the corpses had begun to decay so badly that they had to be taken down.

Failure of the uprisings in November led many East Tennessee Unionists to flee the region. Some were refugees fleeing the destruction of their homes by Rebels. Many others were determined to join the Union army in Kentucky. Refugees utilized an "underground railroad" in the mountains, a network later used by escaped Federal prisoners. To avoid detection by army patrols and by hostile Rebel civilians, they traveled at night over little-used roads and depended on experienced guides or scouts to see them through to Kentucky. Daniel Ellis, a wagon maker from Carter County, became the best known of the scouts. One of Carter's raiders, Ellis helped torch the Holston River bridge in Sullivan County. Later he fell into Rebel hands, then escaped to embark on his long career as a guide in August 1862. Ellis guided several thousand men from East Tennessee to Kentucky. He also led occasional partisan forays against Rebels in Johnson and Carter Counties. Commissioned a captain in the Union 13th Tennessee Cavalry in 1865, Ellis survived the war and escaped the fate of fellow guide Spencer Deaton, who was captured by the Rebels and hanged in 1864. Many refugees did not survive the trip, either. Ellis' discovery of the decomposed bodies of three slain loyalists in August 1863 attests to the danger of the undertaking (Fisher, 65; Ball, 56).

Although Confederate Governor Isham G. Harris had sworn that the Federal army would never get one recruit from East Tennessee, mountaineers in large numbers crossed into Kentucky to enlist. The Federal occupation of Nashville, the first Rebel capital to fall, in February 1862, prompted Lincoln to appoint Andrew Johnson as military governor. Responsible for Federal recruitment in East Tennessee, Johnson encouraged his mountain brethren to enlist. Tennessee loyalists played a significant role in helping to defeat the South, especially after Federal occupation of Knoxville in September 1863 provided them with more material support. Soldiers in Tennessee Union commands often fought actions with Rebel guerrillas.

William Clift, a well-to-do landowner from Hamilton County, raised a Unionist partisan band in the fall of 1861. Confederate forces closed in on him in November, and his group dispersed and hid in the mountains. In May 1862, Brigadier General George W. Morgan's Federal troops occupied Cumberland Gap, and Morgan commissioned Clift to raise the Union 7th Tennessee Infantry Regiment in Scott and Morgan Counties. Clift recruited about 400 men, fortified a base camp near Huntsville in Scott County and made several successful forays into Morgan and Anderson Counties that summer. His men operated in the rear of the Rebel army to disrupt communications and supplies, and they served to protect the loyalist population from Rebel guerrillas. A Rebel force of 1,200 to 2,000 men surprised Clift's camp on August 13, 1862, and routed his command. Clift's soldiers never recovered from the blow, although they remained active, skirmishing with Champ Ferguson's Rebel guerrillas in October. The 7th Tennessee was down to 258 men by the end of the year, and soon the command broke up (Civil War Centennial Commission, 390).

Many East Tennesseans chose to remain in the mountains and wage war as partisans. They ambushed Confederate troops, passed information to the Federals, and harassed Rebel civilians. Loyalist partisans fought an ideological struggle with Rebel guerrillas, fueled by bitter class division.

The goal was political control of East Tennessee; and although outsiders might not see meaning in much of their actions, the conflict made sense in a personal way to the participants. The broader issues between the Union and the Confederacy mattered not as much to the mountaineers as local grievances. Both sides fought with intense ruthlessness, and the guerrilla war in this corner of the Southern Appalachians was particularly fierce. The savage and vindictive nature of this conflict shattered communities and created bitter hostilities that lasted for generations (Fisher, 62–63).

David Beatty, known as "Tinker Dave," was the most active and colorful of the independent Unionist guerrilla chiefs. His enclave, difficult for enemies to penetrate, was a secluded mountain cove on the East Fork of the Obey River in western Fentress County. Beatty had known Champ Ferguson for a long time and was his counterpart in the region. About the same age as Ferguson, Beatty was smaller physically, but he compensated by his cunning and audacity (Sensing, 68, 72).

Beatty recounted that Rebel partisan Scott Bledsoe's men visited his home in January 1862. They looted his property and warned his wife that he had better choose sides or get out of the county. "After this," he said, "they kept running in on us every few weeks, Ferguson, Bledsoe, and others, killing and driving people off" (Sensing, 73).

About three weeks later, Tinker Dave had an encounter with Ferguson. He recalled that Ferguson and about twenty of his band—some wearing Yankee uniforms and carrying a Union flag, some in Confederate uniforms, and others in civilian clothing—rode up to his house while he was working in a field about 150 yards across the river. Beatty called out to them and asked what they wanted, and one of the guerrillas yelled back that they were looking for Captain Beatty to help them chase off some Rebels. Tinker Dave replied that "Captain Beatty" was at a log rolling at a neighbor's farm and volunteered to go fetch him. He left the Rebel horsemen waiting and conveniently failed to return. In the following weeks Beatty and his people exchanged shots with Ferguson and his men several times (Sensing, 75).

Beatty organized a company of scouts, which included his own sons, to patrol Fentress and Overton Counties in search of Confederate guerrillas. Beatty's men never officially entered Federal service, and they received no pay, but Yankee commanders provided them with arms and ammunition. In 1862 the guerrillas intercepted two wagons filled with paper for printing Confederate money being smuggled out of Kentucky, chased off the escort, and confiscated the supplies. They also fought many skirmishes with Ferguson's men. After Burnside's Federal army occupied Knoxville in September 1863, Beatty became more active in operations against Rebel communications and against Rebel guerrillas in White County. Rufus Dowdy, who hailed from the Wolf River section of northern Fentress

County, often cooperated with Beatty in actions against Ferguson's men (Civil War Centennial Commission, 413).

Beatty apparently remembered his friends as well as his enemies. Judge J. D. Goodpasture, a Confederate sympathizer, had defended Tinker Dave in circuit court in Jamestown, the Fentress County seat. Beatty repaid the favor by exempting Goodpasture from attacks by his guerrillas during the war. When Goodpasture ran across the old warrior at the end of the war, he inquired why Beatty had never raided his house. Beatty calmly replied that he simply had no business with Goodpasture (Sensing, 69).

East Tennessee abounds with stories of violent clashes between Unionists and Rebel guerrillas. Sixteen-year-old Julia Marcum of Scott County's Buffalo Creek community survived one bloody encounter when Confederate soldiers broke into her family's home in the early hours of the morning. Armed with an ax, Julia struggled with a burly Rebel soldier. When her father, an officer in the Unionist Home Guard, fired at the marauder and missed, Julia fought for her life. The soldier fired his weapon, shooting off one of Julia's fingers, then jabbed his bayonet into her forehead. Julia lost the sight in one eye, but in the struggle she killed her attacker. It took three months for Julia to recover. Two years later, Rebel guerrillas burned the Marcum home and killed Julia's cousin. This time, a bullet just grazed Julia's hair (Sanderson, 28).

Widespread destruction and suffering plagued East Tennessee, especially during the winter of 1863–1864, when two rival armies struggled for control of the region. Rebel soldiers pillaged relentlessly, but Unionists were dismayed over behavior of the Federals as well. Victimized by both armies, loyalists suffered from foraging, seizing of livestock, and destruction of their homes. "East Tennessee is bleeding at every pore," a Rebel officer reported, "and is literally eaten up" (McKenzie, 205–206). The people were "absolutely starving," wrote a Federal officer after feeding a woman with five children who had not eaten in three days. Conditions actually went from bad to worse in the spring of 1864, when the two contending armies shifted their operations to other areas, Longstreet's Confederates back to Lee's army in Virginia, the Yankees to Sherman's forces invading Georgia. The resulting power vacuum was filled by the partisan bands (McKinney, *Southern*, 22–23).

Occupation by the Union army became a signal to Confederate guerrillas to rise up, as Unionist guerrillas had done while the area was under Rebel occupation. The Rebels became more active by the summer of 1864 as they attacked Unionist households. Rebel guerrillas in the latter part of the conflict adopted the tactic of using neighboring counties across the North Carolina and Georgia lines as "sanctuaries" from which they raided Unionist targets at night (Fisher, 83).

East Tennessee was swept by savage guerrilla violence. In Johnson and Carter Counties in the northeastern corner of the state four separate guerrilla bands operated from the fall of 1863 through the winter of 1864, making life hellish for local residents. In November 1863, a pro-Confederate gang led by W. A. Witcher swept into Carter County and killed nine alleged Unionists before finally moving on. In September and October 1864, Bill Parker's Rebel Home Guards murdered eleven men in Johnson County. Parker also burned barns and homes, shot livestock, and forced scores of women and children from the county. His brutality at last led to retaliation. In the fall of 1864, a Unionist band tracked him down and killed him. But immediately two more Rebel guerrilla bands began operating under B. H. Duvall and R. C. Bozen, the latter of whom was charged with torturing and killing the Unionists he captured (Paludan, 78).

The brutal murders of two Union officers in January 1865 shocked loyalists. A band of 300 Rebel guerrillas rode into Athens, the McMinn County seat, on the night of January 28, held troops of the Federal garrison there at bay for several hours, and captured fifteen prisoners, including Major John McGaughy, the deputy provost-marshal. They stripped McGaughy of his clothing, forced him to march some twenty miles south of Athens, and then killed him. The same night Rebel partisans captured Lieutenant Colonel Joseph Divine, the deputy provost-marshal at Madisonville in neighboring Monroe County. Holed up in a cellar, Divine had killed one Rebel soldier who was sent in to get him. On their promise to treat him as a prisoner of war, Divine surrendered and gave up his weapon. The Rebels led him out of town with ropes around his neck. His mounted captors forced Divine to run from Madisonville to Good Springs in McMinn County while they prodded him with their bayonets and fired their pistols at his feet. The following morning, they beat him to death and tossed his body over a fence into a farmer's field. The killing of McGaughy and Divine were grim reminders that the region was not secure and that Rebel guerrillas were still a real threat (Barker Papers, Vol. 9).

Chapter 6

"There Are Meaner Men"

Did Champ Ferguson become unhinged because Union men brutalized his wife and daughter? The answer will never be known, and whatever dark event triggered his murderous wartime rampage will forever remain a puzzle. By the end of the war his name was better recognized than any other partisan in the Appalachians. And of all the mountain guerrillas, Ferguson was the only one whom Federal authorities would not allow to surrender. He was to be treated as an outlaw.

Ferguson was born on November 29, 1821, to a poor farm family in Clinton County, Kentucky, just a few miles north of the Tennessee line. The oldest of ten children, Champ was named after his grandfather, Champion. He received very little education and remembered going to school for only about three months. He married his first wife, Ann Eliza Smith, when he was 22 years old in 1843. Three years later both Ann Eliza and the couple's only child died. Champ married again in 1848 to Martha Owens, who gave birth to a daughter, a second Ann, 12 years old at the start of the war. According to witnesses, Champ was very loving to his wife and daughter (Sensing, 2).

Ferguson was a rough, muscular mountaineer, over six feet tall, with jet black hair and beard. According to Rebel officer Basil W. Duke, his most striking features were a pair of fierce and penetrating black eyes; the iris and pupil of his eyes were so closely matched in color that they blended, and the resulting appearance was startling (182). Nearly 40 years old when the war started, Ferguson had been a farmer and a hunter all his life and was well acquainted with the Cumberland Mountains along the

Kentucky-Tennessee border. Champ was said to enjoy his liquor, and he could shoot, ride, and brawl with the best of his contemporaries. Loyal to his friends and vengeful to his enemies, he was not the kind of man that one wanted for an adversary. He could hold a serious grudge for a long time, and he was known to have bad feelings toward his younger brother, Jim, who sided with the Union (Sensing, 3, 6, 9–11).

His first documented murder occurred in Clinton County in November 1861. According to newspaper interviews given by Ferguson after his 1865 murder trial, he had received word that a Union sympathizer named William Frogg was out to kill him. Ferguson rode to Frogg's cabin, where Frogg's wife was sitting at the door peeling apples. Ferguson entered the house, found Frogg sick in bed, and calmly fired two bullets into him. No words were spoken. Frogg's wife was unharmed, as was Jack Mace, a witness who happened to be in the house. Ferguson just rode away. He told reporters that he felt totally justified in killing Frogg (Sensing, 82).

Frogg's death was the first of a long string of apparently senseless killings committed by Champ Ferguson during the war. The lack of a clear motive for Frogg's murder—other than Champ's deeming him a Union man—and the fact that he spared Mace, helped give rise to the legend that Ferguson had embarked on a vindictive quest to kill every one of the eleven men who had taken part in the humiliation of his wife and daughter. But whether Frogg—or any of Ferguson's other victims—were among the men that he supposedly targeted for death is not known.

The bloody hand of Ferguson struck out again the following month. At sunset on December 4, 1861, Ferguson and two companions rode up to the home of 60-year-old Reuben Wood near Albany, Kentucky. When they saw Wood, a Union man, in front of the house, Ferguson reined in his horse, accused Wood of being a "damned old Lincolnite," and whipped out his pistol. "Don't you beg," he told Wood, "and don't you dodge." Ignoring the pleas of Wood's wife and daughter, he fired one shot that hit the old man in the stomach and another shot that missed. Clutching his belly, Wood stumbled around the side of the house and through the back door. Ferguson dismounted and ran after him. The two men struggled inside the cabin, and Wood tried to fend Ferguson off with a hatchet. In the scuffle Ferguson lost his pistol and fled, and Wood managed to crawl upstairs. Wood's wife and daughter, who had run away from the house in terror, returned to find the intruders gone and Wood sitting by the fireplace. When his son Robert arrived that night, Wood told him that Ferguson had shot him and that he wouldn't last long. Wood died two days later (Sensing, 83–86).

As the violence of partisan clashes intensified, pro-Union and pro-Confederate citizens on both sides of the border—in Fentress County in Tennessee and Clinton County in Kentucky—attempted to reach an understanding early in 1862 to stop the killing. The agreement broke down, and the entire region was torn by bloody bushwhacking throughout the war. Ferguson played a major part in the violence.

Ferguson killed four members of the pro-Union Zachery family, some of whom served with Tinker Dave Beatty's guerrillas. The first of these victims was 16-year-old Fount Zachery, killed on April 1, 1862, near Albany. The Rebels caught Zachery, who may have mistaken them for Federals, coming out of an ivy thicket. A member of the patrol testified at Ferguson's 1865 trial that after the prisoner had handed over his gun and was removing his shot pouch, someone asked him his name. When he replied that he was Fount Zachery, Ferguson shot him. Zachery fell from his horse, and Ferguson jumped off his horse and finished the boy with his knife (Sensing, 98).

Ferguson gave his version of the incident to newspaper reporters. He confessed to shooting and stabbing Fount Zachery, but he said the Rebs were expecting a fight with Unionist guerrillas that night and had orders to shoot any suspicious person on sight. "I shot him on sight," he explained, "in obedience to orders." Ferguson neglected to mention that Zachery had already surrendered his weapon (Sensing, 99).

On May 2, 1862, Ferguson and his men gunned down Alex Huff across the Tennessee state line in Fentress County. A witness who hid during the gunfire testified that he heard a shot followed by Huff crying and praying for several minutes more while some dozen or more gunshots rang out. He heard voices of several women in the house begging Ferguson and his men not to kill Huff. Then another shot, and there was silence. This seemed to be another Ferguson grudge killing. Preston Huff, the victim's son, recalled an unpleasant encounter with Ferguson earlier in December 1861 in which the drunken mountaineer threatened to kill members of Huff's family. He had never been on close terms with Ferguson, but he had always been cordial with him before the incident. "After that," he said, "I didn't like him much" (Sensing, 105–106).

As border bushwhacking intensified, Ferguson moved his wife and daughter to Sparta in pro-Rebel White County, Tennessee. Meanwhile, he recruited men in Fentress County and became the captain of an independent Confederate command that may have numbered as high as 600 at its peak. Details of his early activities are shadowy. He rode with Colonel John Hunt Morgan's 2nd Kentucky Cavalry on his raids in Tennessee and Kentucky. Ferguson was closely linked with Confederate partisans Oliver P. Hamilton, Willis Scott Bledsoe, and John M. Hughs. These Rebel chiefs fought a vindictive territorial war with Union guerrillas Tinker Dave Beatty, Rufus Dowdy, and Elam Huddleston (Civil War Centennial Commission, 15).

In July 1862 Morgan launched his first cavalry raid into Kentucky. His horsemen left Knoxville on July 4 and two days later reached Sparta, where Ferguson joined them as a guide. While Morgan's raiders hit Union communications lines in Kentucky and Tennessee in July and August, General Braxton Bragg prepared to invade the Bluegrass State. The Confederate offensive began in September but burned out after the inconclusive battle of Perryville on October 8. Basil W. Duke, Morgan's second in command, wrote that Ferguson "had the reputation of never giving quarter, and, no doubt, deserved it (when upon his own private expeditions), although when with Morgan he attempted no interference with prisoners" (182).

Ferguson may have scouted for Morgan, but he was always a lone wolf at heart, and in October 1862, he seemed more inclined toward settling private scores with Tennessee Unionists. Early that month Ferguson and his men conducted a midnight raid on the Unionist Huff household in Fentress County and took three men—John Williams, David Delk, and John Crabtree—captive. As the guerrillas tied the men's hands behind their backs, Delk pleaded for them not to tie him up so tight, that the ropes were hurting him. Ferguson replied, "Damn you, that's what we want to do—we want to hurt you." After looting the home, the marauders rode away with their three prisoners and a black servant girl. They arrived at the home of William Piles, about a mile away, at daylight (Sensing, 121–123).

Piles' wife and daughters watched with dread as Ferguson and his men rode slowly into the barnyard. As they led their captives toward the stable, the guerrillas ordered the women into the house. A few minutes later the Piles women heard three gunshots. The guerrillas told them that they had killed the prisoners, then they rode away (Sensing, 121–123).

The women found the victims' bodies near the stable. A gunshot at close range had taken off part of Williams' skull. Delk was stabbed and shot in the chest. Crabtree lay mutilated with knife wounds, and someone had also shoved a corn stalk into his back. The three prisoners had been tortured before they were killed. It was a particularly cold-blooded and grisly murder (Sensing, 121–123).

George and William Thrasher, two Clinton County men who had joined a Union cavalry outfit, were unlucky enough to fall into the hands of Ferguson and his guerrillas in October 1862. William later testified that Ferguson asked him if he didn't think he should kill him. When Thrasher replied that he thought it would be difficult to shoot an unarmed man, Ferguson responded that it really wouldn't, that in fact it might help to shorten the war if he executed every prisoner he captured. While they were leading the two brothers across Wash Tabor's property, they encountered Tabor himself and took him captive as well. While Tabor was begging for his life, Ferguson drew his pistol and shot him through the heart. When the victim fell, another guerrilla cried, "Damn him, shoot him in the head." Ferguson obliged, leaning down and putting a bullet through Tabor's head. Ferguson later said, "He had killed three of my men a few days previous. . . . He ought to have been killed sooner." The Thrashers were spared a similar fate when a band of eighty Unionist guerrillas led by Elam Huddleston appeared and scattered the Rebels. The brothers escaped in the confusion (Sensing, 118–120).

Unionist partisans wanted to bring Ferguson to bay. Tinker Dave Beatty was a prosecution witness against Ferguson in his 1865 murder trial, but surprisingly Champ seemed to bear no grudge against him even though the two had been mortal enemies all through the war. When asked his opinion of Beatty, Ferguson replied, "Well, there are meaner men than Tinker Dave. . . . I always gave him as good as he sent. I have nothing against Tinker Dave" (Sensing, 71).

But in the kill-or-be-killed mentality of the partisan chiefs, the opportunity to eliminate an enemy was too good to resist. Witnesses accused Ferguson of murdering Tinker Dave's son, Dallas Beatty, in February 1864. Rufus Dowdy testified to a general understanding among the Unionist guerrillas that they would kill Ferguson if they could capture him. But Ferguson struck first. On New Year's Night, 1863, he and his men surprised Elam Huddleston at his home and after a lengthy gun battle shot him in the head and in the back. Ferguson also captured Huddleston's brother and cousin and forced them to lead him to Rufus Dowdy's home. Dowdy, who was away, escaped the fate of Huddleston, but Ferguson and his men killed two more members of the Zachery family who were there, one of them sick in bed (Sensing, 132–137, 163, 204).

In the early part of 1863 Ferguson's guerrillas were steadily drawn into an escalating war of savagery in Kentucky and Tennessee, with neither side giving quarter. At times the guerrillas were said to raise a black flag as a sign that they would take no prisoners. Ferguson's name surfaced frequently in Federal army reports as his activities increasingly led him into skirmishes with Union troops. The Federals played a frustrating game of hide-and-seek with the elusive partisan.

Meanwhile, John Hunt Morgan launched a spectacular but largely fruitless raid into Ohio. On July 2, 1863, he left Burkesville, Kentucky, with around 2,500 men, captured Lebanon on July 5, crossed the Ohio River at Brandenburg on July 9, and raided through the Indiana and Ohio countryside, threatening Cincinnati. The raid ended with Morgan's capture on July 26. He was imprisoned along with most of his men, but in November he staged a daring breakout and returned to Confederate service. The colorful raider was finally killed in a skirmish with Union troops in Tennessee in September 1864.

In the fall of 1863, Ferguson became associated with the guerrilla campaigns of Colonel John M. Hughs. The 32-year-old Hughs, commander of the 25th Tennessee Infantry, was a farmer from Overton County. When the war began he was totally lacking in military training; but he was athletic, a natural leader, and an excellent shot. Like another famous Southern commander, Nathan Bedford Forrest, he enlisted as a private, but soon he became a lieutenant and rapidly advanced to colonel of the 25th Tennessee. He joined Bragg's invasion of Kentucky in September 1862, fought at Perryville on October 8, and a head injury put him out of action at Murfreesboro on December 31. After recovering, Hughs took part in several actions in the summer of 1863 in southeastern Tennessee (Siburt, 87–88).

In August 1863 Hughs began independent guerrilla operations. Bragg authorized him to take twenty men into middle Tennessee "for the purpose of collecting absentees . . . and with authority . . . to enforce conscription." He was supposed to return to Chattanooga when his mission was completed. But in September the Federals advanced into East Tennessee, and in November Grant defeated Bragg and made Chattanooga a Union base. With his command separated from the Confederate army, Hughs concluded, "The least we could employ ourselves at was operating against the enemy, whose presence had greatly emboldened the Union tories, and they were becoming very troublesome—going in bands, robbing and murdering citizens and soldiers. To furnish these villains with a little fighting was necessary" (Nicholson, 47).

Hughs' band of irregulars grew to over 100 men who he later admitted "came and went pretty much as they pleased." He carried out a bold, predawn raid on a Federal army post at Glasgow, Kentucky, on October 6. The Rebels killed 35 enemy soldiers, captured 266 men and 200 horses, as well as a vast quantity of supplies, and destroyed a considerable amount of property. Major Samuel Martin, the Federal commander at Glasgow, accused Hughs' men of looting stores, of robbing a bank of $9,000, and of shooting and killing two unarmed soldiers. Next came attacks on Federal posts at Monticello and Scottsville, where Hughs' men captured 500 stands of arms and other equipment. Federal authorities also accused them of looting stores in Columbia, and Hughs' command was making a bad reputation for itself (Siburt, 88–89, 91–92).

It was about this time that Scott Bledsoe and Champ Ferguson appear to have linked up with Hughs. Bledsoe, a successful 25-year-old attorney from Jamestown in Fentress County, was a seasoned partisan chieftain. His independent command was operating as part of Colonel Baxter Smith's 8th Tennessee Cavalry and had—like Hughs—been separated from the main Rebel army. Ferguson apparently was running amuck with no particular affiliation. Events of the following months led the three Rebel partisan leaders, and a few other guerrilla chiefs as well, to join forces for operations against Federal troops in Tennessee.

The onset of bitterly cold weather brought little respite in the guerrilla war. Hughs faced the increasing aggressiveness of Federal commanders, exasperated by their failure to contain the guerrillas. Brigadier General E. H. Hobson reported from Munfordville, Kentucky, on December 12, that his patrols had fought four engagements with the Rebels and had captured or killed a number of Ferguson's men. "What shall I do with prisoners?" he asked, "They are the meanest of Ferguson's guerrillas. Would it not be well to have them shot?" Hobson felt the "no prisoners" policy brought some results, for he reported on December 22: "I have at last succeeded in alarming the rebels, south of the Cumberland River. My orders to scouting parties sent over the river to take no prisoners has had a good effect. Communication from rebel Colonel Hughs complains of my order, and says that I should not hold him responsible for the conduct of Ferguson, Richardson, and Hamilton, and the cause of his now being in Tennessee is that he cannot get out" (USWD, I, 31, i: 601–602; I, 31, iii: 469).

On January 20, 1864, Bledsoe and his men raided the Federal railroad post at Tracy City in Grundy County and gunned down Captain Stephen P. Tipton, commander of the Unionist scouts stationed there. The raid may have been inspired by the activities of Cal Brixey, an officer of the Union scouts. Brixey, a Tennessee deserter, had terrorized Grundy County for some time doing to Confederates what Ferguson was doing to Union people, killing on the slightest suspicion (Blevins, 64–65).

In February 1864, Federal troops rode into White County, which they considered a Rebel stronghold. Ferguson's home was there, and Morgan used Sparta, the county seat, as a base when he raided into Kentucky. A local woman wrote, "The Rebels are gone and the Yanks are in. They take it time about, and one does about as much good as the other. And we could do very well without either" (DeLozier, 42).

The bluecoats were the 5th Tennessee Cavalry under Colonel William B. Stokes. Called "Wild Bill of the Hills," Stokes lost a hand during the war and replaced it with a brass ball. The 5th Tennessee (also called the 1st Middle Tennessee Cavalry) was chosen particularly for operations against the Rebel guerrillas. The regiment had a good reputation at first, with detachments taking part in fighting at Murfreesboro, Chickamauga, and Chattanooga. Later the 5th Tennessee Cavalry was regarded as an ineffective and poorly disciplined command. In January 1864 Major General George H. Thomas recommended that the regiment be disbanded. Stokes blamed many of the unit's problems on lack of decent mounts and bombarded Brigadier General W. Sooey Smith, the cavalry chief, with requests for fresh horses and rifles. Smith told him, "horses are absolutely out of the question.

You must find and take them in the country you traverse. . . . Now pitch in, Colonel, and help yourself to horses, keep your powder dry, and give the guerrillas thunder wherever you can find them" (Mason, 54–55).

Stokes' troops hit Ferguson's farm near the Calfkiller River, surprising twenty or thirty Rebel guerrillas who quickly scattered. Stokes reported his men "killed 17 of the worst men in the country . . . known to have been engaged in murder, robbery, and rape." After occupying and fortifying Sparta on February 18, Stokes prepared for a Rebel counterattack, reporting, "Colonel Hughs' command is well armed, having secured the best of arms when on their raids into Kentucky. They number at least 600 fighting men" (USWD, I, 32, i: 162, 416).

On February 22, Stokes sent an eighty-man cavalry patrol along the Calfkiller River. Hughs and Ferguson with a force of about forty men awaited them. When they reached Dry Valley, the Federal troopers spotted two Rebel riders ahead of them in the Dug Hill Road. They gave chase, and the Rebels spurred their horses and ran. The bluecoats were drawn into a cunningly prepared ambush. Firing from the cover of rocks and underbrush on the hill overlooking the road, Rebel guerrillas poured a deadly hail of lead down at the trapped Federals. John Gatewood, a particularly brutal guerrilla, was preparing to shoot three Yankee prisoners when his comrade George Carter rode up and stopped him, telling him not to waste precious ammunition. He grinned and handed Gatewood a heavy rock. When Union troops recovered the bodies of their comrades killed by the guerrillas they found thirty men dead of gunshot wounds but three more whose heads had been crushed by stones (Sensing, 165, 168, 169).

A Rebel composer wrote a ballad about the encounter:

> Old George Carter said you better not spend your lead.
> Pick up a rock and knock 'em in the head.   (DeLozier, 43)

Stokes and Hughs pointed fingers at each other about the level of violence at Dug Hill. Stokes charged that the Rebels killed several of his men after they surrendered, adding "Hughs himself does not allow this barbarity, but his subordinate officers practice it." Hughs complained that Stokes' men "had refused to treat us as prisoners of war, and had murdered several of our men whom they had caught straggling from their command." Wild Bill alleged that many Rebels in the Dug Hill ambush had also worn Federal uniforms. He accused the people in White County of being disloyal and of aiding the Rebel guerrillas. And he renewed his request for horses for his command, arguing that the guerrillas had stolen what few were available in the county and they had faster horses than his men (USWD, I, 32, i: 416–417, 55).

The Rebel guerrillas seemed on an offensive. On March 14, Hughs and Bledsoe initiated operations against the Nashville and Chattanooga Railroad. They struck southwest into Franklin County where they destroyed a bridge over the Elk River and caused a train to derail. But on their way back, Stokes' troops surprised them near Beersheba Springs in Grundy County. The Federals overran the Rebel camp on March 18, catching the guerrillas off guard while many of them were sleeping and the rest were cooking breakfast. They killed seven guerrillas and routed Hughs' command. The guerrillas abandoned horses, supplies, and Hughs' personal papers. Stokes gloated, "Hughs' command is scattered over the entire country, no 10 of his men being together. They are merely trying to keep out of my way" (Siburt, 91).

The defeat caused Hughs to reconsider the wisdom of continuing his guerrilla operations. He decided to divide his command into small parties and set out to rejoin Confederate forces across the mountains in Georgia. Hughs and Bledsoe, with as many of their men who could get through, reached Dalton, Georgia, on April 20. Ferguson continued to operate on his own in Tennessee (Siburt, 91).

By August 1864, the Yankees were putting increasing pressure on Ferguson. Rufus Dowdy and his guerrillas raided Ferguson's home near Sparta late in the month and burned it. Ferguson decided the time had come to pull out. Following the example of Hughs and Bledsoe, Ferguson and his men withdrew from White County and reported to General Joseph Wheeler with the Rebel army in Georgia. The guerrilla chief served with Wheeler for less than a month, then he was transferred to southwestern Virginia to join General John C. Breckinridge (Sensing, 176).

Ferguson surfaced again during an October 1864 Federal initiative against Saltville, Virginia. The guerrillas took part in the engagement on October 2, and hard-fighting George Carter was killed. After the Union troops withdrew, their wounded soldiers left on the field fell into the hands of the Confederates.

Emory and Henry College at Emory, Virginia, was converted into a military hospital. Federal casualties were placed on the third and fourth floors. On October 2, Ferguson rode up to the hospital with about a dozen of his guerrillas and entered the building as if they knew exactly where they were going and why.

The guerrillas discovered that armed guards were posted at the foot of each stairway leading to the upper floors. After being turned away by the guard at one stairway, they walked to the other, jumped the soldier stationed there, and disarmed him. Then they ascended the stairs to the ward where a Lieutenant Smith of the 13th Kentucky Cavalry lay wounded. According to witnesses, Ferguson sought out Smith at once, sat next to him on his bed, and pulled out his revolver. "Smith," he said, pointing the gun at him, "do you see this? Well, I'm going to kill you."

Without even waiting for a reply, Ferguson leveled the revolver at Smith's head and blew part of his skull off. Then he calmly walked away. A Rebel quartermaster sergeant, alarmed by the sound of gunfire, rushed in to investigate. Smith was lying dead in his bed, with his brains seeping out onto his pillow (Sensing, 178–182).

Major William Stringfield of Thomas' Legion had stopped at the Emory hospital that day to see his sister Sarah, who was working there. Startled by gunfire coming from the fourth floor, Stringfield and Dr. L. B. Murfree, the chief surgeon, dashed into the building to investigate. Stringfield recalled, "I was soon at the foot of the first stairway confronting several men armed with Colt revolvers." He demanded to know who posted them there, and one of them replied, "Captain Ferguson." Stringfield pushed his way past the guerrillas and raced up the stairs to the fourth floor, where he heard several more pistol shots. Ferguson was there. "I recognized him and at once confronted him," Stringfield related, and told him, "Captain Ferguson, this is hellish work. I know you sir, and I tell you, you can do no more now."

Stringfield ordered Ferguson to leave at once. Ferguson aimed his Colt revolver at Stringfield's chest. Tense seconds ticked away as the unarmed young officer faced down the dangerous bushwhacker. "He looked like a tiger at bay," Stringfield wrote, "then abruptly turned upon his heel and rushed downstairs" (Crow, 98–99).

Ferguson's murder trial never revealed why the ruthless guerrilla had singled out Smith for killing. Some held Smith responsible for the death of Champ's associate, Oliver P. Hamilton, who was shot and killed by his guards—while, trying to escape, according to Smith—in March 1864. Others said Smith had been the leader of the Union men who had invaded Ferguson's home and abused his wife and daughter, a story that was never verified (Sensing, 184).

Prosecution witnesses at Ferguson's trial also accused him of killing twelve white Union soldiers and two black soldiers after the action at Saltville. A Union veteran testified that the morning after the battle, he saw Ferguson shooting wounded soldiers as they lay on the ground. He crawled away and hid, but his mate was not so lucky. In a chilling account of what happened next, he told of how Ferguson walked up to his partner and demanded why he had come to fight with the "damned niggers." He raised his revolver and asked the soldier, "Where will you have it, in the back or in the face?" Ignoring the terrified bluecoat's pleas for mercy, Ferguson leveled his revolver at the man. Ferguson's gun roared, and the soldier was dead (Sensing, 185).

Ferguson denied any part in the massacre of the soldiers at Saltville. But he did admit to the murder of Lieutenant Smith at the Emory and Henry Hospital and said he had a good reason for doing so. He accused Smith of killing several of his band at various times during the war. "I will say this much," he added, "he never insulted my wife or daughter, as reported." Ferguson identified Smith as a kinsman of his first wife and said he had always been courteous to his family. He insisted Smith was the only man he killed at Saltville and repeated, "I am not sorry for killing him" (Sensing, 188).

While many of Ferguson's wartime victims probably were bushwhackers themselves, Lieutenant Smith was a commissioned officer in the U.S. Army murdered while a prisoner of war and while helpless in a hospital bed. Federal commanders especially marked Ferguson after this. Major General Stephen G. Burbridge wrote in February 1865, "Should he or any of the band that accompanied him on this occasion fall into the hands of U.S. forces they will not be treated as prisoners." Major General Lovell Rousseau ordered on May 16, "Champ Ferguson and his gang of cut-throats having refused to surrender are denounced as outlaws, and the military forces of the district will deal with them and treat them accordingly" (USWD, I, 49, i: 765; ii: 806).

After the murder of Smith, Ferguson rejoined Wheeler's cavalry in the Carolinas, but it was not long before Confederate authorities caught up with him. He was arrested for Smith's murder on February 8, 1865, and confined in the Wytheville jail in Virginia for two months. But the Rebels weren't too eager to pursue the matter. As the Confederacy disintegrated, there were more pressing matters to attend to than the case of Champ Ferguson. On April 5, 1865, they turned him loose (Sensing, 14, 189).

Apparently Ferguson operated for a short time in the Old Dominion. George Stoneman reported on April 28, "Champ Ferguson is in command of Southwestern Virginia" (Civil War Centennial Commission, 16). But with the war lost, the bloody guerrilla finally returned to Tennessee and made one more attempt to settle scores with his old wartime nemesis Tinker Dave Beatty. Around May 1, Ferguson and several of his men surprised and captured Beatty at a home in Fentress County. As the party rode away, Tinker Dave suddenly bolted from the group and made his escape in a shower of lead. Wounded three times—in the back, shoulder, and hip—Beatty outrode the Rebels and regained his freedom (Sensing, 76).

Ferguson's reign of terror came to an end on May 26, 1865. Lieutenant Colonel Joseph H. Blackburn of the 5th Tennessee Cavalry captured the unresisting guerrilla at his home near Sparta. Ferguson evidently did not realize he was to be treated as an outlaw and expressed surprise at being arrested. He could have taken to the Cumberland Mountains or gone west.

He boasted later, "I could have kept out of their hands for ten years and never left White County" (Sensing, 1, 13).

Ferguson was taken to Nashville on May 29 and was confined in the military prison there. Tennessee Unionists and Federal soldiers breathed a sigh of relief at the news of his capture. Brigadier General William D. Whipple wrote to General George H. Thomas on May 30, "The capture of Champ Ferguson and surrender of his guerrillas has restored complete quiet to Overton and Fentress Counties" (USWD, I, 49, ii: 931).

Champ Ferguson's trial began in Nashville on July 11 and lasted to mid-September 1865. The trial was covered extensively by the press, and a surprising amount of public support for Ferguson materialized. No matter how bloody his deeds, many in the defeated South saw him as a victim of Yankee vengeance. The chief counsel for the defense was Jo Conn Guild, one of the ablest lawyers in Tennessee. Champ was tried by a military court presided over by Major Collin Ford, with Captain H. C. Blackman of the 42nd U.S. Colored Infantry as the prosecuting attorney. Ferguson was charged with fifty-three counts of murder (Sensing, 25–29).

Looking formidable but hardly the larger-than-life monster of popular lore, Ferguson sat impassively through the trial, while the prosecution produced a string of witnesses that included family members of his victims as well as former antagonists Tinker Dave Beatty and Rufus Dowdy. The prosecutor intended to show that Champ not only committed cold-blooded murders of unarmed prisoners, but that he was in fact an outlaw without any official Confederate army status.

The defense's strategy was to show that Champ Ferguson had been regularly enlisted into the Confederate Army, and therefore his actions had been those of a soldier under orders. Their major witness was former Confederate Major General Joseph Wheeler. Highly credible and respected, Wheeler testified that Ferguson and his men operated under orders as guerrillas and that Champ was a regular Confederate officer with the rank of captain. Wheeler said, "It was customary when a man was authorized to raise a company, and did so, to regard him as an officer" (Sensing, 208–211).

The prosecutor addressed the former general: "You say you heard of him as a Captain as far back as 1862. Will you state whether there were any orders issued by you or your government, to your knowledge, authorizing the shooting or killing of men after they had surrendered or when captured and disarmed?" After the court overruled a defense objection, Wheeler answered, "No, sir, there were no such orders issued" (Sensing, 213).

On October 10, 1865, the court found Ferguson guilty and sentenced him to be hanged. The execution would take place on October 20 in the prison.

During the next few days, Ferguson granted interviews to the press and told his side of the story. Out of curiosity, reporters asked him about his views on religion. He looked up, almost cracked a smile, and asked them if they were joking. "Well," he replied, "I believe that there is a God, who governs and rules the universe, and that we are all held responsible for our acts in this world." The old outlaw maintained that God was on his side and would bring him through his troubles (Sensing, 7).

As his execution approached, Ferguson appeared composed and resigned to his fate. He asked for a bottle of brandy, and for most of the day before the hanging he was allowed to spend time with his wife, Martha, and his daughter, Ann. On the morning of his execution, Ferguson gave his last statement to the press. "I was a Southern man at the start," he said. "I am yet, and will die a Rebel. I believe I was right in all I did." While not denying that he had killed a great number of men, Ferguson maintained that he never killed anyone who was not out to kill him. He insisted that the charge that he never took prisoners was false and that he would have proved it during his trial if he had been given more time. The old guerrilla accused the Federals of killing every member of his band that they captured and said he understood the enemy would shoot him down if they could take him. For this reason, he explained, he killed more men that he normally would have. He concluded by making his last request: that he be buried in White County, Tennessee, in "good Rebel soil" (Sensing, 250–251).

Before he was led away to be hanged, Ferguson shared a brief farewell with his wife and daughter, a moment of unexpected tenderness for one who had shown so little of it during the war. Martha held his hand for a fleeting moment and then turned away. Champ held 16-year-old Ann in his arms, with her head cradled on his chest (Sensing, 250–251).

Although his supporters held out hope for a last-minute reprieve from President Andrew Johnson, it was not to be. Champ Ferguson was hanged on October 20, 1865. To the very end he never showed the least remorse for the things he had done. Before the hangman's rope was placed around his neck, a witness wrote, Ferguson listened impassively as the charges against him were read aloud. The mountaineer nodded in agreement to some of the charges, but mostly he simply stood with his eyes fixed on his boots. At one point in the recitation of charges he mumbled, "I could tell it better than that" (Nashville *Tennessean*, August 7, 1932).

Chapter 7

Community at the Breaking Point

Under the onslaught of military invasion and guerrilla violence, the social and political fabric of the mountain communities broke down. Courthouses were looted or burned, and local justices of the peace suspended their operations indefinitely. Newspaper offices were trashed. Even church services were not immune to violence; armed men sometimes broke in on meetings to seize or kill those they considered their enemies. Government services came to a standstill, and mail was not delivered. Even the few mountain roads deteriorated (DeLozier, 44).

The strain that the war put on the mountain communities stretched them to the breaking point. Although isolated, mountain farms were never completely self-sufficient. Farmers often required the services of millers, blacksmiths, tanners, and shoemakers. When such craftsmen went into the army, the community suffered the loss of their key skills. Since the family was the basic unit of production in mountain communities, the absence of any member of the family brought great hardship. Sons or husbands no longer at home—because they had enlisted or been conscripted, or were riding with guerrillas, or been killed—handicapped the family and the community as well. When a wife died, the results were just as destructive. State resources were not sufficient to relieve the suffering. The community as a whole broke down when the economy ceased to function (McKinney, "Economy," 167–171, 177–178).

The guerrilla war halted the economic progress many communities in the mountains had achieved in the 1850s. Historians Kenneth Noe (" 'Appalachia's,' " 103), Robert Tracy McKenzie (218–219), and Durwood Dunn

(125, 140–141) studied the effects of the guerrilla war on West Virginia and East Tennessee. They believe the destruction brought by the war wrecked the region's economy and laid the groundwork for poverty and commercial exploitation.

The most serious impact the guerrilla war had on mountain society was the creation of bitterly divisive hatreds that shattered families, neighborhoods, and whole communities and led to savage atrocities unknown before. The result was a breakdown of the fine line that separated what was acceptable in conventional war and what was not sanctioned by civilized society. Antebellum Southerners resolved disputes in ways ranging from duels to rough-and-tumble brawls, and they accepted a level of violence in their society that would not be condoned today (Gorn, 18–43). But the excesses of the mountain war intensified a hardness that made killing easy and made possible atrocities like the Shelton Laurel Massacre and the murder spree of Champ Ferguson (Sarris, "Anatomy," 680; Fisher, 62–63).

In a guerrilla war, hatred could consume noncombatants too—men, women, and children. A Tennessee mountain woman, Amanda Burns, wrote, "They who were once united in the strongest bonds of friendship are now ready to kill each other, only waiting for the word from their leaders. God pity the poor soldiers, and forgive those who have caused all this." Another Tennessee woman could not contain her rage and hatred after Rebel guerrillas viciously murdered and mutilated her sweetheart. Livernia Webb wrote, "Now for this, I resolved to have revenge." She sought out the leader of the Confederate marauders. When she finally confronted him at her sister-in-law's home, she produced a pistol, shot the man in the head, and stayed to watch him die. Before she rode away, she told his wife that she did not regret killing him (DeLozier, 44–45).

The mountain war brought some communities together. In the Smoky Mountains, the secluded enclave of Cades Cove, Tennessee, became identified as a stronghold of Unionism. A leading voice in the community was John Oliver, the earliest white settler in the cove. Oliver once had served under Andrew Jackson and clung strongly to the Jacksonian vision of union. A few younger men in Cades Cove, perhaps influenced by pro-Confederate family members still living in Georgia or the Carolinas, decided to support the Rebels. Most of the cove's young men either chose to enlist in the Union army or joined local draft dodgers hiding out in the hills. Unfortunately, this deprived the community of the manpower to defend it from attack (Dunn, 128–129).

Generally the men of some wealth in the community were pro-Confederate. Daniel D. Foute, justice of the peace and postmaster, had guided development of the cove's economy before the war. An open Rebel sympathizer, he now became an object of distrust and hatred to his less well-to-do neighbors. Curran Lemons, also a justice of the peace, was a Rebel supporter, but Dr. Calvin Post, another prominent cove leader, became an outspoken Union man (Dunn, 129–131, 138).

The war brought hardships to the cove, food shortages, and the inevitable Confederate demands for military manpower. In 1863, Rebel guerrillas from North Carolina began raiding the cove from across the border, bringing with them terror and deprivations. The impact of the raids fell harder on Cades Cove than on any other part of Blount County. One resident wrote, "They would make raids into Tennessee for the purpose of robbing the people of their horses, cattle, and goods, and would never fail to murder all the Union men they could find, and appropriate their property for their own use." The cove people were afraid to be seen trying to store food in the daytime for fear that the raiders would confiscate it (Dunn, 128, 131, 134).

Although committed to the Confederate cause, Foute had a hard time justifying the Rebel brutality, and he once stepped in to save a young man from being dragged off by impressment officers. Still the Union people of the cove were shocked when Foute and Curran, their local justices whom they had respected and depended upon, actively aided the Rebel guerrillas (Dunn, 130–131, 139).

Although Union troops had occupied Knoxville, the isolated cove received no help from the Federal army. Maryville, the county seat, was too far away, and the local justice system had ceased to function. The raiders had offered a reward for Union spokesman Calvin Post, dead or alive, forcing him into hiding. Old John Oliver had died after a lingering illness on February 15, 1863. Finally sheer desperation led some of the old men of Cades Cove to resist.

Russell Gregory, a local rancher and herdsman, was one of the cove's most respected Unionists. Too old to enlist in the Union army, Gregory was outraged when his son Charles disgraced him by joining the Confederates. Bitter and in poor health, he became a recluse, resolving to sit out the war in his stone house on Gregory Bald. But when Rebel guerrillas raided the Primitive Baptist Church where he was a member and ran off the minister, it was the last straw for Gregory (Dunn, 134–135).

Gregory and other members of the church took the lead in organizing a Unionist Home Guard in the spring of 1864. They set up a warning system to alert the cove people to the approach of raiders. While the old men drilled, women and children manned lookout posts at the mountain passes where the Rebels would enter the valley. Suddenly the community was pulling together (Dunn, 135).

The strategy paid off. When Rebel guerrillas led by DeWitt Ghormley were spotted entering the cove, Gregory prepared an ambush for the raiders near the forks of Forge and Abrams Creeks. When the raiders reached the site with a herd of stolen horses and cattle, the Union men greeted them with rifle fire from behind a log barricade. The skirmish was over in a matter of minutes. Ghormley and one other guerrilla were wounded, and the raiders withdrew, abandoning their stolen livestock and goods. None of the Union men were hurt.

There also was an ironic twist to the encounter. Russell Gregory did not know that his son Charles was riding with the raiders that day. About half a mile from the ambush site, Charles' sister met the Rebels and pulled her brother aside to ask him about relatives in North Carolina. Although he was eager to catch up with his companions, his sister held tight to his horse's reins, keeping him from being caught in the ambush. When he heard gunfire from the direction of the barricade, the first shot was the unmistakable sound of "Old Long Tom," Russell's rifle. "There goes Old Long Tom," Charles cried, breaking away, "and my old Daddy is at the breech." But when he reached his comrades, the fight was over and they were retreating (Dunn, 135–136).

Cove Unionists were elated, and their spirits soared. They had stood up to the guerrillas and had won. Two local sisters composed a ballad that began:

> I'd rather be a Union man, and carry a Union gun
> Than be a Ghormley man, and steal a cow and run!

> (Dunn, 135–136)

The skirmish with the guerrillas did not end the raids on Cades Cove, but much of the Rebels' boldness had been taken out of them. They were especially anxious to have revenge on Russell Gregory. A couple of weeks later, the Rebels made a nighttime attack on the old warrior's home and killed him as he was getting out of bed. Far from quelling resistance, the murder only made Gregory more of a hero in the eyes of the cove people and inspired them to continue the fight.

As the war turned around for the Union, the cove people reclaimed their community, and Confederate sympathizers left the area. Hatreds generated by the war lingered for years. In his study of Cades Cove, Durwood Dunn views the guerrilla war there as a major testing of the "fabric of the community." As in earlier pioneer times, when neighborhood families helped one another overcome the physical barriers of the frontier, the war brought the families of the cove together to defend themselves against a collective enemy (Dunn, 125, 140–141).

Nestled in the southwestern corner of Virginia lies the Sandy Basin, a mountain region drained by the Big Sandy River's Russell Fork and its tributaries. In the rich lands of the basin some 300 farm families lived much like the first white settlers who came into the area fifty years earlier (Mann, 374, 376).

The first families to settle the Sandy Basin followed migratory routes traced out in Ralph Mann's study of the community. Most of the basin's families were Virginians, with origins in the Clinch River Valley to the south, who settled in the eastern part of the basin in communities like Sand Lick. Pioneer families from the mountains of North Carolina came into the western part of the basin, where they settled in the Holly Creek section. The origins of the families in this case determined the loyalties of the communities during the war. In the eastern part of the basin, largely populated by the Virginians, the area was overwhelmingly Confederate. In the western part, where most of the residents were recent emigrants from North Carolina, the Unionists were in the majority (Mann, 377, 379–380).

Although people in the basin had always cooperated with one another as good neighbors, sharing a frontier environment and the austerity of farm life, things changed when the stress of wartime loyalties interfered. Each neighborhood tended to follow family loyalties. As the Confederates began to conscript men in the basin, these community differences became apparent (Mann, 378).

In the Sand Lick community local Confederate sympathizer Ezekiel Counts raised a military company from among his kin and neighbors. A minority of people in the area favored the Union or neutrality, and during the war many of them were hounded, arrested, or driven out of the region. The Blair family originated in North Carolina like the Holly Creek residents, but they settled in the Open Fork district of the McClure River. Their pro-Union sentiments made them a target for Rebel bushwhackers during the war (Mann, 380–381).

After an initial burst of enthusiasm for secession early in the war, hostility to the Confederacy became more open in the Holly Creek community. Confederate recruiters were fired on by local bushwhackers, and force had to be used to conscript unwilling local men into the Rebel military. Unionists were said to eat "standing up and with their hats on," in case conscription officers should come and force them to flee to the woods. The more radical Unionists formed their own Home Guard company under Alf Killen, connected to the first settlers from North Carolina (Mann, 377, 383).

As in other mountain communities in the Appalachians, antagonism between secessionists and Unionists escalated into violence in the Sandy Basin. Guerrilla warfare flared between Alf Killen's Union Home Guard and locally conscripted soldiers of the 7th Confederate Cavalry on guard in the basin. The Unionists ambushed Rebels and targeted individuals. Rebel guerrillas Jack Frye, John McFall, and Jack Fleming terrorized Unionist homesteads while looking for deserters (Mann, 383–384).

In November 1863, a raiding party of fifty of Killen's Home Guards staged an attack on a Rebel camp occupied by 200 local Confederate troops on the Cranesnest River. Although the Unionists had planned a surprise attack at dawn, the Rebels were ready for them because local secessionists had warned them of Killen's plan. After a brief skirmish, the Union men withdrew, leaving eight dead. The Confederates gained the upper hand in the Holly Creek section, and many of the community's Unionists fled to Kentucky (Mann, 384–385).

The smaller Unionist minority in Sand Lick was similarly crushed, and particular punishment focused on the Blairs, outnumbered by Confederates led by Zeke Counts and Dave Smith. Two of the Blair boys who had deserted from the local Rebel company—accompanied by two more Rebel deserters and a Union army deserter—hid out on Alley's Creek, a tributary of the Cranesnest, during the winter months of 1864–1865. After one of the gang bushwhacked Dave Smith—wounding him in the side as he stood on his front porch and shooting his small son's finger off—Smith and his Rebels retaliated by locating the Blairs' hideout and gunning down all five men. The "Blair Massacre" prompted many Unionist families to move to Kentucky (Mann, 382).

In northwestern Georgia, the thriving town of Rome lay in the southern foothills of the Appalachians, where the Etowah and Oostenaula Rivers join to form the Coosa. A spur line from the Western and Atlantic Railroad connected Rome with growing rail traffic between Chattanooga and Atlanta, and riverboats on the Coosa linked the town with Gadsden, Alabama. Stagecoaches carried passengers and mail to Atlanta, Augusta, and other cities. Because of Rome's excellent location, business boomed in the decade before the Civil War. The city's Noble Foundry manufactured Georgia's first railroad locomotive, boilers and steam engines, and, during the war, cannon for the Confederacy. In 1860, Rome also boasted a flour mill, several grocery stores, three hotels, a jewelry store, four drugstores, three livery stables, a crockery shop, a book store, two schools, four steamboats, and fifty-six lawyers and doctors. The county population was nearly 10,000 whites and 5,300 slaves. But even a growing commercial center like Rome was not immune to wartime devastation and guerrilla violence (Aycock, 63–66).

Because of its industries and railroad, Rome was the target of Union Colonel Abel D. Streight's unsuccessful raid in the spring of 1863. A year later the town had the misfortune to lie in the path of Sherman's army plowing south into the Georgia heartland. Confederate troops evacuated Rome on May 17, 1864, as they fell back to defend Atlanta, and Rebel cavalrymen reportedly looted several stores of $150,000 in property (Battey, 197). Yankee troops moved in. The following six months of harsh occupation left pro-Confederate residents bitter. Mary Noble, daughter of foundry owner James Noble, wrote, "This army—Sherman's—was very undisciplined. . . . The officers, as a general thing, were very gentlemanly, but the privates were the lowest and meanest set of men I ever saw." She had not yet seen the Rebel guerrillas (Lane, 155).

The Rome community became virtual hostage to Rebel freebooters led by Jack Colquitt, a deserter from the 11th Texas Cavalry. Colquitt hid out in Polk County when his regiment withdrew, and he married a local woman whose family lived near Prior's Station nine miles south of Cave Spring. The Texan and his men soon gained a reputation as a particularly ruthless and sadistic gang (Aycock, 125).

On September 18, 1864, Colquitt's guerrillas ambushed a Federal wagon train just south of Rome. The Rebels fired from cover, causing horses and mules to stampede. Several wagons overturned. The guerrillas killed eight or ten soldiers and wounded a number of others; then they melted away into the hills nearby. The Union commander at Rome, Brigadier General John M. Corse, burned the home of Mrs. Pauline Hawkins near the site of the ambush as a reprisal. He feared the Rebels might be preparing for a major attack and put his jumpy troops on alert (Battey, 198, 277).

Federal troops abandoned Rome on November 10 to join Sherman's "march to the sea," but before leaving they set fire to much of the town's business district. Sherman's orders to Corse instructed him to "destroy tonight all public property not needed by your command, all foundries, mills, workshops, warehouses, railroad depots or other storehouses convenient to the railroad, together with all wagon shops, tanneries, or other factories useful to the enemy. Destroy all bridges immediately, then move your command tomorrow to Kingston." By nine o'clock the following morning, the Federals were gone (Aycock, 115).

An almost eerie calm settled over Rome. Worried that pillaging Yankee bands might return, the Rome city council hastily organized a patrol of the forty able-bodied men left in town. And well they should worry. Looters descended on Rome within thirty-six hours of the Federals' departure, but they were Confederates, not Yankees.

At first Rome's townspeople were relieved when the gray-coated riders appeared on the evening of November 12. So overjoyed were they to see Confederates that the young women of Rome ran down to the river bank to welcome them (Lane, 155).

But joy quickly turned to dread as the newcomers, Colquitt's guerrillas, began a reign of terror that same night. The raiders invaded the home of Judge Lewis Burwell. Burwell was physically deformed and stooped forward when he walked, and the marauders threatened to "straighten him out" if he refused to hand over his gold. They hanged him three times by the neck, the noose cutting into his throat until he finally gave the money over. By morning the raiders also had robbed and terrorized several other citizens in the community (Battey, 206).

Several nights later on November 18 the raiders returned. Again they descended on Burwell's house. This time he tried to run, but they chased him down and strung him up to a tree. After hanging him until he passed out, they cut him down and sent him sprawling into a mud puddle. One renegade threatened to cut out his heart if he did not hand over his money. Burwell told them they had already taken everything he had except $500 that he had given to a woman for safekeeping. They forced him to go to Mary Noble's home to retrieve the money that night. Pistol in hand, Mary cautiously opened the door to see Burwell, "very much overcome." Suspecting that Burwell was acting under duress, Mary reluctantly turned over his money when she saw the mortal fear in his eyes. The outlaws were lurking just outside the fence. "I never felt so indignant before," Mary wrote. "My fingers fairly itched to pull the trigger and shoot one at least." When they had what they demanded, the guerrillas released the shaken Burwell. Although his face was badly bruised by pistol whipping and his neck badly chafed by the rope, he was alive (Lane, 155–156).

Rome's volunteer police force was powerless to stop the violence. They had divided into two-man patrols and were making their rounds of the city. Patrolling together, local tailor Nicholas Omberg and Terence McGuire heard a woman's screams near the Buena Vista Hotel on Broad Street. Running toward the sounds of the disturbance, Omberg and McGuire found Mrs. William Quinn desperately trying to aid her husband, who was being hanged by robbers. The two patrolmen were outgunned, and the outlaws captured them. When they ordered Omberg and McGuire to follow them out of town, the two men knew they would probably be killed, so they ran for their lives. The guerrillas opened fire, and although McGuire escaped unscathed, Omberg was hit in the leg. He managed to stagger to the home of his sister-in-law, who hid him from the marauders. None of his neighbors would risk helping Omberg. He died of his wound the next morning, and some even feared to attend his burial (Aycock, 125).

Mary Noble wrote on November 20, "We've seen some sad times. But now the Yankees have left us free once more, yet we are worse off than ever! For there are a set of guerillas infesting the place, who are here robbing, murdering and plundering helpless men and women and we have no protection" (Lane, 154). Rome merchant Reuben S. Norton recorded in his diary, "theft and robbery have become so common that people are compelled to hide their horses and mules in the woods at night, or to sleep in the stables to protect them" (Aycock, 124).

"We are afraid to trust anyone now," Mary Noble wrote. "If a soldier comes to the house, we are afraid of him unless we know him. . . . [W]e almost wish for the Yankees again, since we can't have a Confederate force to protect us. . . . We don't feel safe from one day to another" (Lane, 156).

Colquitt's band finally met their match when they ran afoul of Haden Prior and his sons. The Priors, a prominent clan in neighboring Polk County, owned a large plantation eight miles west of Cedartown. "Hayd" Prior was a Unionist, and his son John was not a strong supporter of the Rebels, although he had served in the Confederate cavalry. But with the breakdown of law and order in the fall of 1864 the Priors were the kind of men Governor Joseph E. Brown wanted on his side, as bands of deserters and renegades pillaged the northwest Georgia countryside. Brown named Hayd Prior commander of the local Home Guard company (Sargent, 376–377).

The irony of a Unionist-led Confederate Home Guard company having to defend a Southern community against supposedly Confederate guerrillas underscores the extent of the breakdown of political and social order in the mountains. Gangs like Colquitt's were a threat to Unionists and Confederates alike.

Eventually Colquitt's men began raiding southwest of Rome into Polk County, and this triggered a response by the Priors. Prior's Home Guards cornered five of Colquitt's band on the road between Cave Spring and Prior's Station. One of the raiders spurred his horse and made a run for it. With a single well-aimed shot, John T. Prior blasted him from the saddle. The other guerrillas surrendered (Sargent, 376–377).

The Priors escorted their prisoners to the jail in Cedartown. Several weeks later the men went free, either through intimidation of witnesses or because of lack of evidence. The incident did not end here though. The Priors, furious that the marauders were loose again to prey on innocent families, vowed to step up their attempts to put Colquitt's gang out of business. The outlaws, in a vengeful mood, threatened openly to kill Haden Prior. John T. Prior, telling his side of the story many years later in a newspaper interview, said, "Colquitt's gang put out the word that they would kill my father for having them arrested, but he never took it seriously" (Sargent, 377–378). The feud between Colquitt's gang and the Priors was far from over. Before the entire drama played itself out, both Haden Prior and Jack Colquitt would lie dead, and a string of bloody revenge killings and gunfights would not end until justice had its day.

Each mountain community was different, yet in many ways the same. The mountain people sought to preserve their dignity, their independence, and their distinctive culture. Whether Unionist, secessionist, or neutralist, they tried to protect their families and possessions from predators and to cope with adversity as best they could until an end of hostilities.

PART III

North Alabama

Chapter 8

"Destroying Angels"

There had always been political and social friction between North and South Alabama, but never was there greater division than during the Civil War. North Alabama counties, populated by struggling poor whites and small farmers, strongly opposed secession in 1861. As in Western North Carolina and in East Tennessee, the Confederate conscription acts brought hardships to the Alabama mountains and stiffened Unionist resistance, and soon there was bloody guerrilla conflict. Neither Alabama Governor John Gill Shorter nor his successor Thomas Hill Watts had the resources to contain the resulting lawlessness in the mountains.

Shorter faced the same problems as Zebulon Vance in North Carolina and Joseph E. Brown in Georgia; but while his fellow governors were mountain bred, Shorter was a secessionist from South Alabama's Barbour County. He had little influence with the mountain people. When he took office in 1861, the mild-mannered new governor hoped to win over the mountain Unionists, describing them as "misguided men." But as conditions deteriorated in North Alabama with Union army occupation of the region, he wrote in September 1862 that the only way to deal with the disloyal mountaineers was to fight fire with fire. He called for the "sternest retaliation" and sanctioned confiscation of Unionists' property as compensation for secessionist farms destroyed by Federal raids (Dodd and Dodd, 100). Although he personally opposed conscription, Shorter enforced it once it became law, enjoining Alabamians to "give no shelter to deserters" and to assist officers "in arresting and coercing those who yield to no gentler means" (McMillan, *Disintegration*, 58–60).

"No gentler means" meant brutal treatment for draft evaders. Makeshift jails set up for captured deserters were really more like concentration camps, where prisoners endured filth and scant rations. After several days of confinement, the recalcitrants usually agreed to "sign up," but occasionally there would be a hard case. After five days in the Jasper jail in Walker County, a prisoner named Bird Norris defiantly refused to serve in the army. He was taken out, tied up, and shot by a firing squad. The guards tossed his body into a ditch. Later a group of soldiers raided the Norris homestead, forced his wife and her five children out, and ransacked the home. A neighbor of Norris, J. R. Rowell, also went into hiding rather than be drafted. Partisan Rangers harassed and threatened his family night after night, and an enraged Rowell finally fired on the group from the woods. Before he could reload his musket, the soldiers rushed him, and after a terrific struggle in which several soldiers sustained injuries, they finally subdued him. The soldiers hung him by his feet from a tree limb, drove sharpened pine splinters into his body, and set them afire. Then they watched him burn to death (Thompson, 68–69).

Organized resistance to the draft was strongest in the northeastern Alabama counties of Cherokee, DeKalb, Marshall, Blount, and St. Clair, and in the northwestern Alabama counties of Lawrence, Winston, Walker, Fayette, and Marion (Martin, 44–46). Winston County, southernmost in the Appalachians and poorest in Alabama, was a favorite hiding place. As one Unionist put it, "There, in the secret coves, far away from the world and vengeance, a deserter might hide forever" (Dodd and Dodd, 100).

In the western part of Winston County, Natural Bridge became a regular meeting site for Unionists banding together for protection from secessionist harassment. The rocky terrain of "The Bridge" provided a natural defensive position, with high bluffs arranged in a half circle around a deep gorge. Rebel forces dared not attack it because the Unionists were well armed, and there was no way to approach the position without being spotted. About 300–400 Unionists and deserters met at Natural Bridge in the fall of 1862 to plan a united course of action. Over 100 of them set out for the Federal lines in North Alabama and put on the Union blue (Dodd and Dodd, 98).

Unionists in northwest Alabama remained fairly passive at first. They preferred hiding out and conducted only a few defensive raids against Rebel conscripting cavalry. In 1863, with Federals in control of the Tennessee Valley, they became bolder and began to go on the offensive. They started to retaliate against the secessionists, and Home Guard leaders who had persecuted them fled rather than risk their wrath.

In the spring of 1863, undisciplined Federal soldiers from Colonel Florence M. Cornyn's 10th Missouri Cavalry ravaged North Alabama's Tennessee Valley. They robbed and terrorized with as much brutality as the Rebel

Home Guards and Partisan Rangers, and frequently they made no distinction between Unionists and secessionists. Cornyn called his raiders "Destroying Angels," and Alabama historians used this term to describe local Unionist guerrillas as well (Dodd and Dodd, 96). Many Unionists took up arms out of desperation. A Confederate officer who had captured some of them in the Tennessee Valley called them "the most miserable, ignorant, poor, ragged devils I ever saw" (Hoole, 6).

Despite the aggressive policies of Confederate Conscript Bureau chief Gideon J. Pillow, whom Shorter supported, the deserter problem in Alabama was getting worse. Pillow estimated 8,000–10,000 deserters hiding out in North Alabama in July 1863. He reported they were as "vicious as copperheads," and some had deserted as many as four times. Pillow conceded, "As fast as I catch them and send them to the army they desert and bring off their arms and steal all the ammunition of their comrades they can bring away. . . . They rob, burn, and murder the unarmed and defenseless population of the country with impunity" (USWD, IV, 2: 638, 680–681).

In 1863, his last year in office, Shorter received mounting appeals from loyal Confederates asking for protection from Unionist raiders. The 9th Alabama Infantry Battalion's Lieutenant Colonel Bush Jones wrote Shorter that fifty of his men had deserted to return to St. Clair County because of letters they had received from their wives there. He told Shorter that gangs "are pillaging, robbing, harassing and intimidating the families of local citizens . . . that many families have fled for protection. . . . In many portions of the country it is unsafe for a soldier loyal to the Confederacy to return to his home, sick or wounded." With state forces unequal to the task, Shorter turned to the Confederate army. On July 29, 1863, he appealed to General Braxton Bragg for military assistance. Alabama, he wrote, "is left powerless to enforce the laws against armed combinations in the sparsely settled districts." He added that, "good men willing to serve their country, will hesitate to leave their families to the tender mercies of these bandits" (McMillan, *Disintegration*, 60–61, 63).

Winston County was the scene of considerable violence. In 1862, secessionists murdered Joel Jackson Curtis for refusing to join the Rebel army, keeping his promise to his dying father to remain faithful to the Union. In 1863, Home Guards shot down his brother, George Washington Curtis, in the presence of his wife and three little children. A third brother, Thomas Pinkey (Tom Pink) Curtis, was probate judge of Winston County. On the night of January 18, 1864, a raiding party of about 100 Confederate cavalry, joined by Home Guards, invaded Curtis' home, forced his wife to give up the keys to the jail where a quantity of salt—selling for $80 a sack by the fall of 1864—was stored, and abducted Curtis at gunpoint. Curtis' body was found five days later, frozen by the bank of a stream. He had been shot in the right eye and in the forehead. Thomas H. Watts, Alabama's new governor, was outraged and called for the guilty men to be punished. "Such conduct," he said, "will do more injury to our cause than a Yankee raid" (McMillan, *Disintegration*, 94).

Unionist partisan leaders defied state law, raided secessionist homes, and became heroes in the eyes of Alabama loyalists. William Looney, the "Black Fox," was a former schoolteacher who owned Looney's Tavern, a frequent hangout for Union men, near Addison in eastern Winston County. Looney gained a reputation as a daring and clever scout who guided hundreds of Alabama Unionists to the Federal lines. An excellent tracker, unsurpassed in evasive skills, he was said to have eluded an entire Confederate brigade for a year. Looney also spied on Rebel troops and reported their positions to the Federals (Dodd and Dodd, 110).

Alabama Federal soldier John R. Phillips accompanied Looney on a recruiting trip to Winston County. Along the way they encountered a man known to Looney as a Confederate. Looney pulled out his pistol, shot the man dead, and left him in the road. After the war, Looney shot and killed a man without any apparent provocation or words being spoken. When asked for an explanation, he said, "He's one of them dam' Rebels who tried to hang me at Decatur durin' the War; and I said then, if I ever laid eyes on him again I'd kill him" (Thompson, 191).

According to a popular story, the "Black Fox" once sought refuge at a friend's house after shooting and killing a secessionist in Winston County. That night a party of Home Guards came to the house looking for him. Looney coolly invited them in. When Looney's friend asked the Home Guards where they were from, one of them responded, "We are from Hell." Looney whipped out a gun he had hidden under his coat and snarled, "Did you see ——— ? I just sent him there!" (Dodd and Dodd, 110)

Following the brutal murder of Tom Pink Curtis, Looney helped facilitate one of the most spectacular Unionist raids of the war, the January 1864 attack on the jail at Jasper, Alabama. Looney rode to Federal army headquarters at Decatur and enlisted eleven men from the Union 1st Alabama Cavalry to ride with him to Walker County. He led the men on an all-night ride in a pouring rain and reached Rocky Plains in Winston County, where they rendezvoused with other Unionists waiting to raid the Jasper jail. The party had to proceed without the "Black Fox," because he was so exhausted that he dismounted, leaned against a tree, and fell sound asleep (Thompson, 94).

The next morning, residents of the little village of Jasper were startled to see a raiding party of about twenty-five whooping Unionists, with bluecoated men in front, thundering down the main street in a V formation. Sergeant Anderson Ward or "Doc" Spain, both on furlough from the Union 1st

Alabama Cavalry, probably led the raiders. Also on hand was Frank Curtis, whose three brothers had been killed by local Confederates. As townspeople scattered, the guerrillas rode up to the log jail where they battered down the wooden door with four blows from a makeshift ram and burst inside. They freed several Unionist prisoners, including another Curtis brother, Jim Curtis. About that time, the jailer, armed with a pistol, came running up, and Jim ordered him to drop it. The raiders forced the jailer to set fire to the jail and then to retreat on foot down the road. He was told not to look back (Dodd and Dodd, 106–107).

The guerrillas torched the brick two-story county courthouse and several other buildings, and they captured arms and ammunition sent by Watts to the local Home Guard unit, disbanded a week earlier. Before returning to Winston, they looked up Dr. Andrew Kaeiser, whom Jim Curtis sought for having had a hand in the murders of his brothers. Accounts differ as to who killed Kaeiser. Some said Jim Curtis gunned him down that night in his home. Another story credited one of "Aunt Jenny" Brooks' sons, who hid in Kaeiser's barn and killed him later in retaliation for the murder of his father (Dodd and Dodd, 106–108).

Atrocity stories circulated about the "Destroying Angels." An especially vicious gang, called the "Buggers" in local lore, terrorized the Shoal Creek area of eastern Lauderdale County. They invaded the home of William Johnson, who had a son in the Rebel army. Warned of the gang's approach, Johnson fled to the woods, thinking the raiders would not harm his wife and daughters, but the night's terrors would show how wrong he was. The marauders hanged Mrs. Eliza Jane Johnson and her two teenage daughters, Alcie and Elizabeth, until the women nearly died from strangulation. Mrs. Johnson gave up about $50 in gold, all the money she had. But the raiders were not through. They stripped all three women, tied them down, and burned their foreheads, breasts, feet, and genitals with blazing pages torn from the family Bible. They dragged them to the basement, hanged all three of them by their hair from a loom, and pistol-whipped them senseless. The horror finally ended when approaching neighbors frightened the raiders away, but the women's mental and physical wounds never really healed. Death mercifully claimed all three of them within a few years (Pruitt, 5–6).

The most feared of the "Buggers" was a swarthy, dark-haired Rebel deserter, Thomas M. Clark, a little man with handsome features that masked a pathologically brutal personality. A suspect in unsolved murders and robberies before the war, Clark bragged that "no one ever ran over him." With his brothers and other allies, he operated from a cave hideout on Shoal Creek and terrorized unprotected Rebel and Union homes alike. Clark once admitted stabbing a baby to death after he had killed the parents. He said it was the only thing he ever felt sorry for; the baby had smiled and cooed as he ran his bayonet through its body. His remorse did not prevent his snatching off a coin worn as a charm around the baby's neck (Pruitt, 84, 91).

Tom Clark and his gang conducted a violent raid near Florence on the night of April 30, 1865. They rode to the plantation of 75-year-old John Wilson, burned and tortured the bed-ridden Wilson to death, and shot his nephew Harvey Wilson in the head. They also shot his grandson and left him for dead, then killed a faithful overseer who came to investigate the disturbance. That same night the raiders tied Florence druggist Joseph Milner to a tree and tortured him as they had done Wilson. Milner survived. Federal troops later caught two of the gang and executed them (Garrett, 111–112).

In Marshall County, Federal guerrilla Benjamin R. Harris became a particular source of fear to local secessionists. The 40-year-old Harris, a native of North Alabama, had been working as an overseer on a plantation in Louisiana, but he made his way back to Alabama in the fall of 1863 to scout for the Union army (Johnston, 30).

At about two in the morning on December 27, 1863, Harris, accompanied by some Union soldiers, rode up to a log cabin on Buck Island, a heavily wooded spot in the Tennessee River near Guntersville where local farmers brought their cattle to graze on the tall evergreen cane. In the cabin were Ben, Porter, James M., and F. M. Roden, and Charles L. Hardcastle, a Confederate soldier home on furlough. Hardcastle was hiding out with the Rodens because he had heard that Harris and his dreaded gang were in the neighborhood. He picked the wrong hiding place, for on that cold, dark winter morning his worst fear came upon him. Harris beat on the cabin door and ordered the five men out. He promised not to kill them if they would help him ferry Ben Roden's cattle to the north bank of the river. The captives agreed to do as he demanded.

Once the cattle were ferried across the river, Harris escorted the five men several hundred yards downriver and then told them he was going to shoot them anyway. The Rodens had known him for years and begged him to spare them, but Harris was adamant as he wanted to leave no witnesses. He gave them a few minutes to pray, then lined them up for execution. Harris and his men emptied their revolvers into each victim point-blank. Hardcastle, the last to be shot, fell to the ground when the first pistol ball hit him, pretending to be dead although only wounded in the right arm.

The guerrillas hauled the bodies to the river and tossed them in. Hardcastle began to choke and cough. The guerrillas tried to finish him off, but their shots missed him, and Hardcastle floated downstream hidden behind a piece of driftwood. When he was sure that Harris and his men had left, he dragged himself up on the riverbank. Exhausted from cold and loss of blood, he struggled to his brother-in-law's home nearby. Hardcastle's chilling eyewitness account of the "Buck Island Massacre" spread terror far and wide in the Tennessee Valley (Duncan and Smith, 74–75).

At the end of January 1864, Colonel James E. Saunders wrote to Major General Joseph Wheeler that conditions in Winston, Walker, and Marion Counties were "becoming bad." Like Governor Watts, he expressed anxiety over the recent murder of Judge Tom Pink Curtis by Confederate irregulars and by their operations against local Unionists in which they acted with "great cruelty toward the wives and families of men suspected of being disaffected to our cause" (USWD, I, 52, ii: 613–614). As the war played itself out, northern Alabama was pillaged by Unionist guerrillas and by Confederate stragglers. One correspondent wrote the governor in February 1864 that law and order was breaking down. "Sheriffs and constables," he said, "are as extinct as geological specimens" (Martin, 154). General James H. Clanton wrote in March 1864 that "our own cavalry has been a great terror to our people. . . . Stealing, robbing, and murdering is quite common" (McMillan, *Disintegration*, 88).

By March 1864, a daring band of Unionist guerrillas led by John Stout raided from their base north of Pikeville in Marion County. Well armed and increasingly aggressive, they intimidated even the local Home Guards. Stout and his men raided the Home Guards' headquarters almost every night and frequently lay in ambush for the Rebels at other meeting places. Several of the Confederates had been killed and some were in hiding. The rest of them feared for their lives (Thompson, 89).

On the night of March 24, Stout's guerrillas raided a secessionist home in Fayette County, but the Confederates drove them off and captured one of them, James Mayfield, a Confederate deserter. Captain D. P. Walston sent the badly wounded Mayfield to Lieutenant Colonel T. H. Baker in Tuscaloosa, along with a report of Stout's activities. Walston described Stout as "a desperate and bad though bold and not unskillful man." Stout's guerrillas, he said, were robbing and pillaging, frequently torturing, abducting, and killing Confederates. Walston estimated that Stout had thirty to fifty, possibly 100, armed men. Four nights later, the guerrillas raided into Marion County and abducted Drury McMinn, a local secessionist. In retaliatio,n Confederates seized Lemuel Burnett, a Unionist, as a hostage and sent him to Baker in Tuscaloosa. McMinn and three other captives were later found tied to trees and shot in the head. A fifth victim was found a few miles away (USWD, I, 32, iii: 746–748).

Alabama's new governor, "Big Tom" Watts, elected by a huge majority, inherited the problem of violence in the mountains. Like Shorter, he was powerless to stop the guerrillas. Confederate forces were spread much too thin. Home Guard units were undisciplined, and by their brutal tactics they contributed to the problem. And Alabama's state militia was an empty

shell. Attempts in late 1863 and early 1864 to create a revamped state reserve force failed to have any impact on the deserter problem. Most members of the local reserve companies were men 50 to 60 years old and boys 16
and younger. Occasionally they rode out on patrols looking for deserters,
but they were so poorly armed and undisciplined that they were practically
useless (Martin, 206–207).

In late April and early May 1864, the Confederacy launched a military
offensive against the guerrillas in northwest Alabama. Taking part in the
expedition were four Confederate army brigades, all of them veterans of
combat. The operation, supervised by Lieutenant General Leonidas Polk,
was conducted like a "deer drive," with Confederate troops sweeping the
countryside in Winston, Walker, Marion, and Fayette Counties, flushing
out the deserters, and driving them north. Unionists who offered armed resistance were to be "killed on the spot." Brigadier General Philip D.
Roddey's Alabama cavalry brigade patrolled the Tennessee River to block
off exit to the Federal army and pick up the deserters. Polk labeled the operation a success and reported that over 1,000 deserters had been returned
to their commands, but rooting the guerrillas out of their hideouts was difficult. Many deserters, including at least fourteen piloted through by Bill
Looney, probably got through (Dodd and Dodd, 114–115).

Of the 2,678 white Alabamians who enlisted in the Union Army, 2,066 of
them served in the 1st Alabama Cavalry, the only white Union regiment
from that state (Hoole, 14). In the summer of 1862 a stream of poor, bare-
footed Unionists from the mountains trickled into the camp of Colonel
Abel D. Streight's 51st Indiana Infantry Regiment near Decatur, asking for
"protection and a chance to defend the flag of their country." One old
woman even volunteered to ride thirty-five miles to bring in new volunteers. Encouraged by this show of Unionist support, Streight left on a recruiting mission to the mountains of Morgan County across the Tennessee
River in July 1862. He wrote, "I am now of the opinion that, if there could be
a sufficient force in that portion of the country to protect these people, there
could be at least two full regiments raised of as good and true men as ever
defended the American flag." The 1st Alabama Cavalry Regiment, U.S.A.,
was organized by the end of the year (McMillan, *Alabama*, 172, 175).

Eighteen-year-old Pinckney D. Hall, from the largely Unionist community at Bull Mountain Creek in Franklin County, may have been typical of
the men who joined the 1st Alabama Cavalry. In the fall of 1862, Hall, Federal recruiter Joseph Palmer, and seven other men made up a nighttime
raiding party armed with rifles, shotguns, and a couple of old muskets.
They sprayed secessionist Marshall McLeod's home with gunfire, and
McLeod packed up and moved out the next morning.

A party of 200–300 Confederate guerrillas came calling on the Bull Mountain Creek community on the evening of February 1, 1863. Hall, out in the barn husking corn, heard gunshots from a neighbor's home nearby. Hall and his father headed for the wooded slope of a hill nearby. His cousin Daniel Barnes, a fugitive soldier who had shot another soldier in the head during an argument, felt the guerrillas would not harm a fellow Rebel and stayed behind. Barnes was wrong. The guerrillas tied him up and took him with them. They set a pack of bloodhounds on the Halls' trail and chased them through the woods until nightfall. The Halls were able to elude the hounds by wading a creek and hiding under a rock cliff. Frightened, cold, and soaked through, they waited until they were sure the Rebels had left, then made their way cautiously back to their cabin (Dodd and Dodd, 272).

The Halls hastily gathered up clothing and a bottle of turpentine and set out that night for the nearest Union lines. Dabbing turpentine on the soles of their shoes to throw dogs off their track, they traveled by night and avoided main roads, stopping only at secluded cabins known to be occupied by Union sympathizers. Along the way they fell in with other Unionists who were headed for Federal lines and eventually reached Camp Glendale near Corinth, Mississippi. A picket took them to the 1st Alabama's camp where, Hall related, "I saw my first genuine Yankee." The Halls and the other members of their party all enlisted in the 1st Alabama Cavalry (Dodd and Dodd, 273).

Like most of the Union commands recruited in the Southern Appalachians, the 1st Alabama Cavalry served mainly as scouts, raiders, recruiters, and flank guards. They rarely saw actual combat, but their knowledge of the country made them useful as scouts. There were conflicting reports as to their reliability under fire.

Two companies of the 1st Alabama Cavalry took part in Colonel Abel D. Streight's daring raid across northern Alabama in April 1863. Streight planned to cut the railroad between Chattanooga and Atlanta and destroy the Confederate arsenal at Rome, Georgia. He led 2,000 handpicked men, Midwesterners from Indiana, Ohio, and Illinois. Captain D. D. Smith led the Alabamians, who served as guides. The main part of the 1st Alabama remained with Brigadier General Grenville M. Dodge's 8,000-man cavalry force sent to divert Confederate troops away from Streight's raiders (Hoole, 25).

Streight and Dodge met at Tuscumbia on April 26. Their two columns left on April 28, Dodge riding eastward toward Courtland in an attempt to draw Confederate General Nathan B. Forrest's cavalry away before doubling back to Corinth. Forrest refused to take the bait and realized quickly what Streight intended.

Streight's raid was one of the more dramatic military operations of the war. Guided by the two companies of the 1st Alabama Cavalry, Streight's troops, mounted on mules because of the rugged terrain, pushed south toward Moulton, then eastward to Guntersville and Sand Mountain. Cold, rainy weather, muddy roads, and flooded streams made the march much more difficult. Along the way, Unionists provided Streight with fresh mounts which they had kept hidden from Confederate impressment agents (Thompson, 72).

Streight's raid lasted four days and covered 150 miles across northern Alabama. Fighting on the run all along the way, closely pursued by Forrest, the "Wizard of the Saddle," Streight zigzagged southwest to Gadsden. He burned the bridge across Black Creek to discourage Forrest's pursuit, but a 16-year-old local girl, Emma Sansom, guided the Rebel general to another crossing, and Forrest gave chase again. The Rebel troopers caught up with Streight's raiders near the little village of Cedar Bluff. Streight had sent an advance party of 200 men eastward to Rome to seize the bridge there; but John H. Wisdom, a driver on the Rome stagecoach line, rode all night from Gadsden and reached Rome in time to warn the Rebels. Rome's Home Guards were prepared when the raiders arrived on May 3. The Federals decided not to risk a fight (A. Moore, 431–432).

Streight was surrounded by Forrest's men near Cedar Bluff. Even though Forrest had only 500 troopers, his men jockeyed one of their two fieldpieces to prominent positions near the Yankee camp to create the illusion that they had more troops. Streight surrendered his exhausted command on May 3. He and 1,300 of his men were taken prisoner, the two companies of the 1st Alabama Cavalry included.

The fate of the captured Alabama loyalists seemed uncertain, since Governor Shorter intended that they should be treated as traitors. Fearing that the Unionists might be executed, Governor Oliver P. Morton of Indiana threatened to hold Alabama Confederate prisoners in his state as hostages to secure the protection of the Unionists. There was a stand-off, and the 1st Alabama men were treated as prisoners of war (Dodd and Dodd, 103–104).

The 1st Alabama Cavalry spent the summer of 1863 raiding and recruiting. The regiment so far had no permanent commander, but in September Captain George E. Spencer, Dodge's assistant adjutant general, became the regimental colonel. Spencer was a 26-year-old New Yorker whose father had been an army surgeon during the War of 1812. After emigrating to Iowa, where he was a lawyer and state senator from 1857 to 1858, Spencer was prospecting in Colorado when the war broke out (Owen, 1606).

In October 1863, Spencer led the 1st Alabama southward on a bold raid of its own. The loyalists were to strike the West Point Railroad near Montgomery, and the Union commanders had high hopes for the raid's success. Major General Steven A. Hurlbut wrote that Spencer's Alabamians "have been in several engagements and behaved well. They are thoroughly acquainted with the country, well mounted and armed; have two light steel guns, take with them as volunteers 6 engineers who can either run or destroy railroads or steamers." But the expedition ended in disaster when Spencer's 650 men were attacked by 2,000 of Brigadier General Samuel W. Ferguson's cavalry at Jones' Crossroads. Twenty of the Unionists were killed, forty were taken prisoner, and the two guns were captured, as well as horses and supplies. Ferguson reported he had "scattered the Alabama Tories over the country" (Hoole, 30).

The 1st Alabama operated in the northeastern corner of Alabama in early 1864 and by June was on the flank of Sherman's Union cavalry moving on Atlanta. They fought occasional minor skirmishes, scouting and foraging in the area between Cedar Bluff and Rome. The 1st Alabama served as Sherman's "headquarters escort" during his "march to the sea" late in 1864. Major General Oliver Howard rebuked Spencer for his men's pillaging private homes and threatened to have him and his officers arrested if the vandalism continued. But Sherman had personally ordered the 1st Alabama to "Burn the country within fifteen miles," and Brigadier General Dodge observed, "it was a license under which other things besides burning could be done" (Hoole, 15, 38–40).

Mortimer R. Flint, a former officer in the 1st Alabama, said years later that it was rumored the Alabama Unionists "believed in the axiom, that self-preservation is the first law of nature and so preserved themselves for the good of their country, by never going hungry in that of the enemy." He added, however, "their love and devotion for the union and the old flag, was not excelled by any who wore the blue" (Hoole, 42). Pinckney Hall was more modest, writing, "While I do not claim the honor for the 1st Ala. Cav. above any other good regiment, I do say they did a great deal of hard service" (Dodd and Dodd, 276).

In spite of the sometimes poor showing of scouts under fire, Federal commanders in northeast Alabama continued to be encouraged by the response of mountain Unionists. Brigadier General Morgan L. Smith reported from Larkin's Landing on February 5, 1864, that Unionists were coming out of their hideouts on Sand Mountain and were organizing companies. One eager mountaineer, with pencil and brown paper, mustered in his own company, took command, and captured some Rebel Home Guards who had moved into the same hiding spots that the Unionists had just vacated! Smith wrote, "the always-loyal people of this part of Alabama have learned from the general good conduct of the men who their real friends are." Major General John A. Logan wrote from Scottsboro that the Alabami-

ans "have shown themselves to be very useful men." He added, "They are
the best scouts I ever saw, and know the country well clear to Montgomery"
(USWD, I, 32, i: 128–129).

Chapter 9

"Prisoners of Hope"

Guerrilla warfare erupted in northern Alabama with Ormsby M. Mitchel's occupation of the Tennessee River Valley in April 1862. On April 28, Mary Chadick of Huntsville noted in her diary, "Mitchell has been in a rage all the week on account of the cutting of the telegraph poles and lines, the tearing up of the railroad tracks, firing into trains, and holds the citizens responsible for the same, having had 12 of the most prominent arrested." She added, "Great depredations have been committed by the Federal cavalry. . . . We are all 'prisoners of hope,' and are in daily expectancy that Gen. Kirby Smith or Gen. Morgan is coming to our relief" (McMillan, *Alabama*, 158).

The only permanent Confederate force in the Tennessee Valley was Brigadier General Philip D. Roddey's Alabama cavalry brigade. A native of Moulton in Lawrence County, Roddey had been a tailor, county sheriff, and steamboat operator. Despite a lack of military experience, the 41-year-old Roddey recruited his own cavalry company. Immediately he showed abilities as a scout and as a partisan, and soon he was in command of his own brigade of cavalry. Always outnumbered, he adopted guerrilla tactics to fight the Federals and became known as the "Swamp Fox of the Tennessee Valley." He often operated under Generals Joseph Wheeler and Nathan Bedford Forrest, but mostly he conducted his own war in the valley (McMillan, *Alabama*, 257).

Confederate troops were stretched much too thin to protect the rural northeastern Alabama mountain counties, leaving local Home Guard companies and small detachments of Rebel cavalry to fight isolated harassing actions against the Federals and Unionist guerrillas. Henry F. Smith was one of the most active Confederate raiders. The young partisan from the Lim Rock community in western Jackson County raised a company that became part of Colonel A. A. Russell's 4th Alabama Cavalry Regiment, which operated in the Tennessee Valley.

Smith's guerrillas were active near Guntersville, a Marshall County hamlet of some 240 people on the Tennessee River. Federal troops shelled Guntersville in July 1862 and burned the town in January 1864, leaving only the two-story Guntersville Hotel and a few other buildings still standing. Yankee soldiers established a post in Claysville on the north side of the river where about seventy of them occupied three houses.

In March 1864 Colonel John M. Oliver with eighty men of the 15th Michigan Mounted Infantry rode into Guntersville to round up Smith's men and the Home Guards there. They arrived about dark on March 2 to find sixty to seventy Rebel troops "drawn up in line on foot, in the shape of a half-moon, at the end of the bridge over New Creek, near the edge of town." After a brief skirmish, the Yankees retreated—without the elusive Smith—and minus five of their own men who were killed or missing (USWD, I, 32, i: 486–487).

With a sixty-five–man party, Smith conducted a bold retaliatory raid on the Federal post at Claysville on March 14. At 3 A.M. he led his men across the Tennessee River at Gunter's Landing, dividing his force into three groups led by Captains William May, Samuel Henry, and himself. Local sympathizers helped the Rebels avoid the Yankee pickets. Smith's men went in firing and yelling, taking the Federals by surprise.

Captain William T. House of the 32nd Missouri Infantry was unable to rally his men, and the fight was over in fifteen minutes. Most of the Yankees panicked and surrendered; others, House said, "fought like tigers." House told them to "save themselves, but not to surrender" and rushed back to his quarters to grab his holsters and slip on his coat and cap. Smith's men quickly cornered him, but he clubbed one Rebel with his revolver and escaped in a hail of gunfire. Smith crossed the river at 10 A.M. and was long gone by the time House returned with reinforcements. Smith captured sixty-six Federal prisoners, as well as supplies and provisions. Each side lost a man killed and several wounded in the action. House reported Smith took a bullet in the abdomen. The Federals would have to wait three more months before they could root Smith and his men out of Guntersville (USWD, I, 32, i: 498, 665).

Some Rebel partisans took up the ways of the guerrilla reluctantly, but once committed, they became dedicated masters of the art. Reverend Milus Eddings Johnston was an opponent of secession who hoped to live out the war in peace. A native of Tennessee, the 39-year-old Methodist preacher had relocated in Madison County with his large family to escape the war's turmoil. But after Federal troops burned the homes of Johnston and his father-in-law in the fall of 1863, he could stand no more. The mild-mannered preacher became one of the occupying Union army's most re-lentless adversaries and was known in the region as "Bushwhacker" John-ston.

Johnston joined Major Lemuel G. Mead's Alabama Cavalry Battalion as a captain in January 1864. Mead, a native of Jackson County, was conduct-ing guerrilla operations north of the Tennessee River and was a real thorn in the side of the Federal army in North Alabama. The members of his com-mand operated in small, semi-independent squads and annoyed the Feder-als with hit-and-run raids against their communication and supply lines. By the spring of 1864 the "fighting preacher" was Mead's most capable offi-cer and was leading cavalry raids against the Yankees.

Johnston knew that Rebels operating inside Federal lines would be con-sidered bushwhackers. He later wrote, "Our home was inside the lines, and we claimed the right to be inside the lines. Hence we went inside the lines, fought inside the lines, and remained inside the lines—only as we saw proper to go out and in as we pleased." He also summed up the objectives of his small squad of Rebel partisans: "to gather recruits and to ascertain important movements of the enemy and to report to the Confederate authorities. And . . . to fight a little, if necessary. We say a little because we did not wish to get into close quarters until we got 'the hang of things' " (44–45).

Johnston's memoirs, written many years after the war, yield many in-sights into the tactics used by Southern partisans in the Tennessee Valley. The preacher posted pickets to alert his band wherever the enemy might approach. If time allowed, he divided his men into three groups to meet the Yankees in front or to strike them in the rear or on their flank. He claimed, "in the greatest victories we ever had we never had more, in direct action, than from twenty-five to fifty men," and "we never fired on any men until we had let them know we were there, and had ordered them to halt and sur-render. . . . We never fired more than two volleys before the order was given to charge. And when we started we went like a whirlwind" (51–53).

On July 8, 1864, Federal troopers of the 12th Indiana Cavalry rode out of Vienna (now New Hope) in the southern part of Madison County in search of the "Old Bushwhacker." Johnston clashed frequently with this unit, and he was waiting for them at Yellow Bank Creek, just a few miles away. His thirty-five dismounted guerrillas had taken cover behind fallen timbers toppled during a past storm. Once in range, Johnston called out for the bluecoats to surrender. When the Yankees realized they had ridden into a trap, whirling their horses about, Johnston discharged his pistol, signaling his men to open fire. There was a brief swirling torrent of smoke, rearing horses, and blazing guns. The troopers withdrew, with nine wounded, leaving one man dead. Johnston's men captured abandoned arms and equipment, including a number of hats left by the Yankees in their haste to get away. Johnston's bold activities gave rise to the tale among Federal soldiers that the clergyman prayed, "Good Lord, enable my boys to take better aim next time that they may kill and not cripple!" (Johnston, 51–53).

Tearing up railroad tracks was a more typical activity for Johnston's guerrillas, and he described a raid on the United States Military Railroad running through North Alabama late in 1864. Dismounting from their horses, the guerrillas filed up to the track "just as thick as we could stand," gripped the crossties, and "raised the yell, 'Turn over the United!' " as they heaved up the rails. Up went the track, cracking and shaking. Johnston wrote, "when we got a long span set on edge, leaning from us, that would half lift what was immediately connected with it; and thus we turned over hundreds of yards at a time, which came down with a mighty crash." The guerrillas piled together steel rails, logs, and other debris and set fire to them; then they bent the heated rails so they could not be used again (124).

Even in the last winter of the war, Johnston and his guerrillas displayed pluck and determination, surprising Union troops with dawn attacks in the snow, burning railroad bridges, and taking prisoners. In January 1865, Lieutenant Colonel Bedan B. McDanald of the 101st Ohio Infantry Regiment, accompanied by Unionist partisan Ben Harris and some of his men, conducted a retaliatory raid in Johnston's pro-Confederate community. The bluecoats burned fifty dwellings suspected of housing Johnston's guerrillas and left their families homeless. They also seized Johnston's wife and confined her as a prisoner in the Huntsville hotel. Mary Elizabeth Findley, a widow, had married Johnston, a widower with five children, in 1859. A preacher's daughter, the brown-eyed, dark-haired woman witnessed her family's home burned three times (Johnston, 95–99, 153–155).

Perhaps the arrest of Mrs. Johnston was a ploy to bring the Old Bushwhacker out of hiding. Ironically, Johnston was scouting just a few miles away, but he was unaware of his wife's fate. He soon made plans to take her back by force. One guerrilla, Captain Robert Welch, threatened to hang Union prisoners unless Mrs. Johnston was released. "I have thirty-five prisoners," he wrote in a message to the Union garrison in Huntsville, "and if you do not set Mrs. Major Johnston at liberty at once, the last one of them will look up a tree!" But retaliation was not necessary. Dr. Thomas A. Wright, a family acquaintance, visited the Federal provost-marshal in Huntsville to secure the woman's release. Motivated by a sense of humanity or fear of retaliation, the provost-marshal, Lieutenant Colonel John W. Horner, ordered Mrs. Johnston released, and she returned to her family (Johnston, 98).

As the war ground to an exhausting close, secessionists in northeastern Alabama had very little left to fight with. In November 1864, Colonel William J. Palmer of the 15th Pennsylvania Cavalry reported that his scouts had just returned from Valley Head and Sand Mountain. They told him that one Home Guard company of sixty men had disbanded and that two other companies near Gadsden posed no threat. Palmer wrote, "Indeed the valley (Lookout) is so well stripped of provisions and forage that a force of any size could not be supported, except on a rapid march through it, and on Sand Mountain there is nothing whatever for man or horse" (USWD, I, 39, iii: 765).

Bushwhacker Johnston, recently promoted to lieutenant colonel, continued playing hide-and-seek with his Union adversaries, but he realized that the game was up. When the Federals agreed to accept his surrender, the old preacher gathered his troops about him and explained to them that the war was lost. On a gloomy May 11, 1865, on a mountaintop just four miles from Huntsville, Johnston's 150 ragged guerrillas huddled in the rain and laid down their arms. Colonel William Given of the 102nd Ohio Infantry accepted Johnston's surrender (Johnston, 163).

One Yankee officer was not so conciliatory toward his former enemies. The 5th Indiana Cavalry's Major Moses D. Leeson described Johnston's men as "some 150 ragamuffins, bushwhackers, guerrillas, horse-thieves, and murderers." But most of the bluecoats were relieved that the fighting was over. The Federals shared brandy with the Rebels, then reissued them their arms on Johnston's promise that he would help police the area and restore order. The war in North Alabama was over (Johnston, 169).

The end of formal fighting brought no resolution of the bitter hatreds and divisions that plagued North Alabama, and memories of guerrilla activities would linger for a long time. The controversy over responsibility and accountability in guerrilla warfare thrust Confederate partisan Frank B. Gurley to the center stage.

When Federal troops overran the Tennessee Valley, Frank B. Gurley was 25 years old. Born and raised on his father's plantation east of Huntsville, he had looked forward to living the life of a prosperous planter. His father was a veteran of the War of 1812, and his grandfather had fought in the Revolutionary War. Like many Alabamians in the valley, Gurley had been lukewarm to secession and supported the Confederacy only after war actually started. In August 1861 he enlisted in a local cavalry company that was absorbed by Colonel Nathan Bedford Forrest's 3rd Tennessee Cavalry Regiment. When the Rebel post at Fort Donelson, Tennessee, fell to Grant on February 16, 1862, Forrest and his men escaped. Ailing with typhoid fever, Gurley returned to Madison County on sick leave (O. Cunningham, 84–85).

While Gurley was home convalescing, Mitchel's Union troops captured Huntsville. Gurley made his way back to Forrest, who ordered him to return to Madison County, collect as many men as he could, and raise a company of cavalry to annoy the Yankees. Commissioned a captain of Partisan Rangers, Gurley led a company of about ninety men and conducted guerrilla operations against the Federals in North Alabama. During the summer of 1862 Gurley's guerrillas harassed Yankee detachments, surprising picket posts and scattering foraging details. Gurley even placed some local Unionists under arrest, but he treated his prisoners decently. Around the first of August, Gurley was joined by Captain Joseph M. Hambrick from his old company, and as senior officer Hambrick assumed command (O. Cunningham, 85–86).

On the morning of August 5, 1862, Hambrick and Gurley received word that Federal cavalry was foraging near New Market, about sixteen miles northeast of Huntsville. The Rebels saddled up and hit the Limestone Road in pursuit. At about 10 A.M. they ran across a baggage train led by blue-coated troopers. Hambrick ordered a charge.

The Federals were actually troops of Brigadier General Robert L. McCook's command. A member of a prominent Ohio family, the "Fighting McCooks," the young general was ill with a severe case of dysentery and was traveling in a small wagon, accompanied by one of his staff officers and a black teamster as a driver. McCook's party had become separated from the rest of his brigade, which he assumed to be about half a mile away. When he saw Rebel horsemen charging down the road toward them, McCook ordered his driver to try to outrun them.

Within moments the Rebels overtook the fleeing Yankees. Hambrick ordered the Federals to halt, but there was so much noise and confusion that McCook and his party may not have heard him. The Rebels opened fire. Nine mounted cavalrymen who were riding with McCook's wagon as his escort panicked and galloped away as fast as they could go, abandoning the general to the enemy. Gurley, in the lead of the attacking Rebels, fired a shot with his service revolver at a sutler named Jacob Aug, who happened to stray into his path. The shot missed Aug, but the frightened sutler lost his balance and toppled off his mule. Meanwhile Gurley was yelling for the "Yankee sons of bitches" to halt. McCook's fleeing wagon hit a low tree branch, which tore off part of the canvas cover and sent the wagon into a ditch.

There were differing versions as to what happened next. McCook's staff officer, Captain Hunter Brooke, testified that he, McCook, and the driver raised their hands to surrender. A Rebel witness said McCook, who was not in uniform but was wearing only a shirt and underwear, grabbed the wagon reins and tried to escape. Gurley, bearing down on the party about twenty-five yards away, fired three shots as he galloped past. One shot missed, the second one went through Brooke's coat, and the third struck McCook in the left side. Without stopping, Gurley rode on with his men after the retreating Yankee troopers. They caught up with soldiers of McCook's brigade about a mile down the road, exchanged gunfire with them, and withdrew to the spot where they had left McCook's party. The badly wounded McCook was carried to a farm close by, and around noon Gurley rode up to the farmhouse to check on his condition. Gurley told McCook that he was sorry for shooting him, that he did not know who he was, and that the general should have heeded the order to stop. McCook seemed to understand and said he had no hard feelings. Gurley, Hambrick, and their men, along with Brooke as a prisoner, rode away. McCook died the next day (O. Cunningham, 86–88).

Gurley considered the incident regrettable but felt he had acted properly. McCook was in the wrong place at the wrong time and out of uniform, and unfortunate mistakes often are made in the heat of battle. But Captain Brooke, after being released by the Rebels, did not forget or forgive. Neither did McCook's family, including his brothers serving in the Union Army. After McCook died, Federal troops burned secessionist homes in the neighborhood nearby in retaliation, including the farmhouse in which the general had been treated for his fatal wound.

When Rebel forces invaded Kentucky in August, Federal troops began a temporary withdrawal from North Alabama, evacuating Huntsville on August 31. Gurley and his men rode into town and arrested two Unionists who were accused of trading with the enemy. Mary Chadick wrote that Gurley "was literally crowned with wreaths of ivy and flowers" by grateful townspeople (McMillan, *Alabama*, 172).

Gurley, Hambrick, and their men moved into Tennessee to rejoin Forrest, raiding after Bragg's army withdrew from Kentucky. In November 1862 their company joined Colonel A. A. Russell's 4th Alabama Cavalry Regiment. Hambrick became lieutenant colonel, and Gurley remained captain of the company he had raised in Madison County. Gurley earned the reputation of being a bold and gritty officer. The same trigger reflexes that had caused him to act so impulsively in the killing of McCook served him well on the battlefield. On December 16, 1862, at Lexington, Tennessee, Gurley and a dozen of his troopers, under heavy fire, rushed a Federal artillery piece and captured it, although his orderly sergeant was killed. Gurley also captured Union Colonel Robert G. Ingersoll of the 11th Illinois Cavalry. Ingersoll, seeing no way out of his dilemma, coolly asked his captors, "Is this your Southern Confederacy for which I have so diligently searched? Then I am your guest" (O. Cunningham, 89).

Gurley seemed to have a promising future ahead of him as a combat officer. But fate had other plans. Within days of the August 5 killing of Robert
McCook, Cincinnati newspapers were carrying accounts of the event and
branding Gurley as a murderer. *Harper's Weekly* in its August 23 issue ran an
inflammatory illustration depicting the general's death and showing an
unarmed McCook being brutally gunned down by Rebel guerrillas. The
case received much publicity in the North, where the McCook family was
popular and respected, and public opinion called for revenge. The Union
army waited for an opportunity to capture Gurley and bring him to trial.

In the late summer of 1863 Gurley was serving with his regiment along
the Tennessee–Alabama–Georgia border area. Union troops were on the
lookout for him and were tracking his activities. On August 26, soldiers of
Colonel Edward M. McCook, Robert's brother, captured eleven guerrillas
near the northeastern Alabama town of Larkinsville. That night they captured one of Gurley's men, identified as being with him when McCook was
killed. But it was really Gurley that they wanted. Finally, on October
20—over a year after the killing of McCook—Gurley, his brother Thomas,
and about thirty of his men were taken by Federal troops after a skirmish in
Lookout Valley in northwestern Georgia's Dade County (USWD, I, 30, iii:
179, 186; 31, i: 707, 770; 31, iii: 573).

Gurley's capture began a long two-year ordeal in which he would be
held in prison, mostly in chains, waiting to be hanged. He had some formidable enemies arrayed against him, including Captain Hunter Brooke, who
now was Acting Judge Advocate for the Army of the Cumberland. Brooke
was eager to see Gurley tried and wrote about him to the Judge Advocate
General, Colonel Joseph Holt, on November 3, "A little over a year ago, I
can positively swear that he was a guerrilla acting without authority from
the Confederate Government, claiming to be a partisan ranger without a
commission and subsisting himself and his band entirely by plunder. He
was the murderer of Brig. Gen. R. L. McCook." Holt responded enthusiastically on November 14, "Frank B. Gurley is clearly triable for the murder of
General McCook, and for any other crime of which he may have been guilty
while acting as a guerrilla and without a commission from the so-called
Confederate States" (USWD, II, 6: 465, 520–521).

Confederate army officers and civilian sympathizers mounted a campaign to save Gurley. Their main contention was that Gurley was not a
guerrilla but a regularly commissioned officer in the Confederate Army
and that the death of McCook was not an act of murder but a legal, though
unfortunate, act of war.

On December 12, 1863, Gurley's old commander, General Nathan B. Forrest, wrote to Major General S. A. Hurlbut, Union commander at Memphis,
on his behalf. Forrest reviewed Gurley's record of service dating from his

1861 enlistment, reiterated that he was acting as a legally commissioned Confederate officer at the time of McCook's death, and offered his own observations on guerrilla warfare:

> Captain Gurley has been from the beginning a soldier in the Confederate service, and I claim for him the treatment due to a prisoner of war. What may have been attributed to him by the press of the country, North and South, is one thing, but actual facts and the muster-rolls in the Department at Richmond is quite another. . . . [A]llow me to say that it is my purpose to drive guerrillas from the country. They must join the service regularly, on the one side or the other, otherwise be disbanded and driven off; and while I deplore the existence of such men and their lawless conduct, I desire respectfully to call your attention to facts self-evident and undenied. The charred walls of many dwellings have met my eyes. . . . It has ever been my desire to see this war conducted according to the rules of civilized warfare, and so far as I am concerned will so conduct it. At the same time I am determined to execute on the spot every house-burner and robber that may fall into my hands, whether he claims to be a Federal or a Confederate. (USWD, II, 6: 691–693)

Forrest wrote a similar letter to Union General Ulysses S. Grant. Confederate Lieutenant General William J. Hardee also appealed to Grant on Gurley's behalf, and Grant replied on December 28, "Captain Gurley being an officer in the Confederate Army does not preclude the possibility of his having committed a foul murder, for which he can be held fully amenable by the laws of war, and if found guilty punished with death. Captain Gurley has been charged with murder not justified by any position he can possibly hold. He will receive a fair and impartial trial" (USWD, II, 6: 771).

President Jefferson Davis, Secretary of War James A. Seddon, and Alabama Governor Thomas H. Watts all were aware of Gurley's case. Seddon said that Gurley was being made "the object of special spite," and Watts wrote Davis that the Rebel officer "ought to be protected by the most prompt and stern retaliation." Watts enclosed an anonymous letter from Madison County, dated December 13, which referred to Gurley as "an honorable, high-toned gentleman, modest, unassuming, and universally popular both as citizen and soldier" (USWD, II, 6: 773, 831–832).

Frank Gurley's trial by a military commission of five officers began in Nashville on December 2, 1863. Gurley was represented by two capable defense attorneys, Bailie Peyton and Jordan Stokes. The court's presiding officer was Colonel John F. Miller, formerly a brigade commander under another one of Robert McCook's brothers, General Alexander M. McCook.

The prosecuting officer from the Judge Advocate's office was Lieutenant H. C. Blackman of the 8th Kansas Volunteers.

The prosecution concentrated on two points in the specification of charges against Gurley: Gurley shot and killed McCook "without any provocation whatever, and while the said Brig. Gen. Robert L. McCook was lying sick and helpless in an ambulance." And, Gurley was not legally a Confederate soldier but was a guerrilla "banded together with certain other citizens for the purpose of killing, robbing, and plundering Federal soldiers and loyal citizens of the United States" (USWD, II, 6: 1029).

Captain Hunter Brooke was the first prosecution witness. Brooke testified to the August 5, 1862, Rebel attack on McCook's party and to the death of the young brigadier. He said that McCook was shot while he had his hands raised in the act of surrendering and positively identified Gurley as the shooter.

Blackman also wanted to establish that Gurley's men acted like guerrillas. Brooke was a prisoner in the Rebels' camp for twelve days, and he observed their informal routine and loose discipline. He testified that Gurley and his men were not uniformed but were dressed in civilian clothing. During the time he was a prisoner he saw a number of men come into camp to join up with Gurley's company, and he testified that they were never formally enlisted but were just told to "go and get your gun and come along." Members of the band would leave camp at night and return in the morning, apparently having spent the night at their homes. He said that Hambrick had told him that they reported to no one, received no pay, and lived off the land (USWD, II, 6: 1030).

Brooke was on the witness stand for two days of convincing and damaging testimony. On Peyton's cross-examination, Brooke admitted that McCook had tried to escape, that it was possible he had not heard Gurley order him to halt, and that Gurley had told Brooke later that "he did not know we had surrendered" (O. Cunningham, 92).

Because the driver of McCook's wagon was a slave, Peyton and Stokes objected to his being allowed to testify, and the court sustained the objection. This left sutler Jacob Aug, the only other prosecution witness. Aug testified that Gurley fired at him and also shouted to his men on seeing McCook lying helpless in the ambulance wagon, "There he lays; kill him." On cross-examination he admitted that there was a great deal of confusion during the attack, that he had hidden in the bushes after he fell off his mule, and that he was not really sure of all the details of the incident. Gurley's lawyers recalled Aug for further cross-examination later in the trial and got him to admit that he had told someone, "If McCook had stopped, he would not have been killed." Aug said he had been drinking with some people in Nashville when he made the statement and had not really meant it. Finally, he did admit hearing one of the Rebels give the order to halt before McCook was shot (O. Cunningham, 92–93).

When the defense opened its case on December 14, the lawyers challenged the prosecution's charge that Gurley was a bushwhacker and put on a series of witnesses to show that he was a legally commissioned Confederate officer when the killing took place. They also wanted to show that Gurley was not the ruthless villain portrayed in the press, and they had witnesses testify to his good character. To add credibility to their case, they brought in Unionist witnesses.

Perry Hawson, a Unionist who lived near Huntsville, testified that he had known Frank Gurley since he was a child, that Gurley was known by the people in Madison County to have been a Confederate officer when McCook was killed, and that he had even been arrested by Gurley, who was wearing a Confederate captain's uniform at the time. He said that Confederate Brigadier General Philip D. Roddey had addressed Gurley as captain. Hawson had even looked for Gurley's commission so he could present it to the court as verification, but he felt the document might have been destroyed when Federal raiders burned the Gurley house (O. Cunningham, 92–93).

Peyton and Stokes even called Union Major General Lovell H. Rousseau as a witness for the defense. Rousseau testified that shortly before McCook's death he had captured some of Gurley's men, and some of their friends produced Gurley's commission as a captain of Partisan Rangers to show that they acted under legitimate authority. The commission was signed by General Edmund Kirby Smith, and Rousseau accepted it as valid. Since dependable local residents also assured him that Gurley's men were not guerrillas, he treated them as prisoners of war and allowed them to be discharged after taking an oath of allegiance (USWD, II, 6: 1030–1031).

Lieutenant R. B. King of Russell's 4th Alabama Cavalry testified that Gurley and his men were officially enlisted into the Confederate army and that Gurley drew captain's pay from May 20, 1862. King also testified that both officers and enlisted men in the Rebel army often wore civilian clothing, since they rarely were issued uniforms (USWD, II, 6: 1030–1031).

The prosecution raised the legal issue of whether Gurley's captain's commission was valid. According to the act that provided for Partisan Rangers, officers' commissions were supposed to be signed by President Jefferson Davis. Gurley's commission had been signed by Kirby Smith and therefore was not legal. The defense countered by calling M. P. Gentry, a former member of the Confederate Congress, who testified that President Davis had delegated authority to Kirby Smith and others to sign the commissions and that Gurley's was in fact genuine (O. Cunningham, 94).

The defense closed its case on January 11, 1864. Peyton and Stokes argued Gurley's case was being pushed forward because of political pressure from the victim's influential family. If Gurley had killed an ordinary enlisted man instead of a well-known general, the case would never have come to trial. While conceding that McCook's death was a regrettable incident in the brutal climate of war, they renewed their argument that Gurley was a member of the Confederate army and not a guerrilla. He should be treated as a prisoner of war. The prosecution reiterated its argument that Gurley had no legal status in the army and that he was an outlaw (O. Cunningham, 95).

The commission rendered a unanimous decision of guilty and sentenced Frank Gurley to hang. Area department commander General George Thomas, the "Rock of Chickamauga," was more sympathetic. He approved the court's verdict but recommended the sentence be commuted to five years in prison because of "the peculiar circumstances and excitement under which the crime was committed" and "the previous and subsequent good character of the prisoner" (USWD, II, 6: 1029).

While Gurley's execution was suspended, Judge Advocate General Joseph Holt became personally involved in the case. Urged on by Brooke and determined to see Gurley hang, he sent President Abraham Lincoln a report of the case in March 1864 and appealed to the president to have Gurley executed. Either because he didn't want to approve the death sentence or possibly because of fear of Confederate retaliation, Lincoln approved the military commission's sentence but never actually authorized the execution to be carried out. Gurley's friends still had not given up on him. In late 1864, during Confederate General John B. Hood's invasion of Tennessee, Major General Benjamin F. Cheatham offered a prisoner exchange deal to the Federals, proposing to swap the Rebel captive for a Union prisoner who was awaiting execution in Columbia, South Carolina. Holt vetoed this plan (O. Cunningham, 97–98).

Meanwhile fate dealt a lucky card to the Rebel prisoner languishing away in the Nashville jail. Through a misunderstanding in communications, the jailer released Gurley in January 1865, along with several other Rebel prisoners, as part of a prisoner exchange authorized by Grant. By the time Holt and Secretary of War Stanton learned about the mistake, Gurley was long gone (O. Cunningham, 98).

The next chapter in the Gurley story unfolded as a new presidential administration became involved. Andrew Johnson, sworn in after Lincoln's assassination, issued orders for Gurley's arrest in the summer of 1865. But first the fugitive Rebel officer had to be located. There were rumors that he was hiding in Tennessee, Georgia, and Louisiana. In fact, Gurley was not hiding out at all but had returned to Madison County. With the war over, he had even signed an oath of allegiance on May 27 and had informed General George Thomas that he was back in Alabama and intended to stay out of trouble. When Gurley was elected county sheriff in October 1865, Holt finally knew where he was. Federal troops arrested Gurley in Huntsville on November 23. Offering no resistance, he was taken in irons to Nashville, where he was given a brief hearing, then was brought back to Huntsville to be hanged. The execution was set for December 1, 1865 (O. Cunningham, 99–100).

Once again Gurley's friends and sympathizers, both Unionist and Confederate, mustered public support for his release. Joseph C. Bradley sent a petition to President Johnson on November 30 asking him to spare Gurley's life. He stressed that the former Rebel officer had been a loyal citizen since the end of the war, living quietly and peacefully at home. "Mr. Gurley is not understood in this community to have been a bitter partisan," he wrote, "he was not an original secessionist, and is known to have rendered valuable assistance in arresting persecution of Union men for their political opinions" (USWD, II, 8: 820–821). Another well-known Unionist, D. C. Humphreys, personally led a delegation to Washington to appeal to Johnson for leniency. Humphreys had once been arrested by Gurley during the war and had even been imprisoned, but Gurley had treated him kindly. He said he believed Gurley's death could serve no useful end. Bradley, Humphreys, and others pointed out to the president that hanging Gurley would only cause more bitterness and hatred. Colonel Lewis Johnson, commander of Union troops at Huntsville, feared an uprising in Madison County if Gurley was executed (O. Cunningham, 101–102).

So once again Gurley's death sentence was suspended, while Andrew Johnson pondered how to handle the situation. Holt stubbornly urged that the execution be carried out. Gurley's advocates continued to pressure Johnson for clemency. While others decided his fate and the ponderous legal drama played itself out, Frank Gurley remained in jail in Huntsville.

The big breakthrough for Gurley came when Humphreys persuaded Ulysses S. Grant to become involved. Humphreys reviewed the entire case with Grant and convinced him that Gurley had suffered enough. Finally, Grant voiced his opinions to President Johnson. The popular general's recommendation was enough for Johnson, who probably was glad to be rid of the case. On April 17, 1866, orders went out from the War Department, and Gurley was freed on April 28. Gurley had to agree not to serve as sheriff of Madison County, had to take another loyalty oath, and had to promise not to take an active part in politics. But he had his life back (O. Cunningham, 102).

It had been almost three years and nine months since the wartime killing of Robert L. McCook. Gurley had spent a total of one and a half years of his life behind bars. It had taken a persistent, determined effort on the part of friends, family, and sympathizers to secure his release. Ironically, former Unionists and former secessionists in North Alabama, who could not resolve their differences except by war, somehow put aside those differences to win Gurley's freedom.

Chapter 10

Blood in the Sky

Few Americans have had to endure the strain and deprivation that the people of the Southern Appalachians lived under for four years. Mountain families coped with hardships from day to day. And for men thinking of enlisting in the Federal army, such a decision was full of peril for their families as well as themselves. Pinckney Hall described the danger they faced: "They were shot sitting by their firesides or walking on the road; they had to leave their families to the abuse of the enemy; had to keep themselves closely concealed like the vermin in the woods until they could make escape through the lines, and then had to share the same hardships of soldiers life that the comrades of the North bore" (Dodd and Dodd, 277).

The price of commitment included separation from one's family, loss of one's property and home, and sometimes the hostility of one's kin. The dilemma is illustrated by the evolution of John R. Phillips from neutralist to deserter to Federal soldier. The 24-year-old Phillips had relocated in Marion County, Alabama, after moving from North Carolina in 1858. At the beginning of the war, Phillips resolved to get along with his secessionist neighbors by keeping quiet and minding his own business. When relations with them began to sour, he and his family moved from the public road to a more isolated location. When conscription went into effect in April 1862, John was drafted into the Confederate army along with several of his neighbors. "I loved my wife and children," he wrote, "and it was almost like death to have to go off and leave them, especially at such a time as then" (Phillips, 22).

As he reluctantly made his way to report for duty, John was torn by inde-
cision. Should he follow his conscience and join the Union army instead?
Finally he just went back home. His neighbors concluded that he had joined
up with the Yankees.

"This meant the confiscation of our property," Phillips grimly wrote in
his autobiography. With livestock amounting to some seventy head of cattle, about the same number of hogs, four horses and mules, and a number of
beehives, the industrious farmer had managed to make his homestead
self-sufficient. The family was out of debt, and an especially good corn crop
had yielded about 1,000 bushels of corn and an abundance of fodder and
hay. Phillips had plenty of Confederate money, but now all this was forfeit.
"Now my liberty was gone," he wrote, "and I could not work for my family
nor enjoy their association, which made my life miserable to me." Soon secessionist raiders began plundering the farm, driving off the cattle, stealing
the horses and mules, and carrying off sacks of meat and corn. They even
stripped the kitchen of plates, saucers, and cups and poured out what little
meal was left on the floor, leaving the Phillips family totally impoverished
(Dodd and Dodd, 97).

When Phillips' Rebel neighbors learned that he was still somewhere
nearby, they set an ambush for him and opened fire on the Union man when
he came home. Phillips escaped and sought refuge in the cliffs near Natural
Bridge in Winston County. Soon he was joined by his friend Bill Dodd, carrying meat, bread, and a quantity of quilts and blankets. Dodd was overage
for the draft under the first Confederate conscription, but when the age
limit was raised he too became a fugitive. On reaching Phillips' hideout, he
"got down on his all fours like a horse . . . and said that he had come to stay . . .
until the grass grew on his back a foot long" (Dodd and Dodd, 97).

Phillips' freedom was short-lived. The Confederates captured him,
along with forty other draft evaders, and held him at Mitchell's Fort in Marion County. "The place where we were confined," Phillips wrote, "was too
filthy for a hog to stay" (Phillips, 25). Each "cell" was a crude one-room hut
made of rough oak logs driven through with large square-cut nails. Several
prisoners might be crowded into a single hut. A large aperture for a door
and a small "privy hole" near the floor were the only openings. Prisoners
were fed once a day, usually some boiled pork or beef. They had to eat with
their bare hands and drink water from a common bucket. There was no bed
or furniture. The captives would stay there until they agreed to serve in the
Confederate army (Thompson, 66–67).

John Phillips finally gave in and joined the Rebel army, but soon he deserted. One of several hundred Unionists who met at Natural Bridge in the
fall of 1862, he eventually enlisted in the Union 1st Alabama Cavalry.

The war generated painful breaches within mountain families. Winston County resident James Bell was a stalwart Unionist, along with four of his sons. A fifth son, Henry, living in Mississippi, pledged his loyalty to the Confederacy. James Bell wrote Henry expressing sorrow to have raised a son "that would secede from under the government that he was born and raised." Henry's mind was made up. He joined the Rebel army in November 1861 and even reported his family to the authorities for their disloyalty. His four brothers enlisted in the Union army. The family was never reunited. Henry died of sickness while serving in the Confederate army in March 1863. Three of his four Unionist brothers died in 1864, one from wounds, one from sickness, and one as a prisoner at Andersonville (Dodd, "Free State," 10).

The mountain war uprooted many families from their homes and forced refugees to relocate to other areas. James Jathan Gregory and his wife had settled on a forty-acre homestead in Bradley County, Tennessee, where they raised a large family. While Bradley County had voted against secession in 1861, Gregory was an outspoken Confederate who spent the early part of the war recruiting for the Rebel army. He also aided in arresting Unionist draft evaders and in raiding their homes. But in November 1863, following the Federal victory at Chattanooga, loyalist residents turned the tables on their Rebel neighbors. Now it was unsafe for Gregory and other Confederate sympathizers to remain, and many of them fled the county. Gregory moved his family to Murray County, Georgia, where he purchased a farm near Holly Creek in May 1864. The family never returned to Tennessee. Family tradition holds that after the war Gregory had to pay for his Georgia farm a second time, because his original payment had been in Confederate currency (Gregory, 11–20).

Four of the Gregory boys served in the Confederate army. Three of them—Stephen, Tapley, and James M.—returned to Bradley County in November 1863 without official leave to help their father relocate to Georgia. Alexander Seth, the youngest son, enlisted in February 1864. Stephen returned to duty in April 1864, was captured by Union forces in July, and spent the remainder of the war in a Northern prison. James M., Alexander Seth, and possibly Tapley joined John P. Gatewood's Confederate guerrillas who operated in the northwestern part of Georgia. After the war, all four brothers settled in Murray County with their father and other relatives. Tapley married and moved to Texas (Gregory, 11–20).

In West Virginia sometime after 1854, Laban Gwinn and his young bride settled on their homestead along the New River in Fayette County. The Gwinn family had originally immigrated from Wales more than 100 years earlier. Laban was 33 years old when the Civil War began, a Unionist living in a largely pro-Confederate area. In August 1862, after being robbed and burned out by Rebel bushwhackers, the Gwinns fled to Burlington, Indiana, and lived there until the end of the war. Gwinn's military pass to Ohio described him as "a good Union man" who was "in reduced circumstances." The war disrupted the lives of other members of the Gwinn clan too. Some became refugees and moved to Indiana and Ohio, and one brother was living in Iowa. Others served in the Federal army (Cox, 227–231).

For family members who remained in West Virginia, life was grim. Laban's younger brother John hoped to ride out the war in Fayette County, but eventually he had to take to the woods to evade enemy partisans. He wrote Laban in July 1863, "We have no peace here. I am still in the brush and expect to remain here untill fall unless accidentally ketched." John expressed delight that Laban was safe, mentioned that their parents were in "tolerable good health" but were concerned about their children being scattered. He went on to write, "I got out no crop this spring with the exception of garden and a small lot of corn and potatoes." Meanwhile, his wife had given birth to a baby girl. John later left Fayette County and relocated to Clinton County, Ohio, where he and his family were taken in by a Quaker couple. He wrote Laban in February 1865 that the Quakers were "first rate folks" and that their new neighbors had been very generous in seeing to their needs (Cox, 231–232, 236–237).

John returned to Fayette County in June 1865, bringing with him the Quaker couple's son who was interested in buying some farm land. He wrote Laban that conditions looked safe enough for him to return to West Virginia, although "Times are pretty hard up there." In the fall of 1865, maybe as late as 1866, Laban moved back to Fayette County. He returned to his farm, where he remained until his death in 1900. Ironically, the Gwinns lived only a few miles from W. D. Thurmond, said to be the leader of the Rebel partisans who burned the Gwinn home in 1862 (Cox, 240–245).

The disruption of everyday life was one of the first by-products of the guerrilla war. The mountain people adapted with stoic resignation. There were horrendous shortages. By the last year of the war, salt had become a luxury item. In the pre-industrial era of the 1860s salt was essential to farm families for preserving meat. Some mountaineers resorted to digging up the floors of their smokehouses. By filtering water through the soil and then boiling the water, one could get what little salt had seeped into the soil. It was filthy, but it could be used. Many other food products were in very short supply. Mountain women used sorghum molasses instead of sugar. They drank sassafras tea and concocted brews made from parched acorns, rye, okra, or corn-meal in place of coffee. Families had to make many everyday items like nails and buttons at home, because general stores ran out of supplies. Medicines were practically impossible to buy (DeLozier, 44).

In the dizzying early months of 1861 when men left to go into the Confederate army, they fully expected the war to be over in less than a year, and few of them gave adequate thought to the long-term needs of their families. Neither did they foresee the deep community divisions, food shortages, and physical dangers their families would confront. With husbands or sons gone, women faced the difficulties of life on the home front in a war that few of them asked for. Women had to cope with the threat of assault, hostility of neighbors, and the very real risk of starvation. Communities, often bitterly divided in loyalties, were no help, and women sometimes could not count on their own families for support. Even churches experienced deep splits, and many simply closed (McKinney, "Women's Role," 38–53).

The inhuman treatment of the Shelton Laurel women in January 1863 was not an isolated case in the mountains. Newspaper reports in February 1865 charged Confederate Home Guards in Wilkes County, North Carolina, with torturing women, some of them pregnant, to force them to reveal the whereabouts of deserters. Every day, women faced threats of physical violence, including the burning of their homes, assault, or actual death. Circumstances forced many women to become refugees. A Unionist woman in Transylvania County, North Carolina, spent two weeks on the run in the wilds with her mother, eight children, and two sisters. "I would get out of heart sometimes," she wrote, "and almost wish I had not started." But she pushed on, "being in dread of my life, they knowing that my husband was with the Yankees" (McKinney, "Women's Role," 44–49).

Despite the many dangers, women often took an active role in the mountain war, hiding deserters, sheltering Federal soldiers on the run from Rebel prisons, and acting as lookouts for guerrilla bands. Some women, like Malinda Blalock, became guerrillas themselves. In Wilkes County, North Carolina, a group of Unionist women in 1864 conducted raids on Confederate homesteads. In 1862 a Haywood County woman led a Rebel detachment into a Unionist ambush. A group of fifty desperate women looted a government warehouse in Yancey County in April 1864 and seized sixty barrels of grain (McKinney, "Women's Role," 43–47).

Historian Gordon McKinney believes the breakup of mountain society—produced by pressures of the war, the crippling of the mountain economy, and fragmenting of communities—left women without a support system and led many of them to abandon hope that the Confederacy could win. In the last two years of the war, women in western Carolina simply quit supporting the war, encouraged their husbands to desert, and unconsciously helped bring on the Confederacy's defeat ("Women's Role," 38).

Ironically, some mountain women attained greater independence during the war, because they were left with the responsibility of managing the family farm. Mary Bell, who lived in the hamlet of Franklin in western

North Carolina's Macon County, handled business transactions for her husband's dental practice as well as the couple's farm while he served in the Confederate army. She also spent a third of the war pregnant, gave birth to two children, and lost one. Like other mountain women, Mary encouraged her husband, Alfred, to get out of the army as soon as possible. She was fortunate, because her community, a base for William Stringfield's troops of Thomas' Legion, was spared the guerrilla raids so many mountain families feared. With the help of a hired slave and a white tenant, Mary kept the farm going and became a skillful manager by the end of the war, achieving a maturity and self-confidence that might not have been possible if not for the war (Inscoe, "Coping," 388–413).

Even for a strong woman, a brush with guerrillas could have grave consequences. Martha Dickson McConnell, a widow, lived in Chattooga County's Broomtown Valley in Georgia. A woman of fierce determination, Martha took her husband's former overseer to court to force him to disclose the location of gold she was sure her husband had buried on the couple's property before his death. Acting as her own attorney, she won a judgment against the man, who eventually left the county. No gold was ever found. Martha McConnell was a strong Rebel supporter, and Unionists raided her farm several times. Finally Martha had enough. When Unionist guerrillas led by John Long and Sam Roberts came once again to the McConnell home in the summer of 1864 to despoil the family of clothes, jewelry, and other personal items, Martha was enraged. She threatened to report the guerrillas' chief to the commander of the Union army garrison at LaFayette. The guerrillas laughed off the threat and warned her that she would regret it if she did (Hall, 13).

Mrs. McConnell did report the incident, and several days later Union soldiers arrested her along with her daughters, Sarah and Martha Ann, and her daughter-in-law, whose husband had been killed in the Confederate army. The women were then taken to Chattanooga, where they were charged with harboring Rebel scouts and engaging in pro-Rebel activities, and they spent the night of July 4 there. The next day the women were shipped to Nashville via cattle car. Sarah McConnell later wrote, "We were tired, hungry and so thirsty that we were thankful to drink out of a canteen politely offered by a filthy jabbering foreign soldier" (Baker, 369).

In Nashville the McConnell women were taken to the Federal military prison and were shown to a bleak cell on the second floor. The prison inmates, mostly captured Rebel soldiers, welcomed them with catcalls, sneers, and shouts of "fresh fish!" While the terrified women, without a decent change of clothing in days, cowered in the cell "alive with bed bugs . . . crawling everywhere," the prisoners banged on their door and showered them with profanity and vulgar threats (Baker, 368–370).

The McConnell women spent over ten months in captivity and were not released until the end of the war. They had to contend with threats of rape, both from their Yankee guards and Rebel prisoners, as well as hunger and indifference. The women eventually were paroled to civilian homes in Nashville. Meanwhile a prison romance ensued between Martha's youngest daughter, Martha Ann, and a Major Fields, a Confederate army doctor being held by the Federals. The McConnell women returned to Chattooga County to find the family homestead devastated. Martha Ann married Major Fields and left for the doctor's home in Texas; she lived with him for four years only to learn the shocking secret that he had poisoned his first wife, to whom he was already married when he and Martha Ann had met (Hall, 14).

Isolated mountain families lived in constant fear of raiding parties. Soldiers of both armies, as well as independent bands of guerrillas and outlaws, foraged freely. They ravaged the farms and fields of the mountain people, taking meat and grain and carrying away horses, cattle, and mules. Often they destroyed or burned what they could not take. They stole furniture, silver, clothes, and personal belongings. Families often were reduced to near starvation.

Family members sometimes took to the woods to avoid bushwhackers. In the Cherry Log community of Georgia's Gilmer County, 16-year-old Henry Pettit helped his mother while his stepfather served in the Confederate army. When his stepfather came home seriously wounded in the fall of 1864, Unionist partisans began to plague the household, and young Henry hid out near a mountain spring several miles away, accompanied only by a bull terrier named Watch. The dog "was as good as his name," Weaver wrote later, sleeping protectively by the boy through the long nights. Henry remained hidden in the woods, lighting no fire for fear the guerrillas might discover him. It was autumn, and severe weather was not yet a problem. When he ran out of food, Henry ventured back to his home. "I crept near enough to stand on the hillside above the house," he recalled, "and toss a pebble on the roof, which was my preconcerted signal. Someone came out and spoke, maybe into darkness, or otherwise gave a prearranged sign in return." Only if safe did he move closer (Ward, 340–341).

African-American families endured their share of privation in the mountains, although scholars have generally overlooked what social scientist Edward J. Cabbell calls "a neglected minority within a neglected minority." Blacks had lived in the mountains long before the first waves of white immigrants; many had come to the region with early Spanish and French explorers. Well-to-do Cherokees owned slaves, and nearly 1,000 black slaves followed their masters on the Trail of Tears to Oklahoma in 1838 (Turner and Cabell, xviii–xix, 4). There were 175,000 blacks living in the Southern Appalachians in 1860, nearly a tenth of the region's total population. More than 90 percent of them were slaves (Stuckert, 145). During the war, there were more slaves in the mountains than normal, because planters in areas under Federal occupation sent their slaves to the more secure mountain areas (Inscoe, "Moving," 165). In some parts of the mountains there were also settlements of free blacks (Eller, 9).

The manpower potential of black mountaineers was not lost on Northern planners. Abolitionist John Brown saw the mountains as the bastion of his proposed slave uprising in 1859, as an escape route for his raiders at Harpers Ferry, and as a stronghold for future operations (Inscoe, "Race," 109–110). After Lincoln opened the Union army to black enlistment in 1863, many black mountaineers served in Federal regiments, often guarding railroads and supply depots threatened by Rebel guerrillas in the mountains (Hattaway and Jones, 357–358).

Slaves were very active in the "underground railroad" that shepherded white Unionists out of Rebel territory. Northern soldiers who escaped from Southern prison camps were especially grateful to black families who hid, fed, and clothed them as they made their way through the mountains to Knoxville and other Federal military posts. John Azor Kellogg, an escaped Union officer crossing northern Georgia in the fall of 1864, found the slaves' knowledge of military activity very helpful. Slaves informed him of the location of Sherman's army, and he could rely on them to disclose which local whites could be trusted and which could not. Another Northern soldier, Albert Richardson, making his way through the western Carolina mountains, wrote that "every black face was a friendly face." Slaves "were always ready to help anybody opposed to the Rebels. Union refugees, Confederate deserters, escaped prisoners—all received from them the same prompt and invariable kindness. But let a Rebel soldier . . . apply to them, and he would find but cold kindness." Some of these Northerners even changed their negative attitudes toward blacks as a result (Inscoe, "Moving,"166–170).

Although the record is nearly silent, blacks did participate in guerrilla warfare in the mountains. A black partisan shot Rebel Colonel William Gibbs Allen in the hand in an ambush near Jonesborough, Tennessee, in November 1864 (Fisher, 73). According to Rebel partisan chief Ben McCollum, a Unionist bushwhacker named Jim Haircrow led a "negro band of thieves and robbers" operating north of Atlanta in the summer of 1864 (McCollum, "Big Shanty," 32). McCollum captured and attempted to hang a black renegade named Alf Donaldson, who had been raiding from a hideout on the northern side of the Etowah River. McCollum had neglected to search Donaldson. The black man whipped out his pocket knife, cut the noose from around his neck, and escaped into the woods (McCollum Papers).

Black families often became refugees, too. Famed educator Booker T. Washington's stepfather found work at a salt furnace in the Kanawha Valley in West Virginia and sent for his wife and children as soon as it was safe for them to leave their plantation in Virginia. It took several weeks for them to make the trip, sleeping in the open at night and cooking over a log fire. The family reached Malden, a salt-mining town five miles from Charleston, where they began a new life. Booker and his brother worked in one of the salt-furnaces, often starting well before sunrise. Like many uprooted families, they had to adjust to new living conditions in a crowded, unsanitary shantytown of black and white workers (Washington, 43–44).

The years between 1880 and 1900 witnessed the disappearance of blacks from ten Southern Appalachian counties, with fourteen more experiencing the same phenomenon by 1920. The lumber and mining industries attracted many to the new company towns. Racism and the hostility of mountain whites drove out others (Stuckert, 145).

The war was devastating to the Cherokee families in western North Carolina, bringing hunger, disease, and the destruction of their farms. A particularly tragic outbreak of smallpox killed 125 people in 1866. There was loss of confidence in the aging Little Will Thomas, who had led the Cherokees to defeat. Plagued by his own financial troubles and declining mental health, Thomas was increasingly unable to manage the Indians' affairs; his unintentional mishandling of their property and business interests opened the door for outsiders to exploit the Indians and rob them of their lands. There was bad blood between the Cherokees who had served the Confederacy and a minority who had fought with Union commands, and power struggles divided their leadership. In 1866 North Carolina's state government confirmed the Cherokees' right to their lands, and in 1868 the United States government formally recognized them as a separate tribe, the Eastern Band of the Cherokees. But poverty, lack of educational opportunity, and despair continued to plague these peaceful mountain people, as in other parts of Appalachia (Finger, 38–39).

The ultimate price paid by mountain families was the death of a family member. It was a price the Shelton Laurel families knew only too well. Sheltons had been the first white settlers of what became known as Shelton Laurel. Their descendants live there to this day. During the Civil War they were poor families. Of the twenty Shelton households that populated the valley in 1860, most owned less than $100 in property, a third of the per capita wealth for whites in the third poorest county in North Carolina (Paludan, 8–9, 26–27).

After the massacre at Shelton Laurel in January 1863, members of the victims' families removed the bodies from the mass grave in which the Rebel soldiers had placed them. They then buried them side by side on a nearby hilltop. Life was hard for the survivors. Mary Shelton, scarred mentally and physically from the torture she had endured, never recovered from the trauma. She had to be cared for by relatives, John and Matilda Shelton, for the rest of her life and suffered a mental breakdown before 1870. Young Martha White, wife of one of the Sheltons who was beaten and tied by her neck to a tree, moved in with her parents. Patsy Shelton was left to raise four children, two older girls who helped with the housework, and two sons too young to take part in the guerrilla war at the time. Patsy's husband, James Shelton, had been killed along with two older sons. In 1860 only one Shelton woman was the head of a household, but by 1870 seven were. The number of Sheltons (widows and children) living in households different from those in which they were born increased by ten between 1860 and 1870 (Paludan, 132–133).

Eight of the Shelton Laurel widows petitioned Congress in 1869 for pensions—eight dollars a month, with a smaller amount going to children under 16—based on the wartime service of their husbands in Union commands. Five of these women had husbands killed in the Shelton Laurel Massacre. Despite the support of North Carolina Governor W. W. Holden and several members of the state legislature, their petition lingered in committee. David Fry lent his voice to the widows' cause. He confirmed that he had enlisted the victims in a Unionist company as early as November 1861. Augustus Merrimon, who had investigated the massacre in 1863, urged the Senate to give the women's petition consideration. But in January 1874, the Senate rejected the petition. America was tired of hearing about the war (Paludan, 126–130).

Death could come suddenly and violently in the mountains. Families in the Unionist Stanley Creek area of Georgia's Fannin County learned this firsthand. A secluded valley not far from Morganton, Stanley Creek was no stranger to violence and had been raided by state troops in May 1864. On September 2, 1864, a Home Guard raiding party ambushed Elisha Stanley, a local gunsmith, near his home on Stanley Creek. Wearing a new pine straw hat with a red calico hat band, which his niece had made for him, and holding his sleeping baby boy in his lap, Stanley was in his work shed taking a break from his chores. Suddenly the calm was shattered by a musket blast, and Stanley toppled out of his chair, the red hat band split in two by a shot to the brain. His wife ran from the house to find Elisha lying dead on the ground, the baby sitting in a pool of his father's blood. Stanley's nephew ran from the house, and the Home Guards hiding in the forest fired on him as well, wounding him in the thigh. He carried the bullet in his leg until the day he died (Stanley, 84).

As the Home Guard party began to plunder the house, Elisha's niece Telitha jerked her recently made quilt from the hands of one of the raiders.

The Rebel smashed her in the side of her head with his rifle butt, destroying her eardrums and leaving her totally deaf and blind in one eye (Stanley, 85).

Elisha Stanley's brother-in-law Evan Hughes was captured at his home nearby, stood in front of a pine tree, and shot. Hughes and Elisha Stanley were later buried in the same grave. Also in the neighborhood two Kelley brothers who were friends of the Stanleys were taken prisoner. One of the brothers was able to escape by plunging into the Toccoa River, but the other was shot and killed. His badly decomposed body was discovered later by Telitha Stanley and her mother, who followed the vultures to the site in the woods where he lay (Stanley, 85).

For some mountaineers, revenge became all consuming. In Polk County, Georgia, the feud between Jack Colquitt's outlaws and Haden Prior's Home Guards reached a bloody climax in the spring of 1865. Although Prior seemed unconcerned with the gang's death threats, his sons John and James took them more seriously. Hoping to seize Colquitt before the situation escalated further, the Prior brothers found the bandit chief one night lying drunk in a Cedartown grocery store. Colquitt woke up cursing and grabbing for his gun. Before he could draw, the Prior brothers fired eight bullets into him. John Prior later wrote, "I was so close when I fired my first shot that I saw smoke coming out of his mouth" (Sargent, 378).

If the Priors expected their trouble with the Colquitt gang to end with the death of their leader, they were to be disappointed. The outlaws waited their chance for revenge. On April 6, 1865, four of the gang, led by a man named Phillips, gunned down Haden Prior and a black teenage servant as they were leaving a home near Prior's Station. Prior fell dead with a bullet through the heart. John Prior received the word of his father's death around noon that day. Just under six feet tall, slightly built but muscular, with piercing gray eyes, John Prior was not one to accept matters and forget. A rage welled up in him that would not be satisfied until he had taken revenge on all of Haden Prior's killers (Sargent, 378).

John gathered up a few friends and rode after the murderers. By midnight they had picked up the outlaws' trail at two homes that had been robbed. Prior tracked the fugitives across the Alabama line to the Piedmont community, but there the killers' trail vanished. Weary but undeterred, John rode south for several miles, then turned back to Piedmont. He spotted some schoolchildren and stopped to ask them if they had seen the men he was tracking. They told him they had seen them traveling north.

About nine miles north, John spied two of the outlaws sitting under some trees at a farmhouse near Coloma, with their horses tied nearby. "I remember the pink and white blossoms of the peach trees," John later recalled. As one of the outlaws reached for his gun, John leapt from his horse and blasted both men with buckshot from a double-barrel shotgun. One of the outlaws fell dead, and the other disappeared around the corner of the house. John drew his pistol, went after him, and found the bandit's dead body where he had collapsed (Sargent, 379).

A third outlaw bolted from the house and made for the woods, firing at Prior as he ran, but John overtook him and killed him too. One of the dead men appeared to be a member of the party that had killed Haden Prior. But Phillips, the ringleader, was not present, and neither were two other members of the gang. John's vendetta was unfinished. He rode home in time to attend his father's funeral.

John Prior searched for Phillips for three more months before he located him in July 1865 at a farm south of Cedartown. Prior, his brother, and two companions surrounded the farm late at night and waited for the outlaw to make his appearance. At daybreak, out came the unsuspecting bandit. As Phillips plowed his field, Prior crept up behind him and emerged from the woods with his pistol drawn. The outlaw fell to his knees pleading for his life, but Prior would not be moved. Phillips sprang to his feet and broke for the woods. Prior shot him in the back. Phillips fell and rolled over, and John calmly walked over to the bandit and fired a bullet into his heart at point-blank range. Phillips' wife and children looked on (Sargent, 380).

There remained two more members of the Colquitt gang involved in the murder of Hayd Prior. John Prior tracked one all the way to Arkansas, then for some reason decided to spare him. When John finally caught up with the last member of the gang, he learned that his quarry had already died of natural causes (Sargent, 380).

In the summer of 1864, many people in the Georgia mountains told of seeing a strange blood-red glow in the atmosphere, a hideous crimson gash across the northern and northwestern sky. "It's a sign," the old folks told their children, "a sign that the North is going to win this war. As long as we see the blood in the northern sky we must hold out some how." And wide-eyed little children drank in the heavenly apparition, and remembered, and many years later spoke of the experience to their grandchildren (Stanley, 75–76).

Great armies were on the move in that summer of 1864, legions of blue-coated and gray-clad men, their tens of thousands of weary feet churning the dirt roads of northern Georgia into dust. And in that hot, dry summer of 1864 a steady breeze that blew from south to north for many days, lifting the dust of the roads and the powder smoke from the guns and channeling it northward, produced a fluke of nature, a red sky in the north at sunset.

The belief in signs was a hallmark of the mountain folk of Appalachia, harkening back to their origins in Scotland, Ireland, or England. To a people close to the land, close to nature, signs in the heavens were to be observed, interpreted, and taken seriously. It had been a hard year for the mountain people. The Confederacy was dying. The war was devouring the young men of the mountains day by day. A series of bad winters and crop failures made life more miserable for poor mountain families. Food was desperately short. When the mountain people wondered at blood in the northern sky in that summer of 1864, with the blood of the Confederacy draining away, some of them read in it hope that the terror would soon end.

Rebel guerrillas in West Virginia mountains. (*Frank Leslie's Illustrated Newspaper,* August 23, 1862)

A Tennessee Unionist family. Daniel Jeffers with his family in Scott County. Jeffers served with a Unionist Home Guard company. (Huntsville–Madison County Public Library)

Victims of guerrilla violence. Union scout Daniel Ellis discovers the skeletons of three men killed by Rebel guerrillas in Tennessee. (*Thrilling Adventures of Daniel Ellis*)

Unionist refugees cross the mountains to the safety of Federal-occupied territory in Tennessee. (*Harper's Weekly*, September 19, 1863)

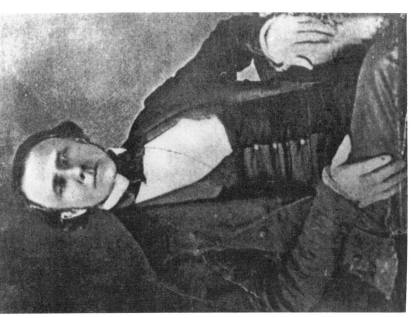

Colonel William H. Thomas, commander of Thomas' Legion, led Cherokees and white mountaineers in guerrilla operations against Federal troops in the North Carolina mountains. (North Carolina Division of Archives and History, Raleigh)

Malinda Blalock posed as a man to join the Confederate army with her husband, Keith, and later fought at his side as a Unionist guerrilla in the North Carolina mountains. (Miscellaneous Photographs, P-4090, photo of Malinda Blalock; from the Southern Historical Collection, Wilson Library, the University of North Carolina at Chapel Hill)

Lieutenant Colonel William W. Stringfield, Thomas'
North Carolina Legion, saw action against Unionist
raiders in the North Carolina mountains. (North
Carolina Division of Archives and History, Raleigh)

Cherokee veterans of Thomas' North Carolina Legion at a reunion in 1901. Lieutenant Colonel
Stringfield is on the far left. (North Carolina Division of Archives and History, Raleigh)

Soldiers of the 15th Pennsylvania Cavalry photographed at Lookout Mountain, Chattanooga, Tennessee, saw considerable action in the war against Rebel guerrillas in the Southern Appalachians. (*History of the 15th Pennsylvania Cavalry*)

Railroad bridge at Strawberry Plains, Tennessee. Union partisans failed to burn this vital bridge across the Holston River in November 1861. (National Archives and Records Administration)

Champ Ferguson, most feared of the Tennessee mountain guerrillas, photographed before his execution in Nashville in October 1865. (Tennessee State Library and Archives, Nashville, Tennessee)

Daniel Ellis guided thousands of Tennessee Unionists to Federal lines. (*Thrilling Adventures of Daniel Ellis*)

The execution of Champ Ferguson in Nashville, October 20, 1865, marked the end of the most notorious guerrilla in the Southern Appalachians. (*Frank Leslie's Illustrated Newspaper*, November 11, 1865)

Federal troops burn Tennessee River Bridge, Decatur, Alabama. Harsh Federal measures against civilians in North Alabama invited retaliation by Rebel guerrillas. (Alabama Department of Archives and History, Montgomery, Alabama)

Captain Frank B. Gurley, Alabama cavalry
officer, was held for eighteen months on charges
that he murdered Union General Robert L.
McCook in a guerrilla action in North Alabama. (Huntsville–Madison County Public Library)

The death of Brigadier General Robert L. McCook, August 1862, as depicted in *Harper's Weekly*. The
Northern press blamed McCook's death on Rebel partisan Frank B. Gurley. (*Harper's Weekly*, August
23, 1862)

Major General George H. Thomas, in conference with staff officers at Ringgold, Georgia, in May 1864. Thomas employed an extensive network of Unionist spies and guerrillas, including partisan James G. Brown. (National Archives)

Benjamin F. McCollum, Confederate partisan, operated in Cherokee County, Georgia, in 1864. (Benjamin F. McCollum Collection, Kennesaw Mountain National Battlefield Park, Marietta, Georgia)

General William T. Sherman. His invading Federal troops were harassed by Rebel guerrillas in North Georgia in 1864. (National Archives)

Lumpkin County Courthouse, Dahlonega, Georgia, c. 1880. The courthouse was headquarters for Confederate partisan Colonel James J. Findley. Captured Unionists Stuart, Stansbury, and Witt were held here prior to their execution by firing squad in October 1864. (Courtesy, Georgia Department of Archives and History)

PART IV

North Georgia

Chapter 11

"Union Men to the Core"

The Georgia mountains were a bastion of Unionist sympathy from the very start of the war. As early as May 1861, loyal Confederates in the region were warning of loyalist unrest. A Dalton resident wrote Confederate Vice President Alexander Stephens, "It will be a very fortunate circumstance, if bands of tories and robbers can be kept down. There are too many spies in our midst." About the same time, members of the Kingston Home Guards wrote Governor Joseph E. Brown that "an armed body of discreet persons" was essential to protect the community from "suspicious characters." A Murray County man hinted of Unionist conspiracy when he wrote the governor on May 21 that a group of dangerous men in the county was forming a "home guard" company. They were about to request arms from the governor, and he hinted that Brown should be conveniently short of guns when they applied (Bryan, 137, 140).

Brown responded to fear of Unionist uprising with diplomacy. He sought to play down potential trouble, hoping that a policy of restraint eventually would win the support of the mountaineers. When Union sympathizers in Pickens County defiantly raised the United States flag in Jasper and kept it flying for several weeks, Brown took no action. When Unionists in Lumpkin County blustered about seizing the Federal mint at Dahlonega, Brown did no more than transfer the facility to state control. He used every means at his disposal to avoid confrontation and gave military companies from the mountain counties preferential treatment whenever he could (Bryan, 140).

Growing reports of trouble in the mountains forced Brown to treat the situation more seriously. Brown's first concern was the security of the Western and Atlantic Railroad—called the Georgia State Road—between Atlanta and Chattanooga. In November 1861, William Carter's bridge raid in East Tennessee sparked genuine alarm, and David Fry and his men tore up tracks in Georgia as far south as Marietta. Early in 1862, Unionists set fire to two of the bridges over Chickamauga Creek.

Federal spy James J. Andrews and a team of eight men failed in March 1862 to burn the bridges on the railroad west of Chattanooga. In April, Andrews embarked on a more daring mission. With twenty-four men he made his way to Big Shanty (now Kennesaw), Georgia, where he commandeered a locomotive on April 12 and drove it northward on the Western and Atlantic, planning to burn the bridges along that line to Chattanooga. The raid was part of a plan to isolate Chattanooga, weakly held by the Confederates, and was not unlike Carter's bridge-burning scheme. Andrews' raid was a failure. Following a wild chase along the railroad line, Georgia troops captured Andrews and twenty-two of his raiders, Ohio soldiers who had volunteered for the secret mission. The prisoners were treated as spies. Andrews and seven raiders were tried by court-martial, found guilty, sentenced to death, and executed. The others remained in prison in Atlanta.

Besides the threat of Unionist saboteurs, Brown contemplated the ever alarming danger of deserter bands forming in the mountains. He was flooded with pleas from loyal people. In the summer of 1862 Gilmer County's Walter Webster Findley wrote that "tories and deserters who have taken up their abode in the mountains" had "burnt up soldiers wives' houses and threatened their lives if molested." He added, "some of our own citizens are with them." And Josiah A. Woody of Lumpkin County wrote Brown, "these blue mountains . . . are being filled with tories and deserters and thieves and runaway Negroes, and they are robbing soldiers' families." Woody said that even preachers had to arm themselves for protection (Sarris, "Execution," 138).

Lumpkin County was the refuge of local hothead Jefferson Anderson, whose gang hid in the mountains, robbed and terrorized, harbored runaway slaves, and grew larger and bolder as time went on. Anderson, a deserter from the 1st Georgia Volunteer Infantry, had been in trouble with the law often. In February 1862 Lumpkin County Sheriff John Early arrested him and locked him up in the jail in Dahlonega. Anderson was tried and convicted of two counts of "Assault and Battery," for which he was fined $50 each, and one count of "Assault and Battery With Intent to Commit Rape," for which he was fined only $10. On a Sunday morning, March 9, 1862, Anderson was in jail waiting to be turned over that day to the military as a deserter. Jeff's brothers, Henry and Doc Anderson, and their friend Bart Edge, had other plans.

Edge and the Anderson brothers rode into Dahlonega early that morning and hitched their horses at the jail. When John McCroskey, the jailer, arrived with breakfast for the prisoner, they asked if they could go inside and see Jeff. McCroskey obliged and opened the prisoner's cell door. Jeff suddenly became "powerful sick" and asked for a doctor. Before McCroskey had a chance to send for the doctor, Jeff suddenly bolted through the door and ran headlong down the front steps and across the town square. Edge stepped in front of McCroskey to slow him down. McCroskey managed to wrest himself loose and run after the prisoner but could not overtake him. Later the Andersons and Bart Edge were charged with aiding in Jeff's escape. They probably had slipped Jeff a file which he had used to cut the log chain securing him to the cell wall, but they denied it and insisted that if they had known what Jeff was planning they would have stopped him. They were never prosecuted (Kinsland, "Civil War," 180–181).

Jeff Anderson joined Unionist saboteurs planning to burn railroad bridges. He was captured, and soon he found himself again behind bars, this time in Atlanta with other bridge burners and survivors of the failed Andrews raid. In the same jail was Tennessee bridge burner David Fry, awaiting execution for his guerrilla activities. Sometime in late 1862 Anderson, Fry, and some of the Andrews raiders broke out of the Atlanta jail. Anderson made his way back to Lumpkin County and continued his activities as a guerrilla leader in the mountains (O'Kelley, 19).

After the bloody Confederate victory at Chickamauga in September 1863, it seemed that northern Georgia might escape most of the ravages of the Civil War. But in November 1863, Federal forces under General Ulysses Grant smashed Braxton Bragg's army at Chattanooga and secured that important transportation center for the Union. Grant now could reinforce Knoxville and push Longstreet's Confederates out of East Tennessee. With Tennessee firmly under Union control, the Federals could use Chattanooga as a springboard for Sherman's campaign for Atlanta, the South's key manufacturing center. In May 1864, the war entered the North Georgia mountains.

With no railroad to anchor them to more populated centers, Gilmer, Fannin, Union, and Lumpkin Counties had always been the most isolated area of northeastern Georgia. By 1864, with Union and Confederate forces focusing all their efforts on the Atlanta campaign, the region was neglected by both warring armies. As civil authority collapsed, this beautiful mountainous part of Georgia was condemned to a living hell of killing and violence. Unionist guerrilla chiefs John Hatley and William Slate were active in Gilmer and Fannin Counties, and redheaded Rebel partisan John Gatewood also operated there on occasion. Raiders crossed the Tennessee line into Georgia via the natural invasion route of the Ocoee-Toccoa River past the Ducktown copper mines and plundered the peaceful mountain valleys unchecked, bringing indescribable misery to a people already exhausted by more than three years of brutal war.

Guerrilla activity also intensified in northwestern Georgia. In Walker County, sandwiched into a "V" between Lookout Mountain and the lower Pigeon Mountain to its south, lay the beautiful farmland valley called McLemore's Cove, named for the McLemore brothers, Cherokee chiefs who lived in the area before the Removal. The valley sheltered Unionist guerrillas led by local boys John Long and Sam Roberts. Sworn enemies of John Gatewood's Rebels who operated in the area, they often left the sanctuary of "The Cove" and crossed Pigeon Mountain to raid homesteads in northern Chattooga County (Baker, 367).

The Long-Roberts gang tracked Ernest and Christopher McSpadden, two popular local Rebel boys, to a vacant house in Dirt Town Valley. Christopher had moved his brother, sick at his mother's home, to the abandoned house because he had received a tip that the Long-Roberts band was after them. In a blazing gunfight in which Sam Roberts had a thumb shot off, the raiders killed Chris, then murdered Ernest, still lying sick in bed but trying feebly to defend himself with his pistol. Later Roberts rode to Mrs. McSpadden's home and presented her with the bloody clothing of her dead sons and told her how he had killed them. He made her serve breakfast to him and his men. A local preacher, T. C. Crawford, retrieved the brothers' bodies and carried them in his wagon for burial in the Bethel Cemetery, but members of the Long-Roberts gang prevented a slave from digging the grave. Crawford finally persuaded the men to allow the brothers a decent burial, finished the digging himself, and laid the McSpaddens in a single grave (Sartain, 124, 237–238).

James George Brown, one of the most active Union partisans in North Georgia, grew up as an orphan in Murray County. Anxious to make something of himself, he studied for the law and married Margaret Leticia ("Letty") Adair, daughter of a prosperous farmer. James borrowed heavily to build a sawmill and then lost the mill when he could not repay the loans. He escaped his creditors by relocating to Holmes County, Mississippi, taking his wife and baby boy with him, and began a new life as a schoolteacher. Letty gave birth to a second child but died sometime near the start of the war. With two small children to look after, James married again, this time to the sister of a well-to-do local landowner. In April 1862, Brown surfaced in Federal-occupied New Orleans, where Major General Benjamin F. Butler recruited him into a team of Union operatives formed to keep tabs on Rebel sympathizers. Brown's relationship with Butler was a rocky one, and by the end of the summer he was behind bars. But Major General Nathaniel Banks, who replaced Butler, found Brown to be a useful agent, and in September 1863 he ordered him released (Davis, "Brown," 18–20).

About 30 years old at the time, Brown was intelligent, articulate, about five feet five inches tall, with a dark complexion, black hair, and black eyes. He was a quick thinker and a glib talker with the ability to promote fanciful ideas. Banks wrote that Brown "knows the character and spirit of the Southern people and I believe any statements he may make upon these subjects, can be relied upon." In January 1864 Brown reported to Secretary of War Edwin M. Stanton in Washington and tried to interest him in a blockade-running scheme to capture Southern cotton and help finance the war. Brown presented Stanton with a written proposal outlining his plan and boasted that he could deliver 50,000 bales of Confederate cotton within three months. Stanton paid Brown $1,000 for the information but did not pursue the matter (Davis, "Brown," 20–21, 29, n. 18).

In February 1864, Brown reported to General George H. Thomas, Federal commander at Chattanooga. Thomas, who utilized an extensive espionage network, appointed Brown his civilian chief of scouts, and James found himself back in North Georgia operating as a Union spy. Brown left Chattanooga on a number of clandestine trips to Dalton, Rome, Atlanta, and other cities behind enemy lines. He took audacious risks, sometimes even wearing a Confederate uniform, and had two narrow escapes, bruising a rib while evading Rebel guerrillas and contracting a minor wound when he had a horse shot from under him. He sent regular coded reports to Thomas, signing them "Letty" after his first wife, and informed Thomas of Rebel troop movements, civilian morale, and friendly and unfriendly guerrilla bands. His observations added to the accuracy of Federal military maps of the region (Davis, "Brown," 22–23).

The existing Unionist network of guides, "safe" houses, and signals used by deserters and refugees in North Georgia came ready-made for Brown, and he established his own web of spies. He had signed up seventeen scouts by March 20, and he made Dalton his base of operations after the mountain town was occupied by Federal troops on May 13. Brown recruited Unionist Home Guard companies in the mountains, cautioning each not to rob and plunder and not to act on personal vendettas. He formed a fifty-man antiguerrilla cavalry company to neutralize Confederate raiders in the area (Davis, "Brown," 23). On May 28, 1864, Brown was in the mountains near Ellijay "gathering information of guerrilla parties" there (USWD, I, 38, iv: 337–338, 423).

In early June 1864, Brown led 200 Federal soldiers on a raid into Pickens County, where he arrested three local secessionists and confiscated horses, corn, bacon, several slaves, and gold from one of the prisoners' farms. But when the Yankees attempted to arrest Rebel sympathizer James Simmons, they ran into Ben Jordan's Confederate guerrillas, who opened fire on the party and chased them out of the county. A Rebel correspondent reported that Brown, "with more brass, impudence and sharpness than intellect," claimed Lincoln had appointed him military governor of Georgia (Macon *Daily Telegraph*, June 11, 1864)!

On August 9, 1864, Thomas authorized Brown to recruit local mountaineers and organize them into the first Federal regiment made up of Georgians. The command would be used to guard Sherman's supply line along the Western and Atlantic Railroad to Chattanooga. Brown wasted no time. With the help of Dr. John A. Ashworth he recruited men from Pickens, Union, and Dawson Counties. At the end of August Brown only had about 300 recruits, not enough for a full regiment but enough for a battalion of four companies that he christened the 1st Georgia State Troops Volunteers, with himself as colonel and Ashworth as lieutenant colonel. Two of his captains, Elias Darnel and George H. Turner, were deserters from Georgia Confederate regiments. First Sergeants Milton Nix, Martin P. Berry, and Virgil D. Monroe were deserters from the 52nd Georgia Infantry, as were a number of other enlisted men. Brown promised his recruits army pay, a $300 bounty, clothing, food, weapons, and ammunition. They had to procure their own horses. They enlisted for three years and were to serve only in Georgia guarding the railroad (Davis, "Forgotten," 271–272).

Leaving Ashworth in charge, Brown traveled to Washington to promote his cotton blockade-running idea. He met with Secretary of State William Seward and requested a meeting with Lincoln to seek an appointment as military governor of Georgia. Brown promised to enlist 5,000–10,000 Unionist troops. On September 29, he wrote Lincoln outlining his plans, but by then Atlanta had fallen. The letter remained unanswered, and Brown never met with the president (Davis, "Brown," 25).

By the time Brown returned to Georgia in mid-October 1864, he found his men under fire for neglect of their duties. Colonel Lewis Johnson, commander of the 44th U.S. Colored Infantry Regiment stationed in Dalton, lodged the most serious charge. On October 13, 1864, Rebel General John B. Hood, having evacuated Atlanta, surprised the Dalton garrison on his march northwest into Tennessee, and Johnson, fearing a massacre, surrendered his command of 751 men. The Rebs focused special abuse on the black soldiers, stripping them of their shoes and clothing and putting them to work tearing up railroad track. When one of the soldiers refused to work, they shot him down on the spot. Five more men who had been sick and were too weak to keep up were also shot and left lying in the road (USWD, I, 39, i: 718–721). A gloating Rebel newspaper correspondent reported, "The negroes . . . will not be treated as prisoners of war, but if any of them should live long they will be reduced to their normal condition" (Macon *Daily Telegraph*, October 21, 1864).

A bitter Johnson blamed Brown's 1st Georgia State Troops. Brown's men, he wrote, had been poor scouts and had failed to give the garrison any advance warning of the enemy. He reported: "These men fled, at the approach of the rebels, to the mountains, as they had done previously on a similar occasion (October 2, 1864), when Wheeler threatened the place and demanded surrender. I furnished these men with such arms as were at my disposal, but I could never even get men enough of these 200 to furnish a picket of only three or four men" (USWD, I, 39, i: 720).

Not only did Brown have to contend with Johnson's charges, but the Rebels also had plundered his home in Dalton. Soon he was at odds with his new commander, Major General James B. Steedman, who replaced Thomas after he was assigned to command at Nashville. While Thomas apparently regarded Brown as an effective scout, Steedman had no use for him. "I consider James G. Brown a very unreliable individual," he wrote in January 1865. "I do not regard Mr. Brown as a fit man to have charge of either soldiers or citizen scouts. His services have not promoted either the interest or credit of the Federal army" (Davis, "Brown," 23–24, 26).

An eyewitness who got a close look at Brown's men in Pickens County sometime during the fall of 1864 left a more favorable account of the Union guerrillas. Colonel John Azor Kellogg of the 6th Wisconsin Infantry escaped from a prisoner of war camp in South Carolina. Hoping to reach Sherman's army, he made his way across Georgia.

Kellogg and two companions had crossed the Etowah River and were near the vicinity of Jasper. As they were making their way around a turn in the road in the wee hours of the morning, they met an armed sentinel wearing what looked like a gray uniform. They struck up a conversation, and after nearly an hour of chatter the wary Kellogg discovered the man actually was a light-skinned slave. When Kellogg described his own predicament, the black man agreed to escort him to the Jasper Home Guard, a band of about 100 Unionist guerrillas under the command of Major George W. McCrary, who was none other than the sheriff of Pickens County as well as an officer in Brown's 1st Georgia State Troops Volunteers.

Kellogg agreed to go with the sentinel but kept a gun handy in case of a trap. The group arrived at a log cabin, knocked at the door, and after a momentary delay a woman opened it a crack. She fed breakfast to the famished Yankee runaways and explained that her husband had slipped out of the house thinking they were Rebels; they would see him at the Unionists' meeting place. After leaving the cabin Kellogg and his party continued down the road until they encountered a mounted picket wearing a gray uniform. At first Kellogg feared he had been betrayed into the hands of the

Rebels, but soon it became clear that the sentinel was indeed a member of a Unionist guerrilla company who guided the men to his camp. Kellogg described what he saw:

> We found perhaps a dozen men, all armed, in and around a small but comfortable log house. The guard reported us to one whom he saluted as Major, who immediately put us through a thorough questioning. We told him who we were, and the rank and regiment of each. We showed him our letters, and, among other things, our compass and map. After undergoing a rigid examination, we were successful in convincing our new-found Union men that we were in very truth Yankees and escaped prisoners, and we were permitted to go where we pleased, being cautioned, however, that it was highly dangerous to stray far from camp. (163)

During his stay, Kellogg noticed that the guerrillas always went about armed, with "muskets, carbines, revolvers, shot-guns—anything that would shoot." He saw several men, each with a musket strapped on his back, digging sweet potatoes. Kellogg learned that the Union men were locked in a death struggle with Ben Jordan's Rebel guerrillas and that both bands conducted periodic raids on the other. He wrote, "When we arrived in camp they were momentarily expecting an attack. The men were stationed where they could overlook the different roads, with orders, if attacked, to fall back slowly to camp, sending in information to the commander, Major McCreary [sic], so that he might put his men in the best possible position to receive the enemy" (165–168).

The guerrillas told Kellogg that a month earlier one of their men had been ambushed and killed by Jordan's band. A Rebel lured the man from his hiding place in the woods under the guise of being interested in joining the Unionist Home Guard. Before the man could reach his cabin, about a dozen more of Jordan's guerrillas came out of cover and jumped him. They tied him up, tortured and mutilated him, and then hung his body to a tree in front of his home. Kellogg wrote, "It was a war of extermination between them. No prisoners were taken by either side" (164, 168).

Kellogg was astounded at the raw poverty and illiteracy he witnessed in the Unionists' camp. Some of the men had never seen a compass, which one open-mouthed mountain man called "that little thing" that he had brought with him when he first arrived at the camp. "But," Kellogg was quick to add, "they were generous, hospitable, brave, and Union men to the core" (168–169, 171–172).

While he was a guest of the guerrillas, Kellogg attended a happier event, the wedding of a local girl named Mary to one of the guerrillas, a young man who happened to be a deserter from the Union army! The ceremony took place in a rustic log cabin, with one small window, and only a bed and a rude pine table and chairs for furniture. A roaring fire blazed in the large fireplace that took up nearly one side of the cabin. The guerrillas attended the wedding armed, and sentries were posted in the woods as lookouts. About thirty to forty men and women crowded together in the cabin, while the bride and groom stood in front of the fireplace. The young bride, Kellogg recalled, was "well-developed" and "looked substantial and durable, rather than beautiful." She wore a simple bright-colored calico dress, woolen stockings, and leather shoes. Her lush hair was held in place with a horn comb. The groom wore a clean white shirt, coat, and pants. While the preacher administered the marriage vows, the guerrillas and their women looked on, some of them standing, others sitting on the bed or in the chairs, others squatting on the floor, but all with their muskets ready. At the conclusion of the ceremony, the young groom kissed his bride lustily and asked her how she liked getting married. Mary replied, "I wouldn't mind gitt'n' married every day" (173–177).

The marriage ceremony was followed by a night of revelry in true mountain style, with singing and music and good-natured horseplay. "Such pulling and hauling and kissing of the bride," Kellogg wrote, "such kissing of everybody who would submit to being kissed, and of some who wouldn't; such screaming and laughing; such jostling and mixing, surely never were seen before." The celebration continued until about one o'clock in the morning before the party finally broke up (177–178).

On the last day of Kellogg's stay with the guerrillas, two of Jordan's men came into the camp under a flag of truce. They offered McCrary an armistice between the two rival gangs. Each band would respect the private property of the other. McCrary spurned the offer. He told them he would agree to a truce only on the condition that they be compensated for their property and possessions already destroyed by Jordan's band. That night, McCrary and ten of his men guided Kellogg and his two comrades to the Union lines at Calhoun and took their leave (Kellogg, 179–181).

Brown did not know it, but his 1st Georgia battalion was on a collision course with Colonel James J. Findley and his Rebel Home Guards from Lumpkin County. On November 5, 1864, while foraging in the Bucktown area of eastern Gilmer County, Lieutenant Colonel Ashworth, McCrary, and twenty-six of their men were surprised by Findley's much larger Rebel force. Nearly all of Ashworth's men were captured or killed. Twelve of them, including 1st Sergeant Milton Nix, were hanged two days later in Gainesville. McCrary was paroled, only to be gunned down about a week later by John Gatewood's guerrillas in Tennessee. Ashworth spent the rest of the war in a Rebel prison camp and died shortly after being liberated at the end of the fighting. Findley's raid dealt a death blow to Brown's guerrillas, already under severe criticism for their failure at Dalton (Davis, "Forgotten," 272–274).

Brown's guerrillas were never officially a part of the Union Army; in fact they had joined with the understanding they were to serve only in Georgia. Since their conduct had been less than exemplary, especially during the Rebel capture of Dalton, Sherman and Secretary of War Stanton declined to admit the 1st Georgia into the Union Army. Brown's troops were ordered dismissed on November 2, 1864. The disastrous clash with Findley's guerrillas came three days later. The ax fell on December 15 when Brown's command was disbanded. His men never received the pay and bounties they had been promised (Davis, "Forgotten," 273). Colonel Lewis Merrill was especially critical of Brown and his guerrillas, calling them "utterly worthless," and "heterogeneous trash." The veteran cavalry officer concurred with Steedman's opinion of the scouts and wrote, "They are simply cowardly thieves—useless, except to keep a community embroiled and encourage guerrillas by running from them whenever attacked. . . . The conduct of these men serves only to embitter the people and prolong the continuance of guerrilla practice" (USWD, I, 49, ii: 606).

The army's disappointment with Brown's 1st Georgia reflected a profound lack of understanding about the realities of the war in the mountains. The Union commanders expected the Georgians to perform like a conventional military unit, protecting supply lines and railroads and providing intelligence as scouts. The guerrillas expected to be armed in order to fight their secessionist enemies, to protect their families, and to retaliate for previous wrongs done to them (Sarris, "Anatomy," 704–705).

After Brown's 1st Georgia was broken up, many of his men enlisted in the 5th Tennessee Mounted Infantry. Others joined the 1st Georgia Infantry Battalion, formed by 23-year-old Major Dewitt C. Howard. A Georgian serving as an officer in the 103rd Ohio Infantry, Howard had tried and failed to raise a brigade of troops from Georgia mountaineers in November 1863. He mustered two companies in October 1864 from Pickens and Dawson Counties. This unit was used to guard the railroad in North Georgia until being discharged in July 1865 (Davis, "Forgotten," 271, 274).

James G. Brown never gave up on his espionage schemes and his attempts to curry favor with the Union army command. He tried to sign on as a spy with Sherman, now in South Carolina, but nothing came of this. Charges began to surface that Brown himself was passing secrets to the Confederates. Colonel H. F. Sikes wrote on March 9, 1865, that Brown was "by no means reliable or free from suspicions." Finally, Brown was court-martialed on April 18, 1865. General Steedman leveled several charges at the former scout: corresponding with known Rebel guerrilla leaders as early as December 1, 1864; being party to the robbery of a Dalton woman of

$1,000; and passing supplies to the Rebels. Brown proclaimed his innocence and accused the prosecution's witnesses of being former Rebels with grudges (Davis, "Brown," 26–27).

The case against Brown broke down when the prosecution failed to provide any testimony that Brown had actually committed any unlawful acts. The only thing that could be proved was that he had written to Henry Stafford, a Rebel guerrilla leader, to thank Stafford for giving protection to his children. There appeared to be nothing sinister in this, and although Brown had been charged with furnishing provisions to Stafford's wife, there were no witnesses to confirm this. Witnesses testified that Brown had provided supplies to several women in Dalton. One witness told of the unarmed guerrilla chief's bravery in facing down a band of Rebels. Another told how Brown once escaped from a group of Rebels by outriding them while under fire. Brown's former benefactor, General George Thomas, testified in a deposition, "his information generally was very reliable. Whilst on a campaign his information was not so reliable but I have no doubt of Mr. Brown's veracity in giving me what he thought was reliable information." Brown wrote, "The testimony of Major General Thomas and the fact that the rebels appeared to have a very decided inclination to kill me is a sufficient answer to the Second Charge & Specification." Brown was released (Davis, "Brown," 27–28).

The survivors of Brown's 1st Georgia State Troops Volunteers and their families fought a largely fruitless battle for fifty years after the war petitioning Congress for some compensation for their service with Union forces. But with most of their officers dead and the original membership roster destroyed in the Rebel raid on Dalton in October 1864, they had little luck. They never received any compensation for their four months of service under Brown (Davis, "Forgotten," 274).

Other Georgia mountaineers—their patience worn thin, unable to evade Confederate conscription any longer, ready at last to follow their conscience, or at least to get revenge on the men who had made life so miserable for their families—also were putting on the Union blue. In the fall of 1864, Colonel Spencer B. Boyd's 5th Tennessee Mounted Infantry Regiment was formed at Cleveland, Tennessee. Recruits came from Bradley, McMinn, Hamilton, and Meigs Counties in Tennessee, and from Fannin, Gilmer, Pickens, Lumpkin, and Dawson Counties in Georgia (Civil War Centennial Commission, 358). Sion A. Darnell, whose father had helped raise the United States flag over the courthouse in Jasper in 1861, enlisted in the 5th Tennessee Mounted in December 1864 after serving in James G. Brown's Pickens County company. Darnell maintained that the 5th Tennessee Mounted consisted mainly of Georgians (Davis, "Memoirs," 113). The regiment's brief period of service was mostly spent in uneventful garrison duty at Dalton and at Marietta guarding railroads.

The most aggressive recruiter for the 5th Tennessee Mounted was Fannin County's William Albert Twiggs. Twiggs had joined the 52nd Georgia Infantry in March 1862. Captured at Vicksburg on July 4, 1863, and paroled three days later, Twiggs finally deserted from the 52nd Georgia in September 1863, after the battle of Chickamauga. Concerned about the safety of his wife and children, he made his way back to Fannin County and then to Cleveland, where Boyd commissioned him to recruit. Twiggs returned to Fannin County in mid-September 1864 and looked up Iley T. Stuart at his home near Higdon's Store. Stuart was also doing recruiting duty in Fannin County, but for a different Union regiment (Kinsland, "Murder," 14, 16).

Iley Stuart was a well-known local blacksmith with strong Union leanings. Somehow he had avoided being drafted into the Confederate army and in September 1863 had enlisted in Colonel Isham G. Young's 11th Tennessee Union Cavalry. Now he was back in Fannin County recuperating from a recent bout with jaundice but armed with papers from Young authorizing him to recruit for the 11th Tennessee Cavalry. Stuart's wife, Margaret, said of him, "He was a Union man from the first and cursed and abused the rebels for the way they did" (Kinsland, "Murder," 14, 16).

For a time Stuart and Twiggs may have flirted with the idea of enrolling their men in Brown's 1st Georgia State Troops Volunteers, where Stuart's brother-in-law John A. Ashworth was second-in-command. But Brown barely had enough recruits to form a battalion and not enough for a complete regiment; Twiggs' and Stuart's men would have to go into another command. Twiggs talked Stuart into merging their two companies into one, Twiggs' Company H of the 5th Tennessee Mounted (Kinsland, "Murder," 16).

Twiggs rode into Morganton on the afternoon of September 25, 1864, accompanied by his recruits. With him were William R. Witt and Solomon Stansbury, two well-to-do Fannin County farmers with large families. Stansbury was actually a deserter from the Union 1st Tennessee Artillery Battalion (Kinsland, "Murder," 15).

The men dismounted at the old Fannin County Courthouse, and Twiggs addressed a gathering of curious onlookers from the steps. He reminded the townspeople of the abuses and injuries they had suffered at the hands of Confederate Home Guards and told them that the Union army would protect them. He appealed to them to join the 5th Tennessee Mounted Infantry. And he went even further. He vowed to lead them in chasing the hated Home Guards out of the county. When someone in the crowd pointed out that neither he nor his men were in Federal uniform and questioned his authority to raise a company, Twiggs faced him down with a threat to conscript local men for service whether they wished to join or not. Slowly, some perhaps reluctantly, twenty new volunteers stepped forward (Kinsland, "Murder," 16–17).

Twiggs stirred up a hornets' nest with his fiery speech. Emboldened by their leader's rhetoric, his recruits struck out in small units from their camp near the Dial community in the southern part of the county. They swept down on Confederate households in the area, sometimes attacking Home Guard bands as well. Groups of independent bushwhackers used the occasion to lash out at old Rebel enemies too in a wave of killing, burning, and looting that invited retaliation from James J. Findley's Rebel guerrillas (Sarris, "Anatomy," 702–703).

Twenty-seven-year-old Robert Porter Woody of Gilmer County joined Twiggs' company of the 5th Tennessee Mounted as a lieutenant on February 1, 1865. He had enlisted in Smith's Georgia Legion in August 1862 but had deserted at Danville, Kentucky, two months later. He also had served briefly in the summer of 1864 in Brown's 1st Georgia State Troops Volunteers. In May 1865 Woody was injured when his horse tripped and fell on him while he was chasing Rebel guerrillas. Woody would become embroiled in a postwar feud with the Findleys that would lead to a famous shootout in Gilmer County in 1884 (Barker Papers, Vol. 5).

Chapter 12

"In the House of Joseph"

Georgia's Governor Joseph E. Brown was the most stubborn advocate of states' rights at the expense of Confederate central authority and a vocal critic of President Jefferson Davis. Throughout the struggle of 1861–1865, he waged a political war with Davis over issues like conscription, draft exemptions, and supply, insisting to the end that Georgia troops be under the control of the governor. Brown attempted several times to create a permanent state army, in part from his desire to protect the northern counties of Georgia from bands of deserters and guerrillas.

Like North Carolina's Zebulon Vance, Joe Brown was a native of the mountains. His hometown was Canton in North Georgia's Cherokee County, and he always sought to identify with the common yeoman farmers of the hills. His conciliatory overtures toward mountain Unionists sprang partly from his own roots and partly from the political necessity of gaining the support of the mountain people. In the end, Brown failed to win over the loyalists and found himself adopting the same desperate measures that fellow governors Vance and Shorter were using in the mountains.

James J. Andrews' raid on the Georgia State Road in April 1862 convinced Brown that an armed force was necessary to protect the railroad from saboteurs. In May 1862 he formed a Bridge Guard Company of 150 men, enlisted from counties through which the railway ran. The new company's headquarters were in Dalton. The unit was exempt from Confederate service and assigned exclusively to guard the nine bridges between Ringgold and Atlanta. Brown's guards were dispersed in squads at the bridges along the railroad. They were issued some arms, but no uniforms.

Brown appointed 52-year-old Captain Edward M. Galt to command the company. Galt came from a respected family in Canton, where his father was a prominent merchant. Galt had worked with his father, but the start of the war found him in Dalton with a farm of his own along with his wife and six children, four slaves and two day laborers. Galt's fellow Bridge Guard officers included Lieutenant Francis M. Cowen, an attorney from Cobb County. Brown, a dyed-in-the-wool prohibitionist, required the Bridge Guard officers to accept an "anti-drinking clause" in their commissions. Galt resented this and said so. Cowen was just thankful to be exempt from duty with the Confederate army. "I had rather have a lieutenancy from the champion of state rights than a captaincy from the fathers of conscription," he quipped. "I had rather be a door keeper in the House of Joseph than to dwell in the tents of Jefferson" (Bragg, 11–14).

In July 1862, Brown raised a second Bridge Guard company and appointed 19-year-old Captain Albert Howell, son of a prominent Fulton County landowner, as its commander. Howell's company guarded the seven bridges on the railroad between Ringgold and Chattanooga and had its headquarters at Graysville near the Tennessee line. Brown was unhappy with reports of lax discipline and drinking in Howell's company and wrote the young officer in September 1862, "I am pained to hear the report that you have not suppressed the drinking of ardent spirits in your company and that probably some of the officers occasionally indulge. This I cannot tolerate." A lieutenant was dismissed from the company for drunkenness, the only known case of a court-martial in the Bridge Guards (Bragg, 14–15).

Disturbed by complaints about Union renegade Jeff Anderson's guerrillas, Brown decided to use military force to break the gang's hold on Lumpkin County. In a letter to political associate Herschel V. Johnson on January 19, 1863, he wrote, "I intend that Georgia shall not be the resting place of deserters. I will hunt them if necessary with the state troops till they are driven from her soil" (Parks, 229). He first requested military aid from Colonel George W. Lee, commander of Confederate troops at Atlanta, but Lee insisted he was unable to spare the men. Then Brown suggested a joint operation by the state and the central government. He wrote Secretary of War James Seddon and proposed that 150 Confederate cavalry be sent to Lee, while Brown would provide state troops. Seddon agreed to dispatch the troopers. And just in time, because Brown had just received word that guerrillas—"a large force flying the Union flag"—were moving against Dahlonega, "laying waste the country" (Bragg, 18).

Brown assigned the state's role in the Dahlonega operation to Captain Galt's Bridge Guard Company. Adjutant General Henry C. Wayne ordered Galt to "scour the mountains for the arrest of deserters and other persons . . . inciting rebellion." He was instructed to use discretion and to execute the mission in the "most quiet way," but to "use all the force necessary for the accomplishment of the object" (Bragg, 18).

After spending eight tedious months guarding railroad bridges, Galt and his men were ready to see some action, though it meant a five-day march through mountain country in freezing January temperatures. The Bridge Guards rode the rails down to Atlanta, where the overland march to Dahlonega would begin. While in Atlanta, Galt learned that Colonel Lee was to command the expedition. He had understood that the Bridge Guards were to be under his command, and he complained to Brown. Brown replied on January 21 that he had just received word that Lee had been ordered to take charge of the expedition. He assured Galt that Lee could handle the job and expected Galt to give him his full cooperation. Brown added that he fully expected the marauders to scatter as soon as the state troops appeared on the scene, so Galt's stay in the mountains would not be a lengthy one (Brown Papers).

Galt swallowed his pride and led his troops north, braving the bitter winter cold, and arrived in Dahlonega, site of the nation's first gold rush, on January 23. As he set up headquarters on the town square, he found Captain Robert A. Graham's Blue Ridge Rangers there. Most of the Rangers were local farmers, but a few of them were gold mine workers, and a couple even owned gold mines. Many were poorly clothed and without arms, but they would help in the roundup of deserters (O'Kelley, 6, 14).

Excellent news greeted Galt on his arrival. Local residents had turned back the freebooters, and several guerrilla leaders were already under arrest. Galt distributed copies of a proclamation by Brown offering limited amnesty to the deserters. Any who voluntarily returned to their units within twenty days would not be prosecuted, but those who still failed to respond would face severe penalties (Bragg, 19).

On January 24, fifty Confederate infantrymen with Lee's supply train reached Dahlonega, and the following day Lee arrived. Lee and Galt took an immediate liking to one another. Galt, who had a low opinion of Confederate army officers, said that Lee "acted the perfect gentleman and showed some common sense." Lee promoted Galt to brevet major, turned over command of his infantry to him and the state companies as well, and returned to Atlanta on February 1, leaving Galt in charge (Bragg, 19, 49).

Galt's soldiers broke up into squads to patrol the mountains in search of more deserters. They were joined on January 28 by Lee's cavalry, four companies of the 16th Georgia Partisan Rangers, who arrived after a rough ride through mud and snow. The expedition ultimately mobilized 500 men, most of whom were Brown's state troops. Citizens of Dahlonega helped by quartering troops in their homes and churches. Many of Graham's men slept in their own homes.

For the remainder of January, the state troops and Confederates searched the mountains. They captured fifty-three guerrillas and sent them in chains to Atlanta. Six hundred deserters were returned to their units. By March 1863 the situation in Lumpkin County seemed to be under control. The expedition was considered a great success and showed that the state and the Confederate government could cooperate and take effective action against deserter-bandits. Lee ordered detachments of state troops to other mountain communities—Blairsville, Clarksville, Gainesville, and Ellijay—as a show of strength and support to the loyal residents (Bragg, 21).

An added bonus to the Dahlonega campaign was the apprehension of "the notorious Jeff Anderson" among the fifty-three prisoners taken by Galt's men. Galt wrote that Anderson's capture had "given more relief to the public mind than all others besides" (Bragg, 21). Anderson's fate is unclear, but his jailbreak days were over. It is likely that Colonel Lee had him executed in Atlanta (O'Kelley, 19).

The success of the Bridge Guards helped Brown secure the Georgia legislature's approval for expanding his little state army to two full regiments, called the Georgia State Line, in February 1863. The 1st Regiment was recruited from companies in northern Georgia, with three reserved for Lumpkin, White, and Gilmer, counties with a potential for more trouble. Graham's Blue Ridge Rangers and the two Bridge Guard companies were included. The 2nd Regiment was composed of companies from southern Georgia (Bragg, 28).

Elections for officers of the two regiments were held on February 20 at Camp McDonald near Big Shanty, and members of the Bridge Guard companies had to rush down from duty at Dahlonega in order to vote. Because of his experience with the Bridge Guards, Galt was elected colonel of the 1st Regiment, defeating James J. Findley, a prominent legislator from Lumpkin County (O'Kelley, 20).

Service of the State Line companies was not confined to the mountains. Nine companies of the 1st Regiment soon departed for duty in Savannah, leaving one company to guard the Western and Atlantic . But the danger of Unionist uprisings in the north was not over. In April 1863 Galt dispatched Captain William Howe with Company C, 1st Regiment, on an expedition to Walker County to help put down a loyalist disturbance there. Brown also was alarmed to learn of Union Colonel Abel Streight's bold cavalry raid across Alabama, which failed to reach the Western and Atlantic Railroad. Brown worried that two regiments of infantry could not protect the railroad from future Federal raids. He wanted a cavalry screen stationed in northwest Georgia, but it was clear he would get no help from President Davis (Bragg, 55).

The summer of 1863 brought new reports of trouble in northeastern Georgia. Colonel Lee telegraphed Brown on June 12 that deserters and Unionists in Fannin County were "plundering and burning." Brown responded that he just didn't have the manpower and that one or two local companies should be formed to deal with the problem (Bryan, 146). On June 22 Brown wrote James J. Findley in Lumpkin County that he was dismayed to learn of new problems with deserters, and he shared with him his latest idea for enlarging the state army: a military force of 8,000 men, exempt from conscription, which would be formed in the mountain counties and stationed there permanently to combat terrorism. He believed local Confederates like Findley were more familiar with the mountains and would be more effective than regular troops (Brown Papers). But Brown was not able to sell this idea to the financially pressed Georgia legislature. In September 1863, Lee mounted another expedition to Lumpkin County and skirmished with guerrillas near Morganton in Fannin County. Part of his command also killed and captured a number of Goldman Bryson's guerrillas in a clash across the Tennessee line (*Southern Banner*, October 14, October 28, 1863).

Unionist guerrilla raids continued, especially in Fannin, Gilmer, and Pickens Counties. In March 1864, Brown formed a State Line Cavalry Company, also known as the "State Scouts," and named Captain Francis M. Cowen to command the new outfit. Enlisted members—100 men drawn from companies already serving in Galt's 1st Regiment Georgia State Line—were assigned special duty cavalry pay and allowances. They had to provide their own horses, however. Cowen was to proceed to Ellijay, where he would set up a command post and conduct operations against the guerrillas in Fannin and Gilmer Counties. He was not able to leave until April 19, because horses were scarce and he had to allow most of his men ten days' furlough to find suitable mounts. Cowen had seventy-nine mounted troopers, ten infantrymen, and ten wagons. His men were well armed with Enfield and Austrian rifles (Bragg, 114–115).

When Cowen and his men rode into Ellijay, with its rectangular brick courthouse standing in the center of town, they found a community in turmoil. The county had been the scene of several violent skirmishes that month between Unionist bushwhackers and Home Guard squads. Cowen remarked that the deserters "are powerful sharp here." On their first night out on patrol his troopers caught only one deserter in Gilmer County. Cowen observed that many local Unionists were moving northward to the Union lines in Tennessee, but his orders were not to interfere with them or confiscate any of the property they left behind (Bragg, 114–115).

One of the targets of the expedition was Fannin County's Stanley Valley, home of the Unionist Stanley clan. Cowen's troops moved into Stanley Valley on May 3. Cowen described it as "the most secluded place as well as the most romantic and picturesque . . . liberally covered with laurel, ivy, and spruce pine" and with "deep dark ravines." Cowen's men took the Stanleys by surprise and after a brief shootout captured two of them along with a couple of deserters (Bragg, 114–115).

The little community of Ducktown just across the Ocoee River in Polk County, Tennessee, also aroused Cowen's attention. Ducktown was the site of a flourishing copper industry before the war, but when the rail line to Cleveland was captured by Union troops in 1863, the mines shut down and the local economy collapsed. Area residents fled the community, and the nearby mountains became a haven for guerrilla bands (Barclay, 100). Cowen led seventy-five of his men in a raid on Ducktown in early May, but the bushwhackers had cleared the ground of timber in front of their camp and were alerted in time to escape. Cowen's men failed to capture any deserters, although they did capture a couple of mules. Overall, Brown was pleased with Cowen's raid, although he felt the officer overstepped himself in going into Tennessee. Cowen could keep the guns and ammunition that he had taken from the guerrillas (Bragg, 115).

Brown's little state army never really had a chance to have a real impact in the guerrilla war. In May 1864, the State Line regiments were transferred to General Joseph E. Johnston's Army of Tennessee preparing to meet Sherman's invasion of northern Georgia. Cowen and his men had to evacuate their base in Ellijay and withdraw from the mountains. Three months later Cowen was dead and Galt was seriously wounded, casualties of the fighting around Atlanta.

By September 1864, newspapers were reporting bands of Unionists boldly operating in the three counties raided by Cowen's men just four months earlier: a company of loyalists in Fannin County, three companies in Gilmer, and one in Pickens. Meanwhile bands of pro-Confederate guerrillas terrorized Unionists in Cherokee and Pickens Counties and in the northwestern counties of the state. But with relentless Billy Sherman's army occupying Atlanta, Brown was powerless to act (Bryan, 152).

Brown's was probably the most ambitious state program to deal with the threat of Unionist guerrillas, but even his iron resolve was not enough to bring the problem under control. The failure of Brown's state troops to pacify the guerrillas is a testimony to the magnitude of the task. For the remainder of the war, responsibility for containing the Unionists fell to Rebel Home Guard companies and independent partisans.

Benjamin F. McCollum's Home Guards, sometimes known as McCollum's Scouts, operated in Cherokee and Pickens Counties, sometimes raiding into neighboring counties. Formed in the spring of 1864 as Sherman's Atlanta-bound army pushed through nearby Bartow County, McCollum's command at first focused on harassing Federal cavalry foraging details and on attacking the Western and Atlantic Railroad, now in Yankee use. McCollum's men, many of whom were deserters themselves, also terrorized civilians (Marlin, 74–75). According to a Rebel correspondent for the February 11, 1865, Augusta *Daily Constitutionalist*, McCollum's men stole livestock belonging to loyal Confederate women. In 1864 McCollum's command was transferred to Confederate service, along with other Georgia Home Guard units (*Southern Watchman*, December 21, 1864).

Ben McCollum came from a well-to-do family in Canton. Educated and articulate, McCollum had a gift for communicating; and after the war he wrote extensively about his guerrilla activities. In June 1861, McCollum joined Canton's Brown Riflemen, part of the 2nd Georgia Infantry Regiment, but the youth was discharged when he was found to be underage. McCollum was probably no more than 18 years old in 1864. Slightly built with a wispy beard and pale blue eyes, he hardly looked the part of a ruthless guerrilla chieftain (Marlin, 74).

McCollum operated from his base camp on the meandering Etowah River three miles north of Canton, the Cherokee County seat. The guerrillas were especially on the lookout for local Unionists acting as guides for Sherman's foraging patrols. When such men fell into McCollum's hands, they were killed without mercy. Often the guerrillas would carry them from their homes in Pickens and Cherokee Counties to McCollum's camp, then would simply shoot the captives off their horses just to watch their bodies plunge into the river and sail downstream (Marlin, 74).

McCollum overtook three Unionist guides who had just left a Yankee foraging patrol and were watering their horses in Sharp Mountain Creek near Ball Ground. One of them, a Cherokee County man, had a roster of names of men in the Union detachment. When McCollum asked him where he got the roster, the man said he had found it in the road. This sounded highly suspicious to the guerrilla chief, and his party set off northward toward Jasper, taking the three captives along. There McCollum made inquiries about the two other captives, both local men from Pickens County, and when an old blacksmith vouched for them, he let them go. The two men were Masons, and so was McCollum. He may have released them for that reason. But he held the man with the Yankee roster. When it was verified that he had been seen with a Federal foraging detachment in Jasper a week earlier, his fate was sealed. The guerrillas took the captive about three miles south of Jasper, strung him up on the top of a hill, and discharged two pistol balls through his heart. The victim's wife arrived the next day. She found her husband's corpse and borrowed a horse and cart from a nearby farmer. The farmer's son helped her cut down her husband's body, and she took it back to Cherokee County (Marlin, 75–76).

McCollum gave a firsthand account of a nighttime raid, probably in July 1864, on the Federal-occupied Western and Atlantic rail line. McCollum and six of his mounted raiders, determined to wreak havoc behind enemy lines, approached Moon Station, a wood and water station on the rail line two miles north of Big Shanty. They were wearing Confederate uniforms, but since the night was cloudy, with only a hint of a moon, they felt the handful of Federals there would not question them if they identified themselves as Yankee cavalry. McCollum claimed to be an officer in the 5th Ohio Cavalry, a Federal unit known to be operating in the area, and said he and his men were returning from a skirmish with Rebel cavalry. He told the bluecoats he was looking for a telegraph office where he could report information on the Rebel army. The ruse worked, and soon the Rebel guerrillas were riding south toward Big Shanty. Along the way they ripped down a mile of telegraph line.

The Rebels halted a couple hundred yards from Big Shanty, and McCollum left his men while he approached alone. It was about one o'clock in the morning. McCollum found that the Yankee guards were sleeping in a small house near the depot with only one drowsy soldier sitting at the hearth, his musket leaning against the fireplace. McCollum quickly returned to collect his men for an attack on the guard post but conceded that "my boys being a little green on the war path, I was somewhat uneasy for fear they would fire on me, so I called out the countersign (Sherman) quick and loud." McCollum gave instructions to his men, who were "in fine spirits and eager for the charge." He told them that "the first duty of a soldier was to obey orders; that if they would follow me and obey orders that we would succeed in capturing the guard and the place" ("Big Shanty," 31).

McCollum and his raiders approached the guard house, and he banged on the door to wake the lone sentinel inside. He identified himself as "Lieutenant Fuller" of the 5th Ohio Cavalry and asked to be let in. When the soldier opened the door, McCollum and his men rushed in and captured the guard post.

The guerrilla leader told the soldiers that there were a hundred Rebel troops surrounding the house and that it was senseless to resist. Then he disarmed the Federals and marched them outside where he left them under the guns of four of his men. McCollum took aside a badly rattled Federal captive who spoke like a "Dutchman" and "told him that if he wanted to live he had better tell me everything he knew." Where was the telegraph office? The "Dutchman" immediately pointed to Lacy's Hotel nearby, and the Rebel chief with his two other guerrillas and the Yankee prisoner descended on their objective only to find the doors locked. After forcing the door, McCollum discovered that the two telegraph operators had fled through an open back window. The Rebels took the telegraph equipment with them ("Big Shanty," 32).

McCollum asked the "Dutchman" if there were any other Federal soldiers staying in the area. He replied that there was one in a house about a hundred yards west of the railroad but that he "would not be taken alive." McCollum suspected the man might be a Unionist scout. He ordered the "Dutchman" to approach the house first and do the talking; if there were any gunplay, he would be shot first. The "Dutchman" did as he was told and called out several times to the man inside the house. At length the man answered, and the "Dutchman" shouted that the house was surrounded.

Instantly the man was at the door with a Spencer rifle at the ready, but McCollum's men quickly overpowered and disarmed him. McCollum wrote, "This man was a regular Western desperado, and all the marks about him pointed him out as a desperate man, and I learned from the other prisoners that he had been selected as a special scout. He was very much chagrined when he found that he had been captured by so small a force." The man had not been alone. McCollum discovered a woman "in her night clothes and cursing the rebels in the best language she could command" ("Big Shanty," 32).

McCollum declined to burn the depot "full of Yankee supplies," because he hoped the Rebel army might recapture it, but his men did sabotage the railroad switches before they left so that the Yankee trains would run off the rails. McCollum gathered his prisoners and spoil before Federal reinforcements could arrive. The party took to horse and withdrew "at double-quick time" ("Big Shanty," 33).

Beset by annoying raids like McCollum's, Federal troops retaliated. Along the road from Cartersville into Cherokee County the Yankees left homes of several Rebel sympathizers in flames (Marlin, 76). And on July 26, 1864, Captain John P. Cummings with 250 troopers from the 3rd Kentucky Cavalry shattered Benjamin F. Jordan's guerrillas—whose membership apparently overlapped with McCollum's to some extent—near the Talking Rock community in Pickens County. Cummings reported his men killed eight of Jordan's men and wounded four, Jordan himself being slightly wounded in the shoulder. Cummings captured five guerrillas, twenty guns and eight pistols, a wagon, eight horses, and twelve mules. The raid was "entirely successful" (USWD, I, 38, ii: 867; 38, v: 274, 299, 315; 52, i: 107).

The Kentucky cavalrymen broke Jordan's hold in Pickens County and helped local Unionists organize a Home Guard company of 125 men that became part of James G. Brown's 1st Georgia State Troops Volunteers (USWD, I, 38, i: 889). Jordan's band never was a significant threat after this, but the guerrilla chief was not destroyed. He clashed frequently with

Brown's partisans and was still operating as of February 1865 (*Augusta Daily Constitutionalist*, February 11, 1865).

One Rebel leader that Union sympathizers had good reason to fear was Colonel James Jefferson Findley, who headed the Home Guard in Lumpkin County. A restless manipulator in pursuit of ambition, Findley was justifiably regarded as an aggressive and relentless officer who ruthlessly went after Unionist guerrillas and deserters. Born in South Carolina in 1829, he became a well-known attorney in Lumpkin County, where he held several political posts before the war. He was also a wealthy property owner with one slave and a gold mine called "Findley's Chute" that yielded $250,000 worth of gold. Findley was said to have brought a gold nugget that weighed eight pounds into Dahlonega one day. Findley served as county sheriff, assistant U.S. marshal in 1860, and judge, and was Lumpkin County's representative in the Georgia General Assembly in 1857 and 1861 (O'Kelley, 106–107).

In March 1862, Findley entered Dahlonega attorney Wier Boyd's 52nd Georgia Infantry Regiment as a second lieutenant and was quickly elected major. The 52nd Georgia served during the summer of 1862 in skirmishes in Kentucky, and in the fall Findley often assumed temporary command since Boyd was sick with typhoid fever. But in November 1862 he abruptly resigned his commission, because he had set his sights on a higher goal. As a state legislator, he was aware of Governor Brown's plans to create a State Line regiment, and he planned to use his political influence to carve out a niche for himself in "Joe Brown's Army." Findley returned to Lumpkin County and began raising a local company, originally called "Findley's Blue Ridge Rangers," for inclusion in the 1st State Line Regiment yet to be formed. He planned to be elected captain of the new company, then use it as a platform to run for colonel of the regiment. From there it would be a clear road to higher command (O'Kelley, 106–107).

Findley's plans failed to come together as he had hoped. When the time came to elect the captain of the Blue Ridge Rangers, Findley was defeated by Robert A. Graham, a local farmer. Undaunted, he placed his name in nomination for colonel of the 1st Regiment Georgia State Line but was defeated by E. M. Galt. His plans frustrated, he pulled political strings to get a release from the State Line, and after a brief hiatus he wrangled an appointment as colonel of the 11th Battalion of Georgia State Guards, the Lumpkin County Home Guard.

In the summer of 1864 the 35-year-old Dahlonega entrepreneur found himself caught up in the mountain counties' relentless struggle with bands of deserters and Unionist guerrillas. When a detachment from the Federal 10th Tennessee Cavalry came prowling into Lumpkin County in September 1864, Findley and his Home Guards intercepted them, killing at least one bluecoat. Findley also was aware of Unionist activity in neighboring Fannin County where William Albert Twiggs was drumming up support for a local company in the 5th Tennessee Mounted Infantry. Findley ordered Captain Francis Marion Williams to Fannin County to deal with Twiggs' Unionist guerrillas, who had been raiding Confederate homes (Kinsland, "Murder," 20).

On October 20, Williams' Home Guard company caught Iley Stuart and eight of Twiggs' recruits at Lewis VanZant's blacksmith shop in the Dial community. The guerrillas had stopped to get their horses shod and were busying themselves when the Rebel Home Guards suddenly appeared and surrounded the building. Although Stuart had posted 17-year-old Willis Gilliam as a lookout, Gilliam was not in a position to see the Rebel horsemen as they rode up from the south. The Unionists were taken completely by surprise, and they had left their firearms outside the forge. When Williams commanded them to surrender, they had no choice. Stuart and his men came out of the blacksmith shop with their hands raised. Williams' men mounted the prisoners on their horses, with their legs tied under the animals' bellies, and led them away (Kinsland, "Murder," 18–20). One of Stuart's men, George W. Wilson, later stated that some of the Rebels wore parts of Federal uniforms (Barker Papers, Vol. 4).

Gilliam, the lookout, was able to escape and make his way back to Twiggs, who quickly assembled a rescue party; but Williams and his captives were long gone. Following the Toccoa River, the Rebel column reached Gaddistown across the Union County line and pitched camp for the night. One of the prisoners, Thomas Anderson, managed to slip away in the darkness and escape. Two days later he reached Twiggs' camp near Dial and reported that the Rebels and their captives were headed into Lumpkin County (Kinsland, "Murder," 19–20).

The Rebels rode into Dahlonega the next afternoon, October 21, and reported to Findley at his headquarters in the brick two-story courthouse on the town square. Findley turned the captives over to Lieutenant N. J. Gaddis, who confined them in the guard house in the same building. Meanwhile Findley examined the papers and documents that Williams had taken from the Unionists. Papers found on three of the captives—Iley Stuart, William Witt, and Solomon Stansbury—gave Findley reason to believe they were Unionist guerrillas. Also, the men were in civilian clothing. Findley suspected them of being deserters at best, and he apparently decided that night to make examples of them and have them executed (Kinsland, "Murder," 21–22).

Findley turned the task of disposing of the prisoners over to one of his officers, Captain William R. Crisson. The 44-year-old Crisson was a justice of the peace and was well regarded in the community. On the morning of October 22 Crisson selected a firing squad, which included his son Corporal Macy W. ("Mac") Crisson, and had the three Union men brought out from their cell. The prisoners were mounted on horses and led out of town along the Cleveland Road. Several miles from Dahlonega the column halted at Bearden's Bridge Hill on the Chestatee River. Crisson had the prisoners dismount, and quickly they were blindfolded and forced to kneel by the edge of the hilltop. The firing squad was formed. One of the soldiers, John Baugus, refused to take part in the execution. He handed his musket to Crisson. Crisson said nothing, simply handed the gun to another soldier. He gave the order to fire and the three victims fell dead. The soldiers tossed the bodies of Stuart, Witt, and Stansbury over the embankment and mounted up for the return to Dahlonega (Kinsland, "Murder," 22).

After the war Crisson and members of the firing squad would be charged with murdering the three Unionists. Crisson would testify, "Colonel Findley ordered me to take the prisoners out and shoot them. I obeyed the order" (Kinsland, "Murder," 26).

Less than two weeks after the execution of the three Fannin County men Findley struck again, this time shattering James G. Brown's 1st Georgia State Troops in Gilmer County. On November 2, Findley received word from one of his officers, Captain R. N. McClure, that John A. Ashworth and a raiding party from Brown's command were heading in the direction of Dawsonville. Early the next morning Findley left Dahlonega with a detachment of his troops and rendezvoused with McClure and his men in Dawson County. Three more companies joined him on the morning of November 4, including Captain Thomas Polk Edmundson's men from Murray County, and Findley now had a respectable force of 128 with which to attack the Unionists.

The Home Guard force left Dawsonville and rode northwest. After covering about nine miles Findley's scouts brought back word that Ashworth and his men were at Alex Spriggs' home nearby. Findley and his troops closed in for the kill only to find that Ashworth had flown the coop just two hours earlier. The Home Guards gave chase, but darkness came quickly, with the threat of an ice storm looming, and the horses were exhausted. Findley ordered the men to make camp for the night at the base of Amicalola Mountain not far from towering, scenic Amicalola Falls.

The morning of November 5 dawned bitterly cold as Findley's weary horsemen climbed out of their bedrolls in the dark. The column made their way slowly across Amicalola Mountain blanketed with an inch of snow at the top, its tree branches loaded with ice. Moving into the rugged eastern part of Gilmer County, the Home Guards made their way up Bucktown Creek. At 10 o'clock in the morning Findley's advance guard located Ashworth's party at the home of Henry Weaver. A newspaper account in the November 30, 1864, *Southern Watchman* described what happened.

Ashworth, George W. McCrary, and twenty-six of their men had stopped at Weaver's house in the Bucktown community for breakfast. Findley's scouts could see smoke curling above the cabin as the Union men congregated around the warmth of the Weavers' fireplace inside. Suddenly gunfire shattered the calm of the cold mountain morning. Findley's troops rode in firing as Ashworth's men scrambled to defend themselves. Badly outnumbered and taken by surprise, the Unionists put up a brief struggle, but when the skirmish was over Ashworth was forced to surrender.

Findley could congratulate himself on a successful operation. Four of Ashworth's men lay dead, and three more were wounded. Findley captured twenty-one Unionists, including Ashworth and McCrary. He also captured twenty-eight horses and mules, "most of which," he wrote, "were stolen from my men, and which I returned to their owners." Also taken were twenty-five rifles, twenty revolvers, and a large quantity of ammunition. Findley's force sustained no casualties. In his report of the skirmish Findley praised the conduct of his men. "Many of them are new troops," he wrote, "and had never been engaged in a fight before. Notwithstanding this, they all acted like soldiers." Findley's men found papers on Ashworth implicating Dawson County Sheriff George R. Robinson and four other prominent local men as Union collaborators. Riding back to Dawsonville with the captives, Findley paid a call on the sheriff and arrested him along with the other civilians listed in the captured documents.

Findley returned to Dahlonega with the prisoners taken in the Bucktown skirmish. Most of them were identified as deserters from Confederate regiments. The lucky ones were simply returned to their commands and forced back into service. But twelve captives fared not so well. On November 7, Findley had these men hanged at Gainesville. Ashworth and McCrary were spared, but neither survived the war, and Brown's command soon disintegrated (Davis, "Forgotten," 272–273).

Among the fortunate Unionist prisoners were James and Bill Weaver, two Bucktown boys. Realizing he could not avoid capture, James had tossed his pocketbook down into the brush under a tree when Findley's troops overwhelmed him at Bucktown. The Weavers were pressed back into service in the Confederate army but soon deserted again. When they returned to Gilmer County in June 1865, James looked for the place where he had left his money. It was still there (Ward, 588–589).

Brigadier General Alexander W. Reynolds, commanding the scattered bands of Confederate soldiers in the Georgia mountains, left Athens on an inspection tour in January 1865. He traveled north to Dahlonega to confer with Findley. Reynolds was not impressed and reported, "Colonel Findlay's [*sic*] command, if he has any, is scattered over the country, as if quartered at home, and it would be difficult to collect the men without considerable delay." He assessed the status of other Home Guard units in North Georgia: 500 men in Gilmer County, 500 in Blairsville, 400 in Hall County, about 100 at Canton under Ben McCollum. Reynolds suspected that many of these men were deserters or draft evaders. Of the various commanders only Colonel Baker, operating on the Coosawattee in Gordon County, and Major Graham, with 400 men near Ducktown, appeared to be doing their jobs. Although a Rebel newspaperman in the Augusta *Daily Constitutionalist* of March 10, 1865, characterized Baker and Graham as guerrillas who preyed on innocent civilians, Reynolds described them as "efficient and energetic young officers" (USWD, I, 49, i: 963).

Reynolds himself came under criticism from an anonymous letter writer who accused him of failing to discipline his troops and of allowing them to victimize the civilian population in the mountains. Reynolds defended his conduct and said that he did the best that he could under the circumstances, with the lack of manpower available to him. He accused the anonymous writer of being a skulker and a coward (USWD, I, 49, i: 974, 977).

As the dreary winter of 1864–1865 unfolded, Joseph E. Brown was showered with appeals like that of Cumming resident F. M. Hawkins beseeching him to "open the way to negotiation and expedite peace" (Lane, 224). Even hard-core partisan James J. Findley could see the handwriting on the wall; on January 26, he wrote Brown urging him to suspend conscription, since efforts to enforce it had become futile (Bryan, 154).

Chapter 13

"The Red-Headed Beast from Georgia"

Sometime in October 1864, in that last autumn of the war when Confederate hopes were fading like the withered leaves, a detachment of Rebel troopers from Colonel George McKensie's 5th Tennessee Cavalry patrolled a dusty road through northwestern Georgia's Walker County. At a turn in the trail, the gray-clad riders reined in at the sight of a decomposing human body hanging on a tree. The victim, a man named Burton hanged by Rebel guerrillas, had been there for days, and animals had devoured his lower limbs. A note left on the corpse defied anyone to cut the body down on pain of similar fate. Why he was killed cannot be known, but the Rebel cavalrymen had no trouble speculating on who killed him, for this country was a haven for the most ruthless guerrilla chief in Georgia. With a war-weary compassion the soldiers cut down the victim and buried him (Sartain, 122).

No matter how savage one terrorist might be, there always was another even more vicious. The name that Georgia mountain folk learned to fear above all others was John P. Gatewood, known as "the long-haired, red-headed beast from Georgia" (Sarris, "Anatomy," 697). Not more than 21 years old in 1864, he was a sadistic sociopath who seemed to enjoy killing for the sheer thrill of it. He was said to brag that he never took prisoners. Unlike Ben McCollum, who wrote of his wartime activities, Gatewood left no such accounts since he was illiterate; one report credits his brother Henry as being in charge of the gang's books and accounts (Battey, 205).

The "red-headed beast" was described as athletic and handsome, six feet tall, weighing about 200 pounds, with piercing blue eyes. His long reddish-brown hair hung shoulder length in two locks down his back. He liked to wear a broad-brimmed soft felt hat casually tipped back on his head. He also liked to carry two pistols, and stories were told that the reckless young guerrilla could handle a revolver in each hand while riding at full gallop (Sensing, 169).

Gatewood hailed from Tennessee's Fentress County on the Cumberland Plateau. In August 1861 he enlisted at the age of 18 in Captain Willis Scott Bledsoe's independent cavalry company, along with his 28-year-old brother, Henry, and other young men from their community. The brothers both reenlisted in May 1862. After seeing considerable action in minor cavalry skirmishes on the Tennessee-Kentucky border, Bledsoe and his men joined Colonel John P. Murray's 4th Tennessee Cavalry in September 1862. Next came fighting at Perryville in October and at Murfreesboro in December. Four companies of the 4th Tennessee went into Colonel Baxter Smith's 8th Tennessee Cavalry when it was formed in January 1863, the Gatewoods included. In September 1863 the 8th Tennessee Cavalry saw action at Chickamauga, and afterwards fought in the Atlanta campaign, but by then Gatewood had taken up a different calling (Barker Papers, Vol. 3).

The reasons why Gatewood, presumably a decent soldier, deserted the army to embrace the life of a guerrilla are lost in obscurity. Some said he began his partisan activities to avenge the killing of his father by Unionists (Battey, 205). Willis Scott Bledsoe, Gatewood's original company commander, also became a well-known Confederate guerrilla, as did George Carter, another officer in the regiment. Champ Ferguson, the most notorious guerrilla in eastern Tennessee, recruited in Fentress County. Gatewood was an associate of Ferguson and was with him on some of his operations before striking out on his own (Sarris, "Anatomy," 700).

Gatewood seems to have made Walker and Chattooga Counties his principal base in Georgia, at least from the latter part of 1864 to the end of the war, but his activities frequently spilled over into neighboring counties, ranging as far east as Gilmer County and as far south as Rome. His raids carved a swath of terror from Gaylesville, Alabama, to Polk County in southeastern Tennessee (Battey, 205).

Some said Gatewood originally intended to protect civilian residents from bands of Yankee looters in the wake of Sherman's army moving through North Georgia. Such admirers referred to his band as "Gatewood's Scouts" and to their redheaded chief as "Captain Gatewood" although he had no official status in the Confederate army. A newspaper account in the November 10, 1864, Macon *Daily Telegraph* referred to the guerrilla leader as "'Gatewood the Regulator" and credited him with protecting Rebel civilians in northwest Georgia. But most felt he was no better than the Union marauders; his victims were as likely to be Confederate as Unionists.

Probably sometime early in 1864 Gatewood carried out a daring night-time raid on a Federal military stockyard at Rossville, Georgia, and captured 2,000 cattle and horses. The guerrillas surprised a squad of Federal soldiers guarding the stockyard and left them with their throats cut. They drove the livestock to Gaylesville, Alabama, where they sold them to the Rebel army (Sartain, 120–121).

The number of men in the Gatewood gang varied. Generally the group averaged about ten to twenty-five, but at times the size of the gang was said to be as high as 300. Gatewood's men traveled on horseback. On a raid they usually separated into small groups of four or five to appear at isolated home sites demanding food. While the terrified women and children prepared them meals, the guerrillas took horses and whatever else they wanted. Some of Gatewood's men may have joined him to avoid becoming victims of the notorious outlaw themselves. When possible they soon separated from him. Gatewood was said to be wary of his own men and sometimes would steal away at night to sleep in an unknown spot where no one could find him (Sartain, 120, 125).

No reliable account exists of the number of men killed by Gatewood's gang, but probability rates the figure as very high. Gatewood's guerrillas murdered William Clayton Fain, the vocal Fannin County Unionist, on April 6, 1864. Fain, a respected Morganton attorney with two brothers in the Rebel army, had served in the Georgia legislature and had spoken out against secession in 1861. Gatewood's men intercepted Fain near Duck-town, where he and several Federal recruits were crossing the Toccoa River. The Rebels surprised Fain's party in midstream and took them prisoner. Fain attempted to escape and was shot off his horse. The guerrillas killed the recruits, including Henry Robinson, who was "tied to a tree and shot 15 or 20 times." Although several witnesses later said the Rebel party was led by a Captain Rogers, the murder of Clayton Fain was laid at the feet of Gatewood (Barker Papers, Vol. 11).

A direct collision between Gatewood and the John Long–Sam Roberts Unionist gang seemed inevitable. According to one local yarn, a bloody face-off occurred near LaFayette sometime in 1864. Reportedly Gatewood often was accompanied by an Indian who acted as his aide and cared for his horse. Gatewood sent the Indian with some corn to be ground into meal at McConnell's Mill on Teloga Creek (near present-day Trion). On the way the Indian fell into the hands of members of the Long-Roberts gang, who killed him. The Unionist guerrillas sent his body strapped to his horse back to Gatewood with a note challenging the redheaded partisan to a showdown at Teloga. Gatewood answered the challenge, and that night the two gangs met near McConnell's Mill and engaged In a gunfight (Baker, 367). Apparently the Unionists got the worst of the encounter. Long and his men withdrew across Pigeon Mountain toward their hideout in McLemore's Cove, and the Rebels gave chase. Long reached the base of the mountain and took refuge at the home of sympathizers where he posted a guard and fell into an exhausted sleep. In the dark Gatewood lost Long's trail, and the Unionist partisan leader was spared an accounting with the "red-headed beast" (Sartain, 121–122).

A turf war also erupted between Gatewood and Green Cordle, leader of a gang that operated in Walker County and northern Chattooga County. Gatewood eliminated Cordle by ambushing him while he was eating supper with friends in a home in Walker County, shooting and killing him as he fled the house. The Cordle gang disintegrated after their leader's death (Baker, 370).

Gatewood, Long, Roberts, and Cordle were not the only guerrilla chieftains operating in the wartime vacuum of northwest Georgia. A shadowy renegade named Doc Morse led a band of marauders that raided to the east in Catoosa and Whitfield Counties and along the Tennessee border. At times they conducted raids into northern Walker County in the Rock Spring community. The allegiance of the Morse gang is unknown, but they were considered a terror to local residents. One report had Morse's men teamed up with Rebel guerrilla leader Tom Polk Edmundson from Murray County (Sartain, 124).

Gatewood's men raided the home of wealthy Unionist Wesley Shropshire in Dirt Town Valley fifteen miles north of Rome on September 15, 1864. The Rebels robbed the family of all their possessions but suspected that Shropshire had money hidden. They hanged him to make him talk, but Shropshire's daughter, Naomi, managed to convince them that there was no hidden gold, and they finally left (Aycock, 125). Federal scouts from the 1st Alabama Cavalry confirmed in a report on September 25 that eleven of Gatewood's guerrillas had been in Dirt Town robbing local residents (USWD, I, 52, i: 639). Gatewood was said to be responsible for a similar attack on Judge A. P. Allgood at his home in Trion (Baker, 366–367).

John W. Maddox, a soldier in the 6th Georgia Cavalry, recalled a skirmish near LaFayette in October 1864 in which Gatewood played a part. The Georgia cavalrymen had been ordered to guard General Joseph Wheeler's left flank while he raided the Western and Atlantic Railroad between Dalton and Resaca. The gray-clad horsemen rode into LaFayette at 10 in the morning, dismounted behind the courthouse, and posted pickets along the roads to the north, east, and west. While the weary Rebel troopers napped on the ground, Gatewood with several of his men rode into town from the east. Bystanders said that Gatewood had just hanged a man named Burton, whose body would be discovered by soldiers later (Sartain, 232–233).

Soon the cavalrymen were called to action by the sounds of bugles and cries to mount up, and Gatewood's guerrillas joined in. Springing into the saddle, the Rebels galloped northward on the road toward Chattanooga and soon met one of their own patrols being chased south by a company of Federal cavalry with sabers drawn, "yelling like mad men." The two columns collided in a clash of steel and whirling dust. The Yankees were overrun and captured (Sartain, 233).

As the prisoners were being rounded up, Gatewood demanded they be turned over to him. The Yankee captives were terrified, expecting to be shot. But Colonel John R. Hart, the commander of the 6th Georgia Cavalry, apparently knew of Gatewood's bloodthirsty reputation. He curtly told the guerrilla chief that the Yankees were prisoners of war and would be treated as such, that he would hold them to be turned over to regular Confederate authorities. The prisoners were visibly relieved. Maddox wrote, "We did not need any guard to keep them, for they stuck to us like brothers." Hart also warned Gatewood not to harm two prisoners he left to care for the wounded Federal soldiers; whether the "red-headed beast" heeded the warning is not known (Sartain, 233–234).

Gatewood's activities soon earned him the attention of Federal commanders in northwest Georgia, and his name began to appear frequently in Union reports. On October 11, 1864, Federal patrols spotted Gatewood and about 150 of his men at Snake Creek Gap near the Walker-Gordon County line. On October 24, Sherman sent this dispatch to Major General David S. Stanley at Gaylesville, Alabama:

There is a gang of guerrillas under one Gatewood somewhere behind us. He has about 100 men and will likely hurry to the north of our road, back to Rome. I wish you to send a brigade, light, to Price's Bridge and across to scout out toward Dirt Town and Coosaville, to make diligent inquiries and to let all know that such fellows will be dealt with summarily. Let the people also understand that when we are in search of such fellows we take no baggage, and therefore live on the country. If they want to save what little corn and potatoes [they have], they must manage to get Gatewood disposed of, for he will bring ruin on them all. (USWD, I, 39, iii: 208, 415)

From Gaylesville, a brigade of mostly Ohio infantrymen under Colonel H. A. Hambright crossed the mountains toward Dirt Town to search for Gatewood but returned empty-handed on October 27 after three days of fruitless activity. Sticking only to the main roads, the slow-moving Federal infantry failed to make contact with the slippery guerrillas (USWD, I, 39, i: 616–619).

Colonel William J. Palmer's 15th Pennsylvania Cavalry was operating in northwestern Georgia, and Palmer reported on November 22 that Gatewood was probably in the lower part of Chattooga County's Broomtown Valley with 75 to 100 men. He also noted the presence in that area, and across Lookout Mountain in Wills Valley, Alabama, of smaller detachments under guerrilla chiefs Davenport, Weatherspoon, Hammock, and Freeman. The Rebel bands were believed to be sending small scouting patrols of five to twenty men north as far as Trenton, McLemore's Cove, LaFayette, and Bailey's Cross Roads, to raid homes of Unionist civilians (USWD, I, 45, i: 980, 990).

Despite the best intelligence available to the able Colonel Palmer, Gatewood was no longer anywhere near Broomtown Valley. The red-haired guerrilla was headed northward on the bloodiest raid of his career. What provoked this, Gatewood's last violent rampage, is unclear; it may have been retaliation for the recent Unionist raids of William A. Twiggs in Fannin County. For some reason Gatewood left Broomtown Valley in late November 1864 and moved north into Tennessee for an incursion into Bradley and Polk Counties. The events of the following days led to what locals would call the Madden Branch Massacre (Sarris, "Anatomy," 700, 703).

At Benton in Polk County Gatewood killed William Kinser after accusing him of being a Confederate deserter. He raided northward into McMinn County then turned southeast toward Ducktown where 19-year-old Alonzo Jones, driving an ox wagon, happened along his path. Gatewood shoved the frightened youth up against a large rock and shot him dead in cold blood. Local residents claimed they could still see Jones' bloodstains on the rock for years afterward. The raiders then hanged Jack and Simon Orr, two more young men who had worked at the copper mines, at Greasy Creek. Closer to Ducktown the marauders accosted George Barnes and shot him in the head, leaving him for dead. Amazingly Barnes lived; although he was left permanently blind in one eye, he became a popular fiddle player (Barclay, 100–101).

Union recruiting officers with the 5th Tennessee Mounted Infantry were active at the time across the Georgia line in Fannin County. William Lillard, a Confederate deserter, recruited aggressively in hopes of receiving an officer's commission in the regiment. In November 1864, he signed up 20-year-old Peter Parris from the Dora community, and Parris enlisted six more young Georgians: Thomas Bell, Harvey Brewster, James T. Hughes, James B. Nelson, Elijah Robinson, and Wyatt J. Parton. They all were young men aged 16 to 22, poor farmers, and Rebel deserters (Sarris, "Anatomy," 683, 688, 690).

Peter Parris had enlisted in the infantry battalion of Smith's Georgia Legion in May 1862. A year later Smith's legion was broken up, the infantry battalion becoming the 65th Georgia Infantry Regiment. By May 1864 Parris had deserted the 65th Georgia and had taken up the familiar lifestyle of so many mountain Unionists. He hid out in the mountains of Fannin County, then joined a local band of Unionist guerrillas—which included his father and brother—and began to raid local Confederate homesteads (Sarris, "Anatomy," 691–693).

On a cold November 29, 1864, Parris and his six fellow recruits set out for a rendezvous with Lillard at Cleveland, Tennessee. They rode along the winding Toccoa River, which became the Ocoee River when they crossed into Tennessee. Soon they came across another small party of young men from Georgia also heading for Cleveland to join the 5th Tennessee Mounted. After sharing lunch with the second party, Parris and his men went on ahead hoping to reach Cleveland before dark, and they were joined by Samuel Lovell, a young man from the second group who was also a deserter from the 65th Georgia Infantry. The eight men continued along the twisting mountain trail called the Old Copper Road, which follows the course of the Ocoee River (Sarris, "Anatomy," 683).

Suddenly as they rounded an abrupt turn in the trail, the Parris party came face to face with the "red-headed beast from Georgia" accompanied by about fifty of his guerrillas. Confronted by the Gatewood gang, the recruits' first impulse was to run. They were completely unarmed except for Parris, who carried a pistol. Immediately they spurred their horses, heading for the hillside and cover of the trees. But Gatewood called out to them to stop, that he and his men were Federal soldiers, that they were friends. The recruits saw that the raiders wore Yankee uniforms although they did not know that this was captured clothing. Gatewood persuaded them that he meant them no harm (Sarris, "Anatomy," 683).

Having cornered the Union men, Gatewood ordered them to dismount, and his guerrillas searched them. Then the raiders lined the prisoners up against the side of the mountain, and Gatewood drew his revolvers. Starting with 16-year-old Lige Robinson, Gatewood shot each man in the face, one by one (Sarris, "Anatomy," 684).

Before their turn with death, Parris and Wyatt J. Parton made a daring getaway and ran for their lives. Parton plunged into the freezing Ocoee River and was swept downstream in the rapid current. Struck several times by Rebel bullets, he survived, and several months later from his hospital sickbed he enlisted in the 5th Tennessee Mounted. Parris escaped up the steep mountainside in a rain of gunfire. He sustained wounds in the left leg, in both thighs, in the right shoulder, and in the right hand, but he too survived and was able to reach a friendly home nearby where his brother James found him later (Barker Papers, Vol. 3).

The guerrillas left the six other Unionists lying in the road.

The next morning a local farmer and his young son were making their way slowly along the Old Copper Road in their ox-drawn wagon. Rounding a bend in the trail, they discovered the bodies of the six victims in the middle of the road. Horrified by what they saw, they placed the bodies in their wagon and drove to the McKissack Cemetery across the creek. And there, after saying a few scripture verses over the dead men, they laid them to rest in a single mass grave (Sarris, "Anatomy," 679).

Federal scouting patrols from the 143rd New York Infantry were next to reach the scene of the massacre that same day. They reported that the victims were killed by Gatewood and his gang (USWD, I, 45, i: 1193). By now the sight of a guerrilla atrocity no longer shocked these veteran soldiers. They had already witnessed their share of violence in the war in the mountains and saw little point in pursuing the matter. The Madden Branch Massacre was just another brutal incident in a dirty little war that the local community would be left to live with.

Gatewood's men caught up with William Lillard on November 30. Gatewood may have obtained information of his whereabouts from the recruits he killed at Madden Branch. Peter Parris' father, Nathaniel, his older brother, James, and younger brother, Alfred, were all at Lillard's home waiting for the Union recruits to arrive, and two other Unionists were busy outside hauling a load of corn. Suddenly one of the women who had been acting as a lookout came running to the cabin yelling that Gatewood's raiders were on the way. The men ran for cover as the guerrillas rode up, and bullets once again flew. Lillard was shot while trying to scale a fence, but he was able to pull himself into a ravine on the other side and escape. The raiders withdrew, but the Unionists anticipated their return. They carried Lillard to a hiding place under a rock cliff in the woods and left him covered with a blanket. Lillard later was taken to a hospital in Cleveland; he did finally receive his commission as a lieutenant in the 5th Tennessee Mounted (Barker Papers, Vol. 3).

Just after the Madden Branch Massacre, Gatewood and his guerrillas caught five more young men from Georgia, ironically including some relatives of the men killed at Madden Branch also on their way to enlist in the Union army. But Gatewood showed uncharacteristic mercy this time. Astonishingly he turned all five captives loose, and as suddenly as he had come he turned south and made his way back into Georgia. Perhaps he was bored with the killing. Or perhaps he was tired. He told the five young Unionists that he had "already killed a lot of men that day" (Sarris, "Anatomy," 699). The Gatewood gang killed twenty-four men during the Tennessee raid, Gatewood himself claiming credit for all but two of them (Barclay, 101).

It is not known whether members of the 5th Tennessee Mounted, which had suffered so much at the hands of Gatewood, actively sought revenge against the red-haired renegade. Lieutenant Charles Stewart reported (in a statement attached to the Widow's Declaration for Pension of George W. McCrary, August 4, 1883) that troops from the outfit pursued Gatewood in November 1864 and chased him back into Georgia. Stewart also confirmed the death of George W. McCrary of James G. Brown's command who was gunned down by Gatewood's guerrillas on their Tennessee raid.

Conducting operations against Gatewood's guerrillas in northwestern Georgia in the early months of 1865, the 5th and 6th Tennessee Mounted Infantry Regiments finally had a chance to even scores with their hated nemesis. On February 1, Colonel George A. Gowin of the 6th Tennessee Mounted picked up Gatewood's trail in McLemore's Cove in Walker County and tracked him to his camp. At ten o'clock that night the bluecoats attacked, taking Gatewood and his seventy-five guerrillas by surprise. Gatewood's band was routed. The Federals killed fourteen Rebels and captured most of their horses and guns. Gowin reported, "I took no prisoners" (USWD, I, 49, i: 33). But the victory was not complete, for the redheaded guerrilla chief escaped. There were still active Confederate forces west of the Mississippi. Gatewood headed for Texas.

Chapter 14

"Guerrilla Holes"

Throughout the summer of 1864, Confederate raiders like McCollum, Jordan, and Gatewood disrupted Federal communications with attacks on the Western and Atlantic Railroad line, and the Yankees responded as they had dealt with bushwhackers elsewhere in the mountains. After a July 2 attack on Colonel Samuel Ross' 20th Connecticut Infantry near Acworth, Brigadier General William D. Whipple instructed him to "guard your post and see that they do not destroy the railroad in your vicinity. If those guerrillas ever fall into your hands take no prisoners." On July 25, Colonel Thomas T. Heath of the 5th Ohio Cavalry was ordered south of the Etowah River to conduct operations against Rebel guerrillas near Dallas, Van Wert (now Rockmart), Stilesboro, and Euharlee. The Yankees were to take as many guerrillas "dead or alive" as possible (USWD, I, 38, v: 27, 254).

Federal commanders became particularly concerned about guerrilla activity near Kingston and Cassville. Because it lay on the vital Western and Atlantic Railroad where a spur line ran westward to Rome, Kingston became an important stop where trains took on passengers, fuel, and water. During the Atlanta campaign in 1864, the thriving commercial center was occupied both by Confederate and Union armies and was used as a supply center and a hospital (Weizenecker, 9). Five miles east of Kingston and just north of the rail line lay the growing town of Cassville, with around 1,800 people and two colleges. Private Jenkins Lloyd Jones, a Wisconsin artilleryman passing through Cassville in July 1864, described it as "a very pretty country town hid away among the hills" (Cunyus, 237).

After the fall of Atlanta in September 1864, the area around Cassville and Kingston was given over to lawlessness as bands of Rebel partisans from General John B. Hood's retreating army raided Yankee supply trains and harassed local Unionists. Many of Cassville's residents had abandoned their homes and fled south as early as May 1864. Life was extremely difficult for those who stayed on, although Colonel S. D. Dean, the Union provost-marshal in Kingston, was a decent man who provided aid to local destitute families as best he could (Mahan, 109).

Cassville came to have a bad reputation with the Yankees. The fact that the Rebels had renamed the county in honor of Colonel Francis Bartow, a Confederate hero killed at Manassas, did not help things any. The town became known as a "guerrilla hole" (Cunyus, 237).

Rebel "scouts" attached to Joe Wheeler's cavalry used Cassville as a base from which they conducted raids on Federal supply trains between Kingston and Atlanta. They tore up railroad tracks when they got the chance, cut telegraph wires, and were a serious nuisance to Yankee troops. Members of the 1st Georgia Cavalry, who received blame for much of this mischief, frequented the homes of Rebel sympathizers in Cassville. Some local girls kept company with them. Sallie W. Howard, daughter of Confederate Captain C. W. Howard of Kingston, was accused of being a Rebel spy and admitted meeting with some of the Rebel scouts (Cunyus, 244–246).

One of Sallie's friends, 20-year-old "Julia" Murchison, even cut her hair short and disguised herself in a Confederate uniform so that she could make runs for the partisans, but on July 19, 1864, she was captured by Union soldiers. The daring female spy and two of her sisters were arrested and shipped north to the Female Military Prison in Louisville, Kentucky, where she fell ill. The Federals released her, but she never saw home again. Somewhere in Tennessee, she died of unknown causes; her body was found by the side of the road (Kennett, 101–102).

Things came to a head in Cassville on the night of October 11, 1864. As a Union wagon train was passing through town, one of the wagons broke down and had to be abandoned. The driver unhitched his horses and prepared to stay with the wagon overnight. Nine Federal stragglers later trailed in and spread their bedrolls on the ground near the wagon. None of these men was seen alive again. In the morning Yankee soldiers found the driver dead, run through with a bayonet. The horses and the nine other soldiers were missing, although their bedrolls still lay on the ground. Shortly afterwards the bodies of the nine victims were found where they had been thrown over a fence into the campus of the Cassville Female College, where Yankee troops were quartered. The Federals had had enough. In retaliation for the murder of the ten soldiers, they burned both colleges in Cassville and several homes in the town (Mahan, 111).

The murderers of the ten Union soldiers were never identified. Whether they were local bushwhackers, scouts attached to Wheeler's cavalry, or members of McCollum's or any of several other guerrilla bands operating in the area probably will never be determined. The Federal reprisals against Cassville apparently did little good because guerrilla raids continued to plague the Yankees. Federal cavalry detachments patrolled north and east of Cassville in a futile effort to track down the marauders (Mahan, 112).

The Yankees were particularly edgy because Hood's Army of Tennessee was on the loose after their evacuation of Atlanta, and the Rebel general's intentions were unknown. He was moving northwest into Alabama and Tennessee preparing to launch his final campaign against the Federal supply base at Nashville in December 1864. He could have attacked anywhere along the railroad line between Atlanta and Chattanooga, so Union posts were on their guard. They were understandably concerned about guerrilla raids, and Sherman was losing patience.

On October 30, 1864, Colonel Heath of the 5th Ohio Cavalry received orders to accompany a foraging party from Cartersville up the Etowah River. His troopers were to burn the homes of several persons identified as being in league with Rebel guerrillas. Then they were to ride northeast to Canton in Cherokee County and burn the town. Finally they were to return to Cassville and burn it too (USWD, I, 39, iii: 513).

The Federals targeted Canton, a small town of about 200 people and no more than fifty or sixty houses, in retaliation for raids by Ben McCollum's band. Heath's troopers probably torched the town on November 4, although the exact date is unclear. They ordered residents to gather up whatever possessions they wanted saved and to evacuate their homes before they were burned. The soldiers set fire to individual homes on each street and may have singled out dwellings suspected of being occupied by guerrilla sympathizers. Although some reports said only one or two houses were left standing, it is more likely that only half the town was destroyed. For those unlucky residents burned out, the approaching cold winter boded for a miserable existence (Marlin, 76–78).

After punishing Canton, Heath's Ohio troopers retraced their route southwest along the Etowah and moved on toward their second objective, Cassville. They carried out their orders on November 5, and this time the Federals finished what they had started on October 12. Virtually the entire town was destroyed. Only three churches and three private homes remained standing after the fires had done their work. One of the spared dwellings housed the seriously ill mother of Confederate Brigadier General William T. Wofford, while another had been used as a hospital by the Yankees (Mahan, 114–115).

By the time the burning was finished, the crisp clear autumn day had turned to clouds, and by nightfall rain mixed with sleet began to fall. The wretched women and children who remained in Cassville were left homeless, huddling together in the cold rain, seeking warmth and shelter, spending a miserable night. Fourteen-year-old J. L. Milhollin watched with his mother and three younger children as the Yankees burned their home across from the town cemetery where his father, a Confederate soldier, lay buried. Mrs. Milhollin and her children ripped planks from a shelter over her husband's grave and fashioned a crude hut, with quilts draped over it, that they could sleep under during the night. The next day, a cold and rainy Sunday, her older son, now the man of the house, looked until he found an unoccupied former slave cabin four miles from town where he moved his family. He never forgot the anguish and humiliation of that previous night (Mahan, 115–116).

An Illinois officer wrote on November 8, "Tuesday morning. Cloudy raining. Orders to march at 6 o'clock A.M. Passed through Cassville. The town was destroyed. Nothing standing but three churches, the chimneys of the burned buildings standing." The displaced Cassville families never received the provisions that Heath had promised. The refugees sought shelter in the homes of friends or family in the county. Many of them never returned to rebuild their homes in Cassville. What once had been a prosperous town never recovered from the devastation of the war (Mahan, 116–117).

That same day, a Federal detachment foraging near Kingston was attacked by Rebel guerrillas who killed one soldier, wounded another, and captured seven. Sherman, in Kingston planning his march across Georgia to the sea, was still concerned about guerrilla activity and was determined to put a stop to it. He did not know that Cassville already had been burned. On November 8, he issued this order to Brigadier General John E. Smith at Cartersville:

> Arrest some six or eight citizens known or supposed to be hostile. Let one or two go free to carry word to the guerrilla band that you give them forty-eight hours' notice that unless all the men of ours picked up by them in the past two days are returned, Kingston, Cassville, and Cartersville will be burned, as also the houses of the parties arrested. I suppose the bandof guerrillas is known to you, and you can know where to strike. (USWD, I, 39, iii: 703, 717)

Colonel Thomas Morgan of the 74th Indiana Infantry made a nighttime raid on November 9 on the area near Kingston where the guerrilla attack had taken place. The bluecoats searched several homes and arrested a number of suspicious characters, including one man who was found armed with a cavalry carbine and "lying on the floor, against his door, completely dressed, and ready to move at a moment's notice." In another home, the Yankees bagged a partisan armed with two revolvers. The prisoner turned out to be Captain James M. Hendricks of the 1st Georgia Cavalry who had led the guerrilla attack the previous day. The Federals burned three homes in the neighborhood and returned to Kingston with their Rebel captives (Kennett, 230).

Kingston was in ruins when the Federal army pulled out, with most of the stores and homes destroyed. The Methodist church was spared, but the town's three other churches went up in flames. Yankee cavalrymen also burned Cedartown, destroying Polk County's two-story brick courthouse and most of the town's stores (Sargent, 373).

Law and order crumbled in northern Georgia in the wake of Atlanta's fall and the withdrawal of Hood's Rebel army. The mountain people were left to the mercy of numerous guerrilla bands who roamed the area unchecked. Even as his government disintegrated, Joseph E. Brown issued a futile proclamation against detachments of Rebel cavalry who claimed to be operating behind enemy lines but who were actually robbing local residents (Macon *Daily Telegraph*, November 25, 1864).

For the people of the area, left in the backwater of Sherman's juggernaut, there was no real law for them to appeal to, and their letters illustrate their despair. A Cumming man wrote of "bands of armed men calling themselves 'scouts' " riding unchecked through the county foraging, stealing livestock, and terrorizing local citizens (Lane, 224). A mountain woman wrote, "The country is plum full of Cavalry just . . . stealing all the time. . . . I believe it will come to . . . guerrilla warfare" (Bryan, 154).

On January 23, 1865, Brigadier General William T. Wofford replaced A. W. Reynolds as commander of Confederate troops in North Georgia. Wofford was assigned 7,000 soldiers—many of whom were deserters themselves—to break up guerrilla bands and restore order in the mountains. There were few officers better qualified for the assignment. The 41-year-old attorney and planter from Cassville had seen combat as an army officer in the Mexican War. He had served in the Georgia legislature, and as a delegate to the state convention in January 1861 he had spoken out vigorously against secession. But when war broke out, Wofford led the 18th Georgia Infantry Regiment, part of John B. Hood's famous Texas Brigade, in Virginia, where he was wounded in action twice (Mahan, 86–87).

The situation in North Georgia certainly warranted attention. Guerrilla chieftains controlled the rural areas and ran roughshod over the mountain people. A newspaper correspondent in the Augusta *Daily Constitutionalist* of February 11, 1865, described the country as devastated, its women and children dirty, ragged, and hungry. He said the country was better off when the Yankees were in control and described Rebel guerrilla leaders McCollum, Baker, and Colquitt and their men as deserters and thieves. Colquitt's raiders robbed people in Whitfield County of $4,000 paid by the state to help soldiers' families. The fierce Gatewood, dreaded by the Yankees, posed as great a threat to Confederate civilians. Only Tom Polk Edmundson in Murray County and Ben Jordan in Pickens County had any real authority to operate in the region.

Time appeared to be running out for the guerrilla commanders. In Murray County, Federal troops were closing in on the last active Rebel partisan, 21-year-old Captain Thomas Polk Edmundson. Edmundson's family was one of the most pro-slavery clans in Murray County, and in July 1861 he joined the 11th Georgia Infantry Regiment. Detached in February 1862 for recruiting duties, Tom Polk drifted into the world of guerrilla warfare and led a band of Rebels operating near Spring Place during 1864. His men skirmished frequently with Federal troops and with Unionist partisans attached to James G. Brown's ill-fated 1st Georgia State Troops Volunteers. Edmundson's command numbered 150 to 200 guerrillas at the end of March 1865 (Murray County History Committee, 72–74).

On the morning of April 1, 1865, Lieutenant Colonel Werner W. Bjerg left Dalton at the head of 300 infantrymen of the 147th Illinois Infantry and 80 horsemen of the 6th Tennessee Mounted. The Federals headed east to Spring Place, camped for the night there, and the next morning made their way southward until they reached the Coosawattee River. On April 3, Bjerg's troops and Edmundson's guerrillas battled along the banks of the Coosawattee in one of the last bloody clashes of the war in the Georgia mountains, and Edmundson was killed. The Federals returned to Dalton with four men wounded in the expedition. Bjerg reported twelve to fifteen guerrillas killed or wounded (USWD, I, 49, i: 508–509; 49, ii: 240). Edmundson's death was a blow to the waning Rebel morale in the area. The remnants of his command were turned over to a Captain Rodgers, who held the guerrillas together for a few more weeks until it was clear that the war was lost (Murray County History Committee, 75).

Wofford was doing all he could do to restore order to the mountains and to rein in the guerrilla bands. In April he reached an agreement with Brigadier General Henry M. Judah, Federal commander at Dalton, for the distribution of 30,000 bushels of corn to the starving people of North Georgia. The 44-year-old Judah, a West Pointer and veteran of the Mexican War, responded with humanity and cooperated with the Rebel commander in feeding the mountain families (Cunyus, 247–248).

Major General Howell Cobb wrote to Wofford on April 21 that an armistice had been arranged between Sherman and Johnston in North Carolina. Cobb wrote, "all military operations have ceased for the present, and will not be resumed except on forty-eight hours notice. In my opinion they will not be resumed at all" (USWD, I, 49, ii: 428).

The shaky detente between Wofford and Judah was threatened when General George H. Thomas received word that Confederate forces in the mountains planned a raid against Federal railroad communications between Chattanooga and Knoxville. On April 18, he warned Wofford that if the attempt were made, he would "so despoil Georgia that fifty years hence it will be a wilderness." Wofford responded on April 24 that the rumor of an impending Rebel raid was false. At the same time he admitted that "there are a number of bad men in the upper counties who have refused or neglected to obey my orders, but that instructions have been given to my officers on outpost duty to arrest and disarm all bodies of men going toward the Federal lines" (USWD, I, 49, ii: 395–396, 456).

Wofford proposed a meeting with Judah on May 8 at Resaca to discuss surrender terms. Writing from Cassville, he explained, "I would have proposed an earlier day, but I am en route to one of the upper counties, where I have an appointment to meet some men who have been bushwhacking, to the terror and injury of our unfortunate people, with the hope of restoring law and order" (USWD, I, 49, ii: 488).

Judah trusted Wofford to help restore order in the mountains. Clearly most of the Rebel soldiers just wanted to go home and remain at peace. Only 500 or so "guerrillas of the Gatewood class," Colonel Lewis Merrill wrote, "who have so far successfully resisted General Wofford's efforts to compel them to submit to his authority," would not surrender (USWD, I, 49, ii: 605–606).

The status of the guerrilla bands was a tricky question. How would they be treated if they laid down their arms? Lieutenant General Ulysses S. Grant responded on May 5, 1865, "I would advise as a cheap way to get clear of guerrillas that a certain time be given for them to come in, say the 20th of this month, up to which time their paroles will be received, but after which they will be proceeded against as outlaws" (USWD, I, 49, ii: 419). In fact many of the guerrillas never surrendered but merely blended back into the shadowy fringes of civilian life. Some of them, like red-haired John P. Gatewood, just disappeared and moved west.

Wofford surrendered the last Confederate troops east of the Mississippi River at Kingston on May 12, 1865. About 3,000 to 4,000 of Wofford's soldiers, guerrillas under McCollum and others, and veterans straggling home from Virginia and the Carolinas all assembled to lay down their arms and receive their paroles. A Confederate soldier described the scene:

I saw the motliest crew I have ever seen before or since. These so-called scouts were strutting around with broad-brimmed hats, long hair and jingling spurs. You could see the old "moss back" who had crept out of his cave. You would find groups of sad-looking men who had followed Lee, Jackson, Johnston, and Wheeler through the war. Some of them carried the mud and dust of 5 or 6 states on their old clothes. (Cunyus, 248–249)

The war was over, and it was springtime, with fragrant flowers in bloom. The women of Kingston asked Judah for permission to decorate the graves of the 275 Rebel soldiers buried there. He agreed on the condition that they decorate the graves of all the soldiers, Federal as well as Confederate. It was the first observance of a Confederate Memorial Day in America (Weizenecker, 10).

PART V

West Virginia

Chapter 15

Death of a Dream

Only in West Virginia did Southern mountain Unionists realize their goal of separate statehood. After Virginia's secession, the Mountain State's "founding fathers" met at Wheeling in June 1861 and formed a "Restored" government with Francis H. Pierpont as governor. As the Federal army secured control of northwestern Virginia, loyalist delegates met again in August, and this time they called for a separate state. Lincoln's commitment to slave emancipation proved to be a political stumbling block. As in East Tennessee, West Virginia Unionists opposed the abolishing of slavery, but a compromise plan providing for gradual emancipation finally satisfied both sides. In June 1863, West Virginia entered the union (McKinney, *Southern*, 20–21).

Like other areas of Southern Appalachia, West Virginia contained a prosperous class of property owners, a mountain variant of the planter class that dominated Virginia politics and society. This mountain elite, often found in county seats, had evolved into a planter-lawyer-merchant class, not as wealthy or influential as the great planters of eastern Virginia, but their ownership of land gave them access to mineral wealth they would exploit after the Civil War. Many of them were slaveowners (J. Williams, "Class," 210–211, 220–221; Eller, 11–12, 58). At the outbreak of the war, the mountain elite supported secession and the Confederacy, despite their other differences with the eastern planters. In secessionist areas of the state, class division increased after the Confederates introduced conscription in 1862, as in other mountain regions. Increasingly, poor mountaineers resented the privileged position of the mountain elite, and many switched sides from Confederate to Unionist (Noe, *Southwest*, 5, 110, 127).

The traditional mountain elite in western Virginia was challenged by a more liberal group of middle-class professionals and yeoman farmers who refused to accept secession and who resolved to stay in the Union. These were the "founders" who seized the opportunity to form a separate state. Leaders of the West Virginia government wrote a new state constitution in April 1862. With it came democratic reforms: universal free education, reorganization of the state's courts, the secret ballot. Circuit-riding preachers took an active role in the movement, condemning slavery and the wealthy mountain elite as well; between 1863 and 1872, twenty-nine evangelists sat in the state legislature. Some preachers took a more active role in the war; in the Kanawha region a number served as scouts and recruiters for the Federal army (J. Williams, "Class," 224).

Although a Union state, West Virginia was not solidly Unionist in loyalty. Without the presence of the Federal army, West Virginia might have gone the way of East Tennessee, where loyalists never were able to gain complete control and form a separate state. Especially in the southern counties, which really had more in common with Virginia than with their neighbors to the north, many mountaineers enthusiastically embraced the Confederacy. They launched a bitter guerrilla struggle in which all of the bloodiest aspects of the war in the Southern Appalachians were present (Noe, *Southwest*, 6).

Rebel partisans ambushed Federal army detachments, destroyed rail and telegraph communications, ruthlessly pillaged Unionist farms, and murdered civilians. In the spring of 1862, Rebel guerrillas murdered a Federal courier, severed his head, and wedged it into what was left of his gutted torso (J. Williams, *West Virginia*, 64–65). One Unionist commented in 1863, "After you get a short distance below the 'Pan Handle' it is *not safe* for a loyal man to go into the interior out of sight of the Ohio River" (McKinney, *Southern*, 24). With an estimated 3,000 men in the entire Virginia–West Virginia area, Rebel partisans dominated the guerrilla war (Castel, 50; G. Moore, 118).

Confederate regulars in southern West Virginia also posed a threat for Unionists, and periodic raids played havoc with the loyal population. In April and May 1863 Brigadier Generals John D. Imboden and William E. Jones pillaged virtually unchecked for three weeks. Fear of Rebel incursions, both from the regular forces and irregular terrorists, prompted many loyal West Virginians, like Laban Gwinn's family in Fayette County, to become refugees until the conflict was resolved (McKinney, *Southern*, 24).

The mountain war in West Virginia produced an abundance of colorful partisans like Perry Conley from the Minnora community in Calhoun County. A rugged 23-year-old mountaineer at six feet, three inches, Conley farmed at the start of the war with his wife, Lucinda, and two children. His brother, James, joined the Union army. In the summer of 1861, Perry formed a Rebel partisan company called the Moccasin Rangers and recruited men from the West Fork of the Little Kanawha River. Conley terrorized Unionists in the central part of West Virginia and became one of the most dreaded Rebel partisans in the area. No one knows for sure how many he killed. Sometimes he cooperated with other Rebel partisan bands from Braxton and Webster Counties. Troops of the 30th Ohio Infantry finally cornered Conley in Webster County in the summer of 1862, and the bushwhacker died in a violent gun battle. After Conley's death, his band collapsed (Stutler, 43–45).

One of Conley's associates was a mountain woman named Nancy Hart. Contemporary accounts paint Nancy as an attractive young lass in her early twenties, lively and spirited, and an ardent Confederate. Sometime in the early summer of 1861, she began riding with Perry Conley's gang. Unionist Home Guards surprised Conley and Nancy at one of their hiding places along the West Fork of the Little Kanawha in the fall of 1861, and Conley escaped in a hail of gunfire, leaving his female companion to be taken by the enemy. Nancy played innocent and convinced the Unionists that she posed no threat to them. After they released her, she made her way back to Conley's camp with valuable information about the local Unionists and regular Federal troops. Nancy married one of Conley's men, Joshua Douglas, who joined the 19th Virginia Cavalry after Conley was killed. While her husband fought in the Rebel cavalry, Nancy continued to act as a Rebel operative in Nicholas County, near Summersville, displaying pluck, resourcefulness, and a talent for acting (Stutler, 43–45).

In July 1862, Federal soldiers of the 9th West Virginia Infantry captured Nancy on a routine patrol. She proved such a charming prisoner that instead of placing her in the county jail, her captors lodged her in one of the spare rooms of the officers' headquarters in Summersville. Nancy flirted with the soldiers and eventually sweet-talked one naive guard into letting her hold his musket. She immediately aimed the weapon at the soldier and shot him dead. Then she bolted from the house, jumped on Lieutenant Colonel William C. Starr's favorite horse, and raced away with soldiers in hot pursuit. Nancy eluded the soldiers, reached the Confederate lines on the Greenbriar River, and returned to Summersville a week later at the head of 200 Rebel horsemen. Taking the Union garrison completely by surprise in the predawn darkness, the Rebels captured Lieutenant Colonel Starr and several of his officers, burned several buildings used as storehouses, and then withdrew (Stutler, 45–47).

There were Unionist partisans in the West Virginia mountains, too. Tough mountaineer John P. Baggs led a company of Unionist scouts called the Snake Hunters, who used methods just as ruthless as the Rebel bushwhackers. In December 1861, they smashed a company of Rebel guerrillas on the Little Kanawha in Roane County, inflicting many casualties. West Virginia Adjutant-General H. J. Samuels considered Baggs' company one of the most effective scout detachments, rating it "highly serviceable" in January 1862. Samuels recommended leaving the Snake Hunters "free to act" in the partisan way (USWD, I, 5: 468; USWD, III, 1: 665, 789).

Many West Virginia Unionists, like their counterparts in Eastern Tennessee and North Georgia, enlisted in the Federal army. They saw considerable action against Rebel guerrillas in the West Virginia mountains. Soldiers of the 1st West Virginia Cavalry and 3rd West Virginia Infantry destroyed a Rebel guerrilla base in Webster County in December 1861. West Virginia troops proved to be effective raiders, as did the East Tennesseans accompanying George Stoneman on his 1865 raid into North Carolina. Seven West Virginia regiments marched with Major General Philip H. Sheridan when he devastated Virginia's Shenandoah Valley in September 1864 (Current, 175, 177–178).

The picturesque valley of the Tug Fork River, separating Logan County in West Virginia from Pike County in Kentucky, would gain national notoriety in the 1880s as the scene of the Hatfield-McCoy feud, which resulted in the deaths of a dozen mountaineers. Civil War animosity was not the direct cause for the clan conflict, which erupted thirteen years later. But guerrilla warfare did scar the Tug Valley in the 1860s, creating the same desensitizing to brutality generated in other mountain communities.

The lure of cheap, plentiful land in the Tug River Valley brought the first white families up from southwestern Virginia into this beautiful region around 1800. Among the first settlers were the McCoys and the Hatfields. The Tug Valley was a region of scenic craggy mountaintops and close dales drained by rocky streams. The rugged terrain offered few opportunities for tilling the soil except along the limited creek and river bottoms. Roads were poor, and the area's remoteness provided a secluded refuge from the outside world for the pioneer families willing to brave the hardships of frontier life (Waller, *Feud*, 19).

The self-reliant Tug Valley people came to cherish their autonomy from the outside world, an independent lifestyle that many historians consider a kind of "pre-industrial" Appalachian ideal, a society based on the yeoman-farmer tradition of Jeffersonian democracy (Noe, " 'Appalachia's,' " 91). It was the preservation of this independence—and not opposition to slavery—that led many mountain communities to support the Union during the Civil War. The Tug Valley was an exception, because most of its people supported the South. In both situations it was their mountain autonomy, and not any ideology or loyalty to nation, that determined the choice. The Tug Valley people simply regarded the Confederacy as their best hope (Waller, *Feud*, 30–31).

Logan County people boycotted the convention for statehood in Wheeling and declined to vote on the new state constitution. Across the river, a majority of people in Pike County, Kentucky, also favored the Confederacy, although support was weaker in the western Pikeville district, an area subjected to raids by Confederate guerrillas (Waller, *Feud*, 30).

Asa Harmon McCoy was one of the few Tug Valley residents to support the Union, an irony since he was also one of the few people in the region to own slaves. In choosing the North, he bucked the wishes of most members of his own family, who favored the Confederacy. His brother Randolph ("Old Ranel") McCoy joined a Rebel guerrilla company called the Logan Wildcats. The Wildcats were led by William Anderson ("Devil Anse") Hatfield (Waller, *Feud*, 17, 30).

Tall, hawk-nosed, black-bearded Devil Anse Hatfield was the leader of the Hatfield clan in Logan County. His mountaineer neighbors acknowledged that he could ride and shoot like an expert. In 1861 he enlisted as a private in the 45th Virginia Infantry Battalion, and by 1863 he was a lieutenant in one of the battalion's companies on duty at Saltville. In December 1863, Devil Anse and two of his brothers deserted and returned to Logan County, perhaps to defend their homes and families from Federal raids in the area (Waller, *Feud*, 2, 17, 31–32).

By 1863, many parts of southern West Virginia were torn by guerrilla warfare. Federal troops burned the courthouse in the little town of Logan. On the Kentucky side of the river there were skirmishes around Pikeville, and Colonel James Garfield, a future United States president, led Union troops in an action in the Tug Valley. With the Confederacy unable to send regular forces to the area, it fell to local men like Devil Anse Hatfield to respond in the mountaineer way, guerrilla style (Waller, *Feud*, 32).

In 1864, Devil Anse formed the Logan Wildcats and waged a bitter partisan war against both the Federal army and Unionist Home Guards from Kentucky. The Wildcats fought skirmishes in Logan County and in neighboring counties. They also terrorized Union people in the region and stole livestock. With the level of violence intensifying, the community's routine was disrupted, as in other mountain areas. Local government services broke down, and the county courts stopped functioning. But the majority of people in the region, who were Confederate, regarded Devil Anse and the Wildcats as local heroes fighting a David-and-Goliath battle against outsiders seeking to destroy their way of life (Waller, *Feud*, 32).

Although Randolph McCoy and many other members of his clan supported the South and served with the Logan Wildcats, Harmon McCoy, the family's dissenting Unionist, joined the Unionist Home Guard company in

Pike County and took part in raids against the Rebel Wildcats. On January 7, 1865, Harmon was shot and killed in a mountain cave after returning home. Rumors held that either Devil Anse Hatfield or his uncle Jim Vance, also a leader in the Wildcats, was the murderer (Waller, *Feud*, 2, 17, 32).

Newspaper writers suggested that the murder of Harmon McCoy by the Hatfields led to the famous feud between the two mountain clans. Altina Waller, in her classic study of the feud, rejects that theory for a number of reasons. Most of the McCoys were pro-Confederate and regarded Harmon as a turncoat. There were no acts of reprisal by the McCoys after the death of Harmon and no serious trouble between the two clans until thirteen years later, when the feud broke out. Members of both clans denied that they feuded because of what happened during the war (Waller, *Feud*, 2).

Waller contends that the murder of Harmon McCoy resulted not from clan friction but from the popular opinion, even among his own family, that he was a traitor to the community who deserved killing. The Tug Valley people were so unified in their support for the Confederacy that even members of Harmon McCoy's own family could not bring themselves to defend him or to condemn his killers, who were seen as fighting to preserve the community's autonomy against outsiders (Waller, *Feud*, 17).

The Tug Valley folk were destined to lose the independence they fought so hard to preserve, but the poor mountaineers who fought for the Union would see their autonomy slip away as well. Neither would benefit from the war economically, and both would begin a slide into increasing poverty, despair, and hopelessness. As industrialization took hold in the years after the Civil War, the Southern mountains would become what Ronald Eller calls "a rich land inhabited by poor people" (xxv).

In an equally ironic turn of events, the planter-merchant oligarchy who had shared in the Confederacy's defeat profited the most from the economic transformation which swept the mountains after the Civil War. By the end of Reconstruction in 1870, West Virginia's mountain elite, who had favored secession before the war, regained control of the state's government, following a political pattern seen in other Southern states as conservative Democrats returned to power. While new state constitutions and new land laws benefited the wealthy, West Virginia's mountaineers struggled with bitter divisions, uprooted families, and baffling economic changes (J. Williams, "Class," 210–211, 228; Eller, 58; Noe, *Southwest*, 139–140).

As America's industrial revolution gained momentum in the years after the Civil War, eastern corporations realized the potential wealth of the Southern Appalachians and were anxious to purchase timber and mineral rights. "It is a race for the prize," wrote New York journalist Charles Dudley Warner in 1889. As early as 1864, West Virginia lawmakers, looking to attract eastern investors, were promoting the "boundless natural resources" of their state. Other mountain states were soon to follow. Little Will Thomas had envisioned the mountains as an industrial core for the Confederacy. Now Southern promoters, with the same vision for the Appalachians, saw a "New South" based on modern industrial power, as well as a chance to profit personally. The mountain elite who reemerged as the governing power in West Virginia had been pro-secession, but they also had been pro-modernization. With their access to mineral wealth, they became the driving force in speculation and promotion. Many were former soldiers like John D. Imboden—whose troops had raided into West Virginia during the war—men who had served in the mountains and realized their potential (Eller, 40–49).

Railroads paved the way into the mountains. By 1873 the Chesapeake and Ohio had reached the Ohio River, opening central and southern West Virginia to development, and the Norfolk and Western Railroad unlocked vast coal riches in the 1880s. As absentee businessmen bought up the land and mineral rights, sawmills, coal mines, and boom towns were soon to appear. Railroad branch lines in the 1880s opened the timber lands of Western North Carolina, East Tennessee, and North Georgia as speculators sold to eastern capitalists (Eller, 65–67, 97–101, 132).

West Virginia became the nation's largest coal producer. The Mountain State experienced a rapid metamorphosis unmatched anywhere else in the southern Appalachians. The population in the southern West Virginia coalfields increased fourfold between 1890 and 1920, creating boom towns like Logan, company towns run by eastern coal barons. And with these company towns came an end of the mountaineers' dream of independence and an end of their way of life as they had known it (Eller, 132, 133–140).

The Civil War devastated agriculture in the mountains. As farming became less profitable in the postwar years, many landowners turned to other activities to supplement their income. Devil Anse Hatfield operated a successful part-time timber business after the war, but he lost his timber lands in 1888. The pattern was typical all across the Southern mountains, as local landowners, lacking the capital to develop the minerals, sold their land to eastern corporations that could (Salstrom, 123–124).

Eastern coal barons replaced the traditional mountain elite. While the old elite utilized kinship and familiarity with voters as their means of controlling local politics, the coal barons used their economic power over jobs. The average mountaineer was left more isolated from the political process, as citizen participation dropped. As the coal barons bought up the mountain land, they also displaced many of the mountain folk from their family homes. Many stayed on as sharecroppers or migrated into the new industrial centers to find work there, but the gap between poor and rich became greater. What had been one of the most self-sufficient regions of America had indeed become "a rich land inhabited by poor people" (Eller, xxi–xxv, 199–210).

Because they were growing poorer as farmers, the mountaineers became coal miners. At first it was a part-time activity to supplement their decreasing farm income. Often they saw mining as a temporary measure, but for most their new way of life became permanent. The mountain people had little choice but to abandon the family farms. Despite their poverty compared to workers in other parts of America, West Virginia coal miners earned three times the average yearly income of farmers in that state in 1900. Like thousands of other West Virginians, the proud mountaineers of the Tug Valley lamented the loss of their autonomy after the Civil War; and as they migrated from their family farms to company towns, their grandchildren would grieve over the loss of a way of life. They could never go back (Salstrom, 42, 53).

Chapter 16

Legacy

Colonel John S. Mosby, the most famous Civil War guerrilla of all, wrote, "The military value of a partisan's work is not measured by the amount of property destroyed, or the number of men killed or captured, but by the number he keeps watching" (Wert, 96–97). In August 1864, General William T. Sherman had 72,000 soldiers on the Georgia fighting front and 68,000 in the rear guarding his supply and communication line through the mountains. An average of 233 soldiers per mile of track was required to watch the vulnerable Western and Atlantic Railroad (Kennett, 96). Federal troops were constantly harassed by partisans who cut telegraph lines, sabotaged the rail lines, and sometimes even derailed trains.

But Albert Castel, in his study of the guerrilla conflict, points out that Federal troops stationed to guard rail lines and supply depots were more likely to be militia or "Home Yankees" like Kirk's partisans, the 5th Tennessee Mounted, or the 1st Alabama Cavalry. There were still many regular Union soldiers available for duty at the front. And Confederate troops sent to the mountains to catch deserters and deal with Unionist guerrillas only subtracted from the Rebel army's manpower at the front (Castel, 50). Of the thousands of Rebel guerrillas operating in the South, only Mosby's Rangers in Virginia had any real impact in delaying Confederate defeat, and the partisans of the Appalachians seemed to have more in common with Quantrill's notorious marauders in Kansas than with the dashing Mosby.

Confederate politicians and generals were nearly unanimous in condemning guerrilla warfare as a counterproductive evil. The guerrillas' lack of discipline made them undependable troops who did more harm than good. Guerrilla warfare brought misery to the Southern people, generated ongoing local feuds, and gave rise to postwar outlaws of the Jesse James mold (Castel, 50). In February 1864, the Confederate Congress disbanded the Partisan Ranger units they had authorized in April 1862, exempting only Mosby's and John McNeill's commands in northern Virginia (Wert, 69–70, 140).

Partisan conflict had a more significant influence on tactics in the war. Guerrilla operations influenced the normal routine of both armies and had a pronounced psychological impact on soldiers and civilians (Fisher, 92–95). And the experience of guerrilla fighting in the mountains influenced the adoption of the Union high command's strategy of total war against the South in the last two years of the contest.

The South could have used guerrilla warfare to prolong the war, and the experience of the American Revolution proved that Southerners were capable practitioners. Federal commanders certainly were uneasy about the prospect. But although they toyed with the idea in 1865, Southern leaders in the end discarded such notions. Partisan conflict in the mountains could have extended the war for decades, prolonged Federal military occupation and reprisals, and would have to be waged from an area where Unionists derived their greatest strength. If the South still failed to win, all that would remain would be a legacy of bitterness, brutality, and destruction (Castel, 49–50).

For the mountain people the war did leave a legacy of bitterness, brutality, and destruction. The guerrilla war had an enormous psychological impact on Appalachia, and decades would pass before the scars began to heal.

The first thing to be done was to restore some semblance of law and order to the mountains. An end to the war did not mean an end to the lawlessness. In May 1865, a Wilkes County, North Carolina, man wrote, "All we dread here now is robbers & no doubt there will be plenty of them this summer." A gang of about thirty renegades already had gathered at "Fort Hamby," a two-story log blockhouse on the Yadkin River, from which they terrorized nearby communities. Local citizens made three unsuccessful attacks on Fort Hamby in May, one of them led by Harvey Bingham. Finally they laid siege to the hideout, set it afire, and executed four of the outlaws (Van Noppen and Van Noppen, 12–14).

A judge wrote Georgia's Governor Charles J. Jenkins in March 1866 that "murderers, bushwhackers, robbers, and thieves" controlled Fannin County. He continued, "I am now a refugee from my home having been shot—by a man by the name of James Morrow, leader of the band, who swears he will kill me if I do not die of the wounds he has already inflicted—I have to ask you to give me that protection to life and property which governments afford to their citizens. This band numbers more than two hundred—They speak openly and boldly of the men they intend to kill" (Jones, 34).

County courts were crowded with murder cases, and lawsuits stemming from wartime incidents dragged on for years. Such actions fanned the flames of bitterness that still lingered. An even worse legacy of the war was the proliferation of vendettas and feuds.

In Madison County, North Carolina, Kirk's raiders had shot and killed three of widow Nance Franklin's four sons in front of her home as she looked on. When she tried to stop them, one of the soldiers fired his weapon, snipping off a lock of her hair. After the war the same former soldier was helping to rebuild Mars Hill College a few miles from Shelton Laurel, and he joked with some of the students about the time during the war when he shot off part of a woman's hair. When James Norton heard the story from one of the students later, he offered him a five-dollar gold piece if he would point out the man. When the meeting took place, Norton told the ex-soldier, "That was my sister you shot the hair off of, and one of her boys you murdered was named James after me." Norton pulled out a revolver and shot the man in the stomach. He was arrested and tried for murder. The jury acquitted him (Paludan, 21–22).

A Union soldier at a refugee camp in Stevenson, Alabama, recalled bitter mountain women nurturing the spirit of revenge: "I heard them repeat over and over to their children the names of men which they were never to forget, and whom they were to kill when they had sufficient strength to hold a rifle" (Paludan, 23).

Several years after the war, a group of travelers in Walker County, Alabama, fell in with some strangers whom they helped free a cow from a bog. When the men introduced themselves, one of them said, "My name is Hulsey." Instantly another man, named McCavenger, produced a pistol and jammed it into the other man's face. "Is it Whit?" he demanded. "No," the terrified man recoiled, "I'm Bill Hulsey." "Well," McCavenger replied, "that's all in the world that kept you from getting your brains blown out. I've always said that if I ever saw that Whit Hulsey—that home-guard leader again, I'd kill him if it is the last thing I ever do." Suddenly turning on Hulsey again, he growled, "You look like the same Hulsey to me." Hulsey was saved only when his companions convinced McCavenger that he was who he claimed to be (Thompson, 191).

The origins of many feuds are difficult to trace. The famous feud between the Hatfields and McCoys actually stemmed from an incident in 1878 in which Old Ranel McCoy accused Floyd Hatfield, a cousin of Devil Anse Hatfield, of stealing one of his hogs. Altina Waller contends Civil War enmity had nothing to do with the start of the feud, but there is evidence that once underway it may have been egged on by Pikeville Unionist Perry

Cline, who may have borne a grudge against Devil Anse Hatfield for his guerrilla activities during the war. The feud evolved into an extension of the wartime animosity between pro-Union Pikeville and the pro-Confederate Tug Valley (*Feud*, 2, 194).

Some grudges smoldered for years, only to be released violently and without warning. In November 1876 Anthony "Tone" Goble murdered Wofford L. Brown after a drunken argument in Ellijay, Georgia, in which Brown alleged that Goble's father had stolen meat from his father during the Civil War. Brown later was found on a nearby mountain with his head crushed and his body mangled beyond description. Goble was tried and was sentenced to be hanged. Sheriff William Jones resigned rather than hang the prisoner and face retaliation from Goble's family. Goble was publicly hanged in June 1877 in the only legal execution in the history of Gilmer County (Davis, "Goble," 51–55).

The gunfight between Robert Porter Woody and Walter Webster Findley in Gilmer County provides another example of animosities that may have come out of wartime antagonisms. These men had served on opposing sides during the Civil War. Woody had ridden with James G. Brown's partisans and then was a lieutenant in the 5th Tennessee Mounted Infantry. Findley had been a lieutenant in the Confederate Home Guard in Gilmer County, and his brother was James Jefferson Findley, the relentless Rebel partisan of Lumpkin County. Woody and Findley once had been friends before the tragic events of the war in the mountains divided their community (Davis, "Gunfight," 61).

After the war Web Findley participated in a number of raids with Federal agents on illegal mountain distilleries. He also cooperated with some of his moonshiner friends on the other side of the law. In April 1880, after federal agent John A. Stuart and his men raided fourteen stills in North Georgia, Findley and the moonshiners struck back by attacking Stuart's farm and wounding his son. Arrested and indicted for his part in the attack, Findley was tried in federal court in Atlanta and was convicted in October 1882. Sentenced in February 1883 to two years in prison, he applied to President Chester A. Arthur for a pardon. Findley's supporters, including Georgia's two U.S. senators and several state legislators, signed a petition requesting his release (Davis, "Gunfight," 61–62).

Robert P. Woody, who had aided federal prosecutors in their case against Findley, spearheaded a counterpetition signed by many mountain residents asking that Findley not be released. The president eventually granted the pardon, and Findley was a free man. He never forgot that Woody had played a leading role in trying to keep him locked up. Findley and Woody lived in the same eastern Gilmer County community, but they refused to speak to each other in public or greet each other civilly in passing. The smoldering feud finally boiled over on September 28, 1884, at the Mount Pleasant Church at Doublehead Gap on the Fannin-Gilmer County line (Davis, "Gunfight," 63).

Arriving for a church meeting that Sunday night, Woody was helping his wife, Elizabeth, down from his ox-drawn wagon, when Findley, standing nearby, cracked, "By God, roll her out, Woody." Woody whirled around. "By God," he replied, "I'll roll you down." As the two men exchanged more angry words, bystanders began to scatter, and Elizabeth Woody grabbed her baby and jumped out of the wagon to try to contain her enraged husband. Findley invited Woody to settle their differences right there. The two men both hauled out their pistols and opened fire. William Kimsey, unable to get out of the way, was struck by a stray bullet and was killed. Remarkably, although they blazed away at each other at close range, neither Woody nor Findley was killed. Woody emerged from the shootout with wounds to his hand and stomach, while Findley was hit in the head by a rock thrown by a bystander. (Davis, "Gunfight," 63–64).

Woody and Findley both were charged with the murder of William Kimsey but were acquitted. Woody served a year in the state penitentiary for his attack on Findley. Findley was instrumental in getting Woody's Union disability pension revoked on the basis of fraud. But after the gunfight at Doublehead Gap, there was no more trouble between the two former adversaries. Reportedly, Woody insisted that if Findley would not be courteous and speak to him in public, they could settle the feud for good. In any event, the two men apparently fought no more (Davis, "Gunfight," 64).

A popular perception of Appalachia as a poverty-stricken region—with people inclined to violence, feuding, and clannishness—may have originated in the 1880s. Altina Waller showed that the Hatfield-McCoy feud of the 1880s was not in fact characteristic of mountain society as a whole. Twelve people died in twelve years of feuding, and out of the entire populations of Logan and Pike Counties only eighty people took part. Most Tug Valley residents did not accept the feud as "normal" and were shocked by the violence. One woman explained, "We didn't know we lived in a place where such things could happen" (Feud, 10).

While many vendettas undoubtedly had wartime origins, Waller sees a string of well-publicized Appalachian feuds in the 1880s—the Hatfield-McCoy feud and similar feuds in Perry, Harlan, and Bell Counties in eastern Kentucky—as a power struggle between local rural farmers, determined to resist outside ideas, and local businessmen determined to foster economic development by bringing in railroads, modern government, and taxation. "Progress" was perceived by many mountain people as an attempt by outsiders to take over their local economy, government, and courts. Industrialization created a class of restless, frustrated young men with no future in farming, since available land was being bought up by powerful outside business interests, and such young men were more inclined to turn to violence as a solution to their problems ("Feuding," 366–367). Amidst the burst of growth in the publishing industry in the 1880s, eastern newspapermen were more than willing to provide their readers with stories about the "violent, feuding," mountain people (Eller, xv–xvi).

The outside world that saw Appalachia as backward and violent ignored the sweeping economic and social changes that created the image. Such changes, accompanied by the hatreds and dislocations caused by the war, destroyed much of Appalachian culture, turned formerly independent farmers into wage-laborers, and created poverty, isolation, and distrust (Noe, *Southwest*, 139–142). Many mountain people reacted by closing themselves to outsiders and their ideas. Class conflict emerged in the growing mountain industries that benefited a wealthy few at the expense of the impoverished masses. The unstable social and economic environment nurtured feuds and unrest. Poverty and isolation, while not particular mountain characteristics before the war, now intensified (Noe, " 'Appalachia's,' " 102–105; Dunn, 140–141). To many mountaineers isolation became a way to ensure cultural survival. Historian Rodger Cunningham suggests that mountain culture survived and became even stronger—more distinctly Appalachian—after the war (100).

The violence surrounding moonshining is a familiar part of mountain culture and illustrates some misconceptions held about the region. The phenomenon emerged after the Civil War when the federal government began to implement new revenue laws requiring the licensing of alcohol manufacture. Many mountaineers in the postwar world of Southern Appalachia supplemented their scant income by making whiskey, just as they had done for generations before the tax laws became a reality. They could not afford to purchase the costly licenses required for legal production of alcohol, so they continued the practice illegally. Many mountain Unionists now found themselves at cross-purposes with the same government they had fought for during the war.

Federal revenue agents collected fees based on the number of arrests they made and the number of illegal distilleries seized, and this practice encouraged unscrupulous agents to inflate their fees by making false arrests. They also utilized, and paid, local residents who acted as spies and informed on suspected moonshiners. Many a man was turned in by these "reporters" because of a wartime grudge. Revenue agents acted with brutal fanaticism and earned the hatred of mountain people. Suspected moonshiners were thrown in jail and treated as guilty until proven innocent. Families were forced to spend everything they had to pay the legal expenses of freeing a loved one. The sudden appearance of hostile armed men outside one's cabin in the middle of the night was disturbingly reminiscent of wartime guerrilla violence (Davis, "Moonshine War," 214–215).

The mountain people resisted such harsh and unfair tactics in the only way they could, the same way they had always done. As in the war, they resorted to private justice. Secret societies, vigilante gangs, and armed bands of determined mountain men struck back, intimidating potential informers and sometimes even killing revenue agents. Between 1875 and 1881, the mountains of North Georgia witnessed the greatest number of attacks against Federal agents in the Appalachians. The federal government responded by sending U.S. troops to the mountains. In 1876 and 1877, Federal soldiers became embroiled in an ugly civil conflict between revenue agents and moonshiners in Gilmer County that left several mountaineers and one army officer dead. The experiment was so counterproductive that in 1879 Congress banned the further use of Federal troops in local disturbances (Davis, "Moonshine War," 216, 222).

Similar bands of "Night Riders" fought revenue agents in North Georgia's Pickens County from 1889 to 1891. In "weird and terrifying black cloaks and hoods," the Night Riders roamed the county using methods similar to those of the Ku Klux Klan, although their targets were the hated Federal revenue men, not blacks (Davis, "Night Riders," 336–339). But in Cherokee County in 1915, as part of a "white backlash" against the loss of jobs, another band of "Night Riders" intimidated employers who hired blacks. These activities provide harsh reminders of the strong tradition of guerrilla warfare in the mountains (Buffington and Jackson, 41–42, 48–49).

The guerrilla war had a pronounced effect on mountain communities. Cades Cove, Tennessee, emerged from the war a changed place. Old leaders like Daniel D. Foute and Russell Gregory were dead, and the younger men who took their place—forced to grow up fast in the chaos of the war—were less informed and less imaginative in their vision for community growth. Foute's bold plans for the cove's economic development died with him. The brutal guerrilla war left bitter hatreds that took many years to heal, and many Confederate sympathizers were forced to leave the community for good. The Union majority in Cades Cove became increasingly provincial and hostile to outsiders and to new ideas. During the war, the close family ties and mutual community interests of the cove people had helped them to stand together against Rebel guerrillas. Ironically, these same qualities led to distrust of strangers and of change in the years following the war. Durwood Dunn finds the cove's society increasingly a closed society, with only 45 surnames in a population of 449 in 1880, as opposed to

86 out of 671 before the war. Few new families moved into the area, where only people who were already kin were likely to be accepted (140).

Altina Waller observed similar dynamics at work in the Tug Valley. The largely pro-Confederate valley people, on both the West Virginia and Kentucky side, had sought to preserve their autonomy from the outside world. When the war was lost, they became more hostile to outsiders and to new ideas. Although their new state constitutions prohibited former Rebel soldiers and officials from voting, many valley residents defied the law and continued to vote and to hold local offices. Community animosity developed between the pro-Rebel Tug Valley, where most people voted Democratic, and pro-Union Pikeville, which became a largely Republican enclave. Pikeville generally favored economic development and growth, while Tug Valley people remained firmly opposed to change. A type of "siege mentality" developed in the valley, which became increasingly isolated from their states and from the nation as a whole (*Feud*, 33, 195).

Ralph Mann observed that the guerrilla war also brought changes to the Sandy Basin area of southwestern Virginia. As in Cades Cove, old community leaders either had died or moved away. Union guerrilla leader Alf Killen had been killed in Kentucky, and other prominent Union men who had fled the area chose not to return. Rebel guerrilla chief Jack Frye disappeared. After the war, Ike Blair confronted Rebel leader Ezekiel Counts and was killed, and Counts moved to Minnesota. The only wartime leader to remain in the basin was Dave Smith, and more moderate leaders canceled out his voice in local politics. Bitterness divided the community for years, and many Unionists who had been forced to leave never returned. After the war many new families settled in the basin, following the same migration patterns as before the war. Many from the basin also moved west. In 1866, former residents of the basin settled New Virginia Township in frontier Minnesota, and amazingly the new colony included both ex-Union people and ex-Confederates (387).

Former Unionists tended to become Republicans and former Confederates Democrats, a political phenomenon that would continue to be standard in many areas of the mountain South well into the second half of the twentieth century. Shelton Laurel was so staunchly Republican that when two Democratic votes surfaced in an election in 1910, local folk regarded it as a remarkable fluke (Paludan, 126).

While most communities devastated by the war recovered slowly and prospered again after decades of hard work, some of them never bounced back from the effects of the guerrilla struggle. Of the North Georgia towns burned by Sherman's raiders, Canton rebuilt from the ground up. The Atlanta *Constitution* remarked twenty years later, "Its backwoods atmosphere is now gone, and Canton is a town of new and modern appearance. Most of its buildings are of brick" (Marlin, 80). Cassville never really recovered. Most of the people burned out of their homes chose not to return to build a new life there (Mahan, 116). Kingston rebuilt, enjoyed a brief period of revival with the railroad, and even survived a great fire in 1911. By 1915, Kingston was a bustling town with several hotels, banks, and forty businesses. But when passenger traffic on the rail line dried up, Kingston declined, residents moved away, and the community became a virtual ghost town (Weizenecker, 11).

The guerrilla war had shattered what economic growth the mountain communities had made in the 1850s, leaving only destitution, despair, and violence. Historians Ronald Eller, Kenneth Noe, Durwood Dunn, and Paul Salstrom argue that Appalachia's poverty and backwardness were byproducts of the postwar industrial era when the region came to be exploited by outside corporate interests. Industrial exploitation transformed Appalachian society from the agrarian Jeffersonian dream to one beset by poverty, dependency, and powerlessness (Noe, " 'Appalachia's,' " 91–92, 103; Eller, xv-xviii, xxi–xxv, 3–6, 227–232; Salstrom, xiii, 8–9).

The mountain war, in which guerrilla destructiveness played such a large role, devastated agriculture and manufacturing in the Southern Appalachians, and the mountaineers never fully recovered (C. Williams, 25). Dunn (140–141) and Noe (*Southwest*, 4–5, 140–142; " 'Appalachia's,' " 102–105) stress the extent of damage done to the economies of East Tennessee and southwestern Virginia, while Stephen Hahn notes similar conditions in up-country Georgia's agriculture. Livestock and crops were destroyed, and to add to the problem a series of droughts wreaked enormous damage in the postwar years. Former Georgia governor Joseph E. Brown reported the corn crop in North Georgia "almost an utter failure" in September 1866, and in 1867 a resident of Cherokee County cited "Hundreds of Widows and orphans on the verge of starvation." By 1870, North Georgia's farm production in corn, cotton, grain, and livestock had dropped 35 to 45 percent (Hahn, 139–141).

Robert Tracy McKenzie and Paul Salstrom contend that mountain economies had already begun to decline before the Civil War, which simply accelerated the process. McKenzie notes the severe material destruction in East Tennessee during four years of occupation by both armies, the loss of livestock in the region, and the cruel irony that Unionists won the war but suffered economic ruin in the process (200, 203, 206–207, 217). Salstrom observes a steadily declining production in Appalachian farms between 1860 and 1880. Appalachian self-sufficiency perished, and as outside industrialists began coal mining and lumber operations, the mountaineers—finding it harder and harder to make a decent living farming—provided cheap labor that could be exploited (Salstrom, xiii, xviii, 9, 42, 53, 122–124). Stephen

Hahn showed similar circumstances plaguing North Georgia farmers, increasingly captive to hard times created by falling cotton prices, farm tenancy, and the fluctuations of an international economy. "Once the domain of yeoman freeholders," Hahn writes, "the Upcountry was fast becoming a territory of the dispossessed" (4, 151–152, 165–168).

The guerrilla war caused economic disruption and left a heritage of distrust of outsiders and a fostering of extralegal vigilantism. It left the mountain people impoverished and even more isolated from the rest of the nation. Hatreds engendered by the war lingered for decades. But perhaps what is ultimately more important is what the guerrilla war failed to destroy: the mountain people's love of family, their independent spirit, their reverence for tradition, and a charitable nature that could still allow them—even in the lean postwar years—to offer hospitality to travelers, even when it meant that they themselves must do without. The mountain folk emerged a distinct and unique people, embodying the best in the American character.

Appendix

Survivors

LAWRENCE M. ALLEN, Colonel, 64th North Carolina Infantry, C.S.A., never faced charges in the Shelton Laurel Massacre. With his wife and a daughter born after the massacre, he moved to Arkansas and spent the next twenty years farming. As his health deteriorated, he sought a more beneficial climate, moving to Colorado in 1884, then to Arizona. In 1885, Allen fought a duel in Sonora, Mexico, and killed a man who had compared Southern women to common streetwalkers. In 1892, he returned to Marshall and spent his declining years writing a defense of his conduct during the war. He never addressed his part in the Shelton Laurel Massacre (Paludan, 120).

DAVID "TINKER DAVE" BEATTY, Tennessee Unionist partisan, lived out his life in Fentress County, where he was an active community leader during Reconstruction. Popular with his Unionist neighbors and remembered for his affable hospitality, Beatty died in 1883 (Hogue, 37–38).

KEITH AND MALINDA BLALOCK, North Carolina Unionist partisans, resumed a semi-normal life after the war in present-day Avery County. Keith shot and killed John Boyd, who had betrayed Keith's stepfather, in 1866 but received a pardon from pro-Union Governor W. W. Holden. Malinda died in 1903. Keith perished in an accident in 1913, when his railroad handcar left the track at a steep turn and plummeted into a ravine (Trotter, 155).

WILLIS SCOTT BLEDSOE, Major, 4th Tennessee Cavalry, C.S.A., served with his regiment in North Carolina in 1865. Since Unionists had the upper hand in Fentress County after the war, Bledsoe moved to Texas, where he lived out his days in affluence and respectability (Hogue, 18, 35).

JAMES GEORGE BROWN, Colonel, 1st Georgia State Troops Volunteers, U.S.A., settled in Gilmer County with his wife and two children. Details of his final years are unknown, as he apparently drifted into obscurity. He died in Gilmer County of unknown causes sometime before April 1867 (Davis, "Brown," 28).

WILLIAM B. CARTER, Tennessee Unionist partisan, died in 1901. He never revealed the names of his bridge burners of 1861 (Ball, 56).

THOMAS M. CLARK, Alabama Unionist partisan, dropped out of sight at the end of the war, and his gang scattered. He is believed to have hidden out in Jackson County, but in September 1872 he returned to Lauderdale County with two colleagues for one last robbery spree. The three outlaws were caught and placed in the jail at Florence, where a vengeful mob stormed the building, dragged Clark and his accomplices out, and hanged them. The memory of Clark provoked such outrage that local women denied him burial in the town cemetery. The sadistic outlaw who once bragged that "no one ever ran over him" was buried where everyone could run over him—in the middle of the road in front of the main gate to the cemetery (Pruitt, 90–92).

ROBERT T. CONLEY, Lieutenant, Thomas' North Carolina Legion, C.S.A., was in business after the war with other former legion members. He moved to Talladega, Alabama, around 1870, and he died in 1892 (Crow, 143).

WILLIAM R. CRISSON, Captain, Georgia Confederate Home Guards, Lumpkin County, took up gold mining after the war and wrote a modest book on the subject in 1875. Although Federal military authorities sought punishment for Crisson—and other members of the execution squad that killed Union soldiers Stuart, Stansbury, and Witt—the 1866 grand jury in Lumpkin County refused to indict him. Crisson died in 1907 (Kinsland, "Murder," 30).

NANCY HART DOUGLAS, West Virginia Confederate partisan, welcomed her husband, Joshua, home from the war, and the couple farmed together on Spring Creek in Greenbrier County until Nancy's death in 1902 (Stutler, 47).

DANIEL ELLIS, Tennessee Unionist partisan, wrote a popular autobiographical account of his activities, trumpeting his own exploits and heaping blame on the secessionists for the violence of guerrilla warfare in the mountains (Trotter, 202–203).

JAMES J. FINDLEY, Colonel, Georgia Confederate Home Guards, Lumpkin County, lived a prosperous life in Dahlonega after the war, enjoying profits from his gold mine, Findley's Chute. He also was a deputy U.S. marshal. He died in 1888 (Kinsland, "Band," 15, 16).

EDWARD M. GALT, Colonel, 1st Regiment Georgia State Line, C.S.A., developed a serious lung ailment after being wounded in the fighting around Atlanta. His health failed to improve, and he died in January 1866, in Acworth, Georgia (Bragg, 126).

JOHN P. GATEWOOD, Georgia Confederate partisan, refused to surrender in May 1865. His gang disbanded, and the "red-headed beast" made his way to Texas. In March 1871 he died in a gunfight in Waco (Barclay, 101).

FRANK B. GURLEY, Captain, 4th Alabama Cavalry, C.S.A., resumed the life of a farmer and kept a low profile politically in Madison County after his release from prison in April 1866. He never married. After a two-year illness, he died at the home of his sister in 1920 (O. Cunningham, 102–103).

BEN HARRIS, Alabama Unionist partisan, died of pneumonia at Huntsville in March 1865 (Johnston, 76).

WILLIAM ANDERSON "DEVIL ANSE" HATFIELD, West Virginia Confederate partisan, entered the realm of popular legend. He received so much national attention from the famous Hatfield-McCoy feud that when he died in 1921, a throng of 400–500 people attended his funeral (Waller, *Feud*, 238).

HENRY HETH, Major General, C.S.A., attempted a number of business ventures—coal mining, life insurance, railroads—after the war. Success seemed to elude him until he was appointed a special agent for the Bureau of Indian Affairs, where he demonstrated unusual compassion for the Indians. He retired in 1889, wrote his memoirs, and died in 1899 (Paludan, 119–120).

ALBERT HOWELL, Lieutenant Colonel, 1st Regiment Georgia State Line, C.S.A., went into the grocery business in Atlanta and became a close associate of newspaperman Henry W. Grady. After a long and productive life in business and in city politics, Howell died at the age of 84 in 1927 (Bragg, 126–127).

JOHN M. HUGHS, Brigadier General, C.S.A., was reassigned to Lee's army in Virginia, where he led his old brigade in a heroic defense of Fort Harrison in September 1864. He asked leave to return to Tennessee to conduct independent guerrilla operations, but Lee turned down his request. Hughs resigned in March 1865. Next to nothing is known of his life after this (Siburt,

92–95). According to one source, he was a U.S. marshal in Tennessee during the 1880s (Sensing, 166).

MILUS E. "BUSHWHACKER" JOHNSTON, Lieutenant Colonel, 25th Alabama Cavalry Battalion, C.S.A., returned to preaching after the war. Reportedly, he welcomed former Unionists to his church as well as Confederates. Partial deafness forced him to leave the pulpit after thirty years of ministry, and he turned to writing his memoirs. He died at the age of 92 in 1915 (Johnston, Introduction).

BENJAMIN F. JORDAN, Georgia Confederate partisan, was indicted for robbery and murder in Pickens County but was never tried. He was reported killed in Florida following the war (Davis, "Memoirs," 99 n. 22).

JAMES A. KEITH, Lieutenant Colonel, 64th North Carolina Infantry Regiment, C.S.A., took his family to Arkansas and never returned to North Carolina. He sold his property in Madison County through an attorney in 1871 (Paludan, 120).

GEORGE W. KIRK, Colonel, 3rd North Carolina Mounted Infantry, U.S.A., became an ally of North Carolina Republican Governor W. W. Holden, who called the old raider back to duty in 1870, as Ku Klux Klan violence—nighttime raids on homes of white Unionists and black freedmen, torture, and murders—brought back bitter memories of the war years in the Carolina mountains. Once again Kirk rode, at the head of 600 Unionist mountaineers, sweeping through Caswell and Alamance Counties to restore Republican control. Kirk occupied the Alamance courthouse, sacked the town, and arrested some 100 people. Kirk's ruthlessness and the negative impact of the "Kirk-Holden War" led to Holden's impeachment. Kirk relocated to California and died there in 1905 (Crow, 257 n. 66).

JOHN LONG, Georgia Unionist partisan, murdered a man on Lookout Mountain in Alabama. Tried and convicted, he received a life sentence in an Alabama prison. Pardoned after serving thirty years, he died soon afterward (Sartain, 124).

JAMES R. LOVE, JR., Colonel, Thomas' North Carolina Legion, C.S.A., resumed an active life in business and politics in Jackson County, served in the state legislature, and married Julia Reagan of Sweetwater, Tennessee, in an 1869 wedding ceremony performed by William Stringfield's brother James. The Loves, Stringfields, and Thomases remained closely associated. Love died in 1885 (Crow, 142).

BENJAMIN F. MCCOLLUM, Georgia Confederate partisan, practiced law in Canton, where he wrote his own version of his activities during the war. Indicted in 1865 and 1866 for robbery and murder, along with other former members of his gang, McCollum never was brought to trial (Tate, 213–214). He relocated to Hampton, Georgia, where he was an attorney. McCollum was killed in a shoot-out with a local policeman and died from wounds inflicted by a double-barreled shotgun at close range (Marlin, 77).

RANDOLPH (OLD RANEL) MCCOY, West Virginia Confederate partisan, failed to receive the notoriety that his rival Devil Anse Hatfield attained. He settled in Pikeville, Kentucky, where he operated a ferry. In 1908, his clothes caught fire while he was cooking, and he died at the age of 88 (Waller, *Feud*, 238–239).

JAMES G. MARTIN, Brigadier General, C.S.A., was plagued by poor health and financial troubles. He was an attorney in Asheville, North Carolina, where he died in 1878 (Crow, 144).

PETER PARRIS, 5th Tennessee Mounted Infantry, U.S.A., resumed his life in Morganton, Georgia, where his family acquired some land. His brother Alfred was in a shoot-out with Federal soldiers in 1866 in a dispute stemming from his involvement with the wife of an officer. Parris tried to secure federal pensions for himself and for the families of the Madden Branch Massacre victims. He got into trouble with the law when it was discovered that he had forged muster rolls to show that the victims were already enlisted members of the 5th Tennessee Mounted at the time of the massacre. The victims' families never received compensation (Sarris, "Anatomy," 709–710).

JOHN T. PRIOR, Georgia Confederate Home Guards, Polk County, was never charged with any wrongdoing for the deaths of the Colquitt desperados. He settled into a peaceful and unremarkable life. In 1905 he and his daughter moved to Oregon to live with his son, quitting the family property at Prior Station. John Prior died a tranquil death at his daughter's home in 1910 at the age of 70 (Sargent, 380).

ALEXANDER W. REYNOLDS, Brigadier General, C.S.A., left the United States in 1869 and became an officer in the Egyptian army. He died in Alexandria in 1876 (Warner, *Generals in Gray*, 255).

PHILIP D. RODDEY, Brigadier General, C.S.A., became a businessman in New York. He died while on a trip to London in 1897 (Warner, *Generals in Gray*, 262).

HENRY F. SMITH, Captain, 4th Alabama Cavalry, C.S.A., was active in local politics and served as a state representative from Jackson County, 1865–1866 (Kennamer, 202).

GEORGE E. SPENCER, Colonel, 1st Alabama Cavalry Regiment, U.S.A., returned to his law practice in Decatur, where he played a conspicuous role in carpetbag politics in Alabama. Elected as a Republican to the U.S. Senate, he was accused of misconduct—vote buying, bribery, and mishandling of state funds—in 1875 by a largely Democratic Alabama legislature that called for his removal. Spencer retained his Senate seat until 1879, was named a commissioner for the Union Pacific Railroad in 1881, and spent his later years as a rancher and miner in Nevada. He died in Washington, D.C., in 1893 (Hoole, 138–141).

GEORGE STONEMAN, Major General, U.S.A., left the army in 1871 and retired to Los Robles, his ranch near Los Angeles, California. He played an active role in state politics and served as governor, 1883–1887. He died in 1894 (Warner, *Generals in Blue*, 482).

WILLIAM STRINGFIELD, Lieutenant Colonel, Thomas' North Carolina Legion, C.S.A., was released from the military jail in Knoxville, Tennessee, on May 24, 1865. He returned to Strawberry Plains to farm, but bad feelings with his Unionist neighbors compelled him to sell his home and move to Rogersville, Tennessee. He and Maria Love finally married in 1871. Later the couple moved to Waynesville, North Carolina, where they managed the White Sulphur Springs Hotel, on the site of the last skirmish of the war in which the legion had taken part. Active in Confederate veterans' organizations and in state politics, Stringfield served in the North Carolina legislature. He became strongly associated with the Cherokees, as Thomas had before him. Willie and Maria had seven children. After Maria's death in 1909, Stringfield grieved for her for the remainder of his life. He died in 1923, at the age of 85 (Crow, 142–143).

WILLIAM H. THOMAS, Colonel, Thomas' North Carolina Legion, C.S.A., was never the same after the war. He lost everything to his creditors, and he suffered a mental breakdown in 1867. Thomas' remaining years were sad ones, and he drifted in and out of institutions. After his wife, Sarah, died in 1877, his mental state worsened. Little Will died at the age of 88 in 1893 (Crow, 142). At the very end, he would sometimes lapse into the Cherokee tongue and recall with warmth the golden days of his youth spent with the people he had loved (Frome, 131).

WILLIAM ALBERT TWIGGS, Captain, 5th Tennessee Mounted Infantry, U.S.A., emigrated to Arkansas in 1869. He died at the hands of a mob during a bitter political dispute in 1892. His body was discovered riddled with buckshot and rifle balls, and both of his hands had been shot off (Barker Papers, Vol. 4).

WILLIAM T. WOFFORD, Brigadier General, C.S.A., was elected to Congress in 1865, but Radical Republicans refused to seat him. He made money in the railroad business and became an active voice for public education. Wofford died in Cassville in 1884 at age 61 (Warner, *Generals in Gray*, 344).

ROBERT P. WOODY, Lieutenant, 5th Tennessee Mounted Infantry, U.S.A., won an appointment as U.S. postmaster at Dial, formerly Van Zant's store, in Fannin County, Georgia. He died in 1901 (Davis, "Gunfight," 64).

Works Cited

Ash, Stephen V. "Poor Whites in the Occupied South." *Journal of Southern History* 57 (1991): 39–62.

Augusta *Daily Constitutionalist* (1865).

Aycock, Roger. *All Roads to Rome.* Roswell, GA: Wolfe Associates, 1981.

Baker, Robert S. *Chattooga County: The Story of a County and Its People.* Roswell, GA: Wolfe Associates, 1988.

Ball, Alan R. "Night of the Burning Bridges." *America's Civil War* (January 1997): 50–56.

Barclay, Robert E. *Ducktown Back in Raht's Time.* Cleveland, TN: White Wing Publishing House & Press, 1974.

Barker, Robert B., Papers. C. M. McClung Historical Collection, Knox County Public Library, Knoxville, TN.

Battey, George M., Jr. *A History of Rome and Floyd County.* Atlanta, GA: Cherokee Publishing Co., 1979.

Blackmun, Ora. *Western North Carolina: Its Mountains and Its People to 1880.* Boone, NC: Appalachian Consortium Press, 1977.

Blevins, Jerry. *Sequatchie Valley Soldiers in the Civil War.* Huntsville, AL: By author, 1990.

Bragg, William Harris. *Joe Brown's Army: The Georgia State Line, 1862–1865.* Macon, GA: Mercer University Press, 1987.

Brown, Joseph E., Papers. Felix Hargrett Collection, University of Georgia Library, Athens, GA.

Bryan, T. Conn. *Confederate Georgia.* Athens: University of Georgia Press, 1953.

Buffington, Herbert, and Olin Jackson. "The Life and Hard Times of Augustus L. 'Gus' Coggins." *North Georgia Journal* 8.2 (1991): 40–50.

Castel, Albert E. "The Guerrilla War, 1861–1865." *Civil War Times Illustrated* (October 1974): 1–50.

Civil War Centennial Commission. *Tennesseans in the Civil War: A Military History of Confederate and Union Units with Available Rosters of Personnel*. Part I. Nashville, TN: By author, 1964.

Cox, William E. "The Civil War Letters of Laban Gwinn: A Union Refugee." *West Virginia History* 43 (1982): 227–245.

Crawford, Michael. "The Dynamics of Mountain Unionism: Federal Volunteers of Ashe County, North Carolina." In Kenneth W. Noe and Shannon H. Wilson, eds., *The Civil War in Appalachia: Collected Essays*, 55–77. Knoxville: University of Tennessee Press, 1997.

Crow, Vernon H. *Storm in the Mountains: Thomas' Confederate Legion of Cherokee Indians and Mountaineers*. Cherokee, NC: Museum of the Cherokee Indian, 1982.

Cunningham, O. Edward. "Captain Frank B. Gurly, Fourth Alabama Cavalry, C.S.A.: Murderer or Victim?" *Alabama Review* 28 (1975): 83–103.

Cunningham, Rodger. *Apples on the Flood: The Southern Mountain Experience*. Knoxville: University of Tennessee Press, 1987.

Cunyus, Lucy J. *History of Bartow County, Formerly Cass*. Easley, SC: Southern Historical Press, 1976.

Current, Richard N. *Lincoln's Loyalists: Union Soldiers from the Confederacy*. Boston: Northeastern University Press, 1992.

Davis, Robert S., Jr. "Anthony 'Tone' Goble, and the Brown Murder of 1877." *North Georgia Journal* 8.2 (1991): 51–55.

———. "The Curious Civil War Career of James George Brown, Spy." *Prologue: Quarterly of the National Archives* 26 (1994): 17–31.

———. "Forgotten Union Guerrillas of the North Georgia Mountains." In Olin Jackson, ed., *A North Georgia Journal of History*, Vol. 1, 270–300. Alpharetta, GA: Legacy Communications, 1989.

———. "Gunfight at Doublehead Gap." *North Georgia Journal* 8.3 (1991): 61–64.

———. "Memoirs of a Partisan War: Sion Darnell Remembers North Georgia, 1861–1865." *Georgia Historical Quarterly* 80 (1996): 93–116.

———. "The Night Riders of Pickens County." In Olin Jackson, ed., *A North Georgia Journal of History*, Vol. 1, 336–340. Alpharetta, GA: Legacy Communications, 1989.

———. "The North Georgia Moonshine War of 1876–1877." In Olin Jackson, ed., *A North Georgia Journal of History*, Vol. 2, 214–222. Alpharetta, GA: Legacy Communications, 1991.

DeLozier, Mary Jean. *Putnam County, Tennessee, 1850–1970*. Nashville, TN: Putnam County Publishers, 1979.

Dodd, Donald B. "The Free State of Winston." *Alabama Heritage* 28 (1993): 10–19.

———. *Historical Atlas of Alabama*. University: University of Alabama Press, 1974.

Dodd, Donald B., and Wynelle S. Dodd. "Winston: An Antebellum and Civil War History of a Hill County of North Alabama." *Annals of Northwest Alabama*. Ed. Carl Elliott. Vol. 4. Birmingham, AL: Oxmoor Press, 1972.

Duke, Basil. *A History of Morgan's Cavalry*. Bloomington: Indiana University Press, 1960.

Duncan, Katherine McKinstry, and Larry Joe Smith. *History of Marshall County, Alabama, Vol. I: Prehistory to 1939*. Albertville, AL: Thompson Printing, 1969.

Dunn, Durwood. *Cades Cove: The Life and Death of a Southern Appalachian Community, 1818–1937*. Knoxville: University of Tennessee Press, 1988.

Eller, Ronald. *Miners, Millhands, and Mountaineers: Industrialization of the Appalachian South, 1880–1930*. Knoxville: University of Tennessee Press, 1982.

Ellis, Daniel. *Thrilling Adventures of Daniel Ellis*. Freeport, NY: Books for Libraries Press, 1971.

Fellman, Michael. *Inside War: The Guerrilla Conflict in Missouri During the American Civil War*. New York: Oxford University Press, 1989.

Finger, John R. "Cherokee Accommodation and Persistence in the Southern Appalachians." In Mary Beth Pudup, Dwight B. Billings, and Altina L. Waller, eds., *Appalachia in the Making: The Mountain South in the Nineteenth Century*, 25–49. Chapel Hill: University of North Carolina Press, 1995.

Fisher, Noel C. *War at Every Door: Partisan Politics and Guerrilla Violence in East Tennessee, 1860–1869*. Chapel Hill: University of North Carolina Press, 1997.

Fleming, Walter L. *Civil War and Reconstruction in Alabama*. Spartanburg, SC: Reprint Company Publishers, 1978.

Frome, Michael. *Strangers in High Places: The Story of the Great Smoky Mountains*. Garden City, NY: Doubleday, 1966.

Garrett, Jill Knight. *A History of Lauderdale County, Alabama*. Columbia, TN: By author, 1964.

Gorn, Elliot. "Gouge and Bite, Pull Hair and Scratch: The Social Significance of Fighting in the Southern Backcountry." *American Historical Review* 90 (1985): 18–43.

Gregory, Conway, Jr. "The Civil War History of the James Jathan Gregory Family." *Whitfield-Murray Historical Society Quarterly* 16.4 (1997): 11–20.

Grimsley, Mark. *The Hard Hand of War: Union Military Policy Toward Southern Civilians, 1861–1865*. New York: Cambridge University Press, 1995.

Groce, W. Todd. "The Social Origins of East Tennessee's Confederate Leadership." In Kenneth W. Noe and Shannon H. Wilson, eds., *The Civil War in Appalachia: Collected Essays*, 30–54. Knoxville: University of Tennessee Press, 1997.

Hahn, Steven. *The Roots of Southern Populism: Yeoman Farmers and the Transformation of the Georgia Upcountry, 1850–1890*. New York: Oxford University Press, 1983.

Hall, Herb. "The McConnell Family History—Settlers of Broomtown Valley." *Chattooga County Historical Society Quarterly* 5.2 (June 20, 1993): 13–14.

Hattaway, Herman, and Archer Jones. *How the North Won: A Military History of the Civil War*. Urbana: University of Illinois Press, 1982.

Hogue, Albert R. *History of Fentress County, Tennessee*. Baltimore, MD: Regional Publishing Co., 1975.

Hoole, William Stanley. *Alabama Tories: The First Alabama Cavalry, U.S.A., 1862–1865*. Tuscaloosa, AL: Confederate Publishing Co., 1960.

Horn, Stanley, ed. *Tennessee's War, 1861–1865. Described by Participants*. Nashville: Tennessee Civil War Centennial Commission, 1965.

Howe, Barbara J. "The Civil War at Bulltown." *West Virginia History* 44 (1982): 1–40.

Inscoe, John C. "Coping in Confederate Appalachia: Portrait of a Mountain Woman and Her Community at War." *North Carolina Historical Review* 69 (1992): 388–413.

———. *Mountain Masters, Slavery, and the Sectional Crisis in Western North Carolina.* Knoxville: University of Tennessee Press, 1989.

———. "Moving Through Deserter Country: Fugitive Accounts of the Inner Civil War in Southern Appalachia." In Kenneth W. Noe and Shannon H. Wilson, eds., *The Civil War in Appalachia: Collected Essays*, 158–186. Knoxville: University of Tennessee Press, 1997.

———. "Race and Racism in Nineteenth-Century Appalachia: Myths, Realities, and Ambiguities." In Mary Beth Pudup, Dwight B. Billings, and Altina L. Waller, eds., *Appalachia in the Making: The Mountain South in the Nineteenth Century*, 103–131. Chapel Hill: University of North Carolina Press, 1995.

Jackson, Olin, ed. *A North Georgia Journal of History.* 3 vols. Alpharetta, GA: Legacy Communications, 1989, 1991, 1995.

Johnston, Milus E. *The Sword of "Bushwhacker" Johnston.* Ed. Charles E. Rice. Huntsville, AL: Flint River Press, 1992.

Jones, Ethelene Dyer, ed. *Facets of Fannin: A History of Fannin County, Georgia.* Dallas, TX: Curtis Media Corp., 1989.

Kellogg, John Azor. *Escape and Capture: A Narrative of Army and Prison Life.* Madison: Wisconsin History Commission, 1908.

Kennamer, John Robert. *History of Jackson County.* Winchester, TN: Southern Printing & Publishing Co., 1935.

Kennett, Lee. *Marching Through Georgia: The Story of Soldiers and Civilians During Sherman's Campaign.* New York: HarperCollins, 1995.

Kinsland, William S. "A Band of Brothers: The Men and the Legend of the 52nd Georgia Regiment." *North Georgia Journal* 2.2 (1985): 9–18.

———. "The Civil War Comes to Lumpkin County." In Olin Jackson, ed., *A North Georgia Journal of History*, Vol. 1, 179–184. Alpharetta, GA: Legacy Communications, 1989.

———. "Murder or Execution? A Tale of Two Counties." *North Georgia Journal* 1.2 (1984): 13–30.

Lane, Mills, ed. *Times That Prove People's Principles: Civil War in Georgia, A Documentary History.* Savannah, GA: Beehive Press, 1993.

Lonn, Ella. *Desertion during the Civil War.* New York: American Historical Association, 1928.

McCollum, Benjamin F. "The Second Battle of Big Shanty." Comp. B. C. Yates. *Georgia Magazine* (February–March 1962): 31–33.

———, Papers. Kennesaw Mountain National Battlefield Park, Kennesaw, GA.

McKenzie, Robert Tracy. "Oh! Ours Is a Deplorable Condition: The Economic Impact of the Civil War in Upper East Tennessee." In Kenneth W. Noe and Shannon H. Wilson, eds., *The Civil War in Appalachia: Collected Essays*, 199–227. Knoxville: University of Tennessee Press, 1997.

McKinney, Gordon B. "Economy and Community in Western North Carolina, 1860–1865." In Mary Beth Pudup, Dwight B. Billings, and Altina L. Waller, eds., *Appalachia in the Making: The Mountain South in the Nineteenth Century*, 163–184, Chapel Hill: University of North Carolina Press, 1995.

————. *Southern Mountain Republicans, 1865–1900: Politics and the Appalachian Community*. Chapel Hill: University of North Carolina Press, 1978.

————. "Women's Role in Civil War Western North Carolina." *North Carolina Historical Review* 69 (1992): 37–56.

McMillan, Malcolm C. *The Alabama Confederate Reader*. Tuscaloosa: University of Alabama Press, 1963.

————. *The Disintegration of a Confederate State: Three Governors and Alabama's Wartime Home Front, 1861–1865*. Macon, GA: Mercer University Press, 1986.

Macon *Daily Telegraph* (1864).

Mahan, Joseph G., Jr. "A History of Old Cassville, 1833–1864." Master's thesis, University of Georgia, Athens, 1950.

Mann, Ralph. "Family Group, Family Migration, and the Civil War in the Sandy Basin of Virginia." *Appalachian Journal* 19 (1992): 374–393.

Marlin, Lloyd G. *History of Cherokee County*. Atlanta, GA: Brown Publishing Co., 1932.

Martin, Bessie. *Desertion of Alabama Troops from the Confederate Army: A Study in Sectionalism*. New York: Columbia University Press, 1932.

Mason, Robert L. *Cannon County*. Memphis, TN: Memphis State University Press, 1982.

Mitchell, Reid. *Civil War Soldiers*. New York: Simon & Schuster, 1988.

Moon, Anna Mary, ed. "Civil War Memoirs of Mrs. Adeline Deaderick." *Tennessee Historical Quarterly* 7 (1948): 52–71.

Moore, Albert B. *History of Alabama*. Tuscaloosa: University of Alabama Press, 1934.

Moore, George Ellis. *A Banner in the Hills: West Virginia's Statehood*. New York: Appleton-Century-Crofts, 1963.

Murray County History Committee. *Murray County Heritage*. Roswell, GA: Wolfe Associates, 1987.

Nashville *Tennessean*, August 7, 1932.

Nicholson, James L. *Grundy County*. Memphis, TN: Memphis State University Press, 1982.

Noe, Kenneth W. " 'Appalachia's' Civil War Genesis: Southwest Virginia as Depicted by Northern and European Writers, 1825–1865." *West Virginia History* 50 (1991): 91–108.

————. "Exterminating Savages: The Union Army and Mountain Guerrillas in Southern West Virginia, 1861–1862." In Kenneth W. Noe and Shannon H. Wilson, eds., *The Civil War in Appalachia: Collected Essays*, 104–130. Knoxville: University of Tennessee Press, 1997.

————. *Southwest Virginia's Railroad: Modernization and the Sectional Crisis*. Urbana: University of Illinois Press, 1994.

Noe, Kenneth W., and Shannon H. Wilson, eds. *The Civil War in Appalachia: Collected Essays*. Knoxville: University of Tennessee Press, 1997.

O'Kelley, Harold Ernest. *Dahlonega's Blue Ridge Rangers in the Civil War*. Gainesville, GA: Georgia Printing Co., 1992.

Otten, James T. "Disloyalty in the Upper Districts of South Carolina During the Civil War." *South Carolina Historical Magazine* 75 (1974): 95–110.

Owen, Thomas M. *History of Alabama and Dictionary of Alabama Biography*. Chicago: Clarke Publishing Co., 1921.

Paludan, Phillip S. *Victims: A True Story of the Civil War*. Knoxville: University of Tennessee Press, 1981.

Parks, Joseph H. *Joseph E. Brown of Georgia*. Baton Rouge: Louisiana State University Press, 1977.

Phifer, Edward William, Jr. *Burke: The History of a North Carolina County, 1777–1920*. Morganton, NC: By author, 1977.

Phillips, John. "The Diary of a Union Soldier from Alabama." *Alabama Heritage* 28 (1993): 22–25.

Pruitt, Wade. *Bugger Saga: The Civil War Story of Guerrilla and Bushwhacker Warfare in Lauderdale County, Alabama*. Columbia, TN: P-Vine Press, 1977.

Pudup, Mary Beth, Dwight B. Billings, and Altina L. Waller, eds. *Appalachia in the Making: The Mountain South in the Nineteenth Century*. Chapel Hill: University of North Carolina Press, 1995.

Roland, Charles P. *The Confederacy*. Chicago: University of Chicago Press, 1972.

Royster, Charles. *The Destructive War: William Tecumseh Sherman, Stonewall Jackson, and the Americans*. New York: Alfred A. Knopf, 1991.

Salstrom, Paul. *Appalachia's Path to Dependency: Rethinking a Region's Economic History, 1730–1940*. Lexington: University Press of Kentucky, 1994.

Sanderson, Esther Sharp. "Guerrilla Warfare During the Civil War." *Tennessee Valley Historical Review* 1 (1972): 25–33.

Sargent, Gordon D. "The Asa Prior Family." In Olin Jackson, ed., *A North Georgia Journal of History*, Vol. 3, 372–381. Alpharetta, GA: Legacy Communications, 1995.

Sarris, Jonathan D. "Anatomy of an Atrocity: The Madden Branch Massacre and Guerrilla Warfare in North Georgia, 1861–1865." *Georgia Historical Quarterly* 77 (1993): 679–710.

———. "An Execution in Lumpkin County: Localized Loyalties in North Georgia's Civil War." In Kenneth W. Noe and Shannon H. Wilson, eds., *The Civil War in Appalachia: Collected Essays*, 131–157. Knoxville: University of Tennessee Press, 1997.

Sartain, James Alfred. *History of Walker County, Georgia*. Carrolton, GA: A. M. Mathews and J. S. Sartain, 1972.

Sensing, Thurman. *Champ Ferguson: Confederate Guerrilla*. Nashville, TN: Vanderbilt University Press, 1942.

Shaffer, John W. "Loyalties in Conflict: Union and Confederate Sentiment in Barbour County." *West Virginia History* 50 (1991): 109–125.

Siburt, James T. "Colonel John M. Hughs: Brigade Commander and Confederate Guerrilla." *Tennessee Historical Quarterly* 51 (1992): 87–95.

Sondley, F. A. *A History of Buncombe County, North Carolina*. Spartanburg, SC: Reprint Company Publishers, 1977.

Southern Banner, Athens, GA (1863).

Southern Watchman, Athens, GA (1864).

Stanley, Lawrence L. *A Rough Road in a Good Land*. N. p.: n. p., 1971.

Stuckert, Robert P. "Black Populations of the Southern Appalachian Mountains." *Phylon* 48 (1987): 141–151.

Stutler, Boyd Blyn. *West Virginia in the Civil War*. Charleston, WV: Education Foundation, 1963.

Tate, Luke E. *History of Pickens County, Georgia*. Spartanburg, SC: Reprint Company Publishers, 1978.

Thompson, Wesley S. *The Free State of Winston: A History of Winston County, Alabama*. Winfield, AL: Pareil Press, 1968.

Trotter, William R. *Bushwhackers: The Civil War in North Carolina. The Mountains*. Winston-Salem, NC: John F. Blair, 1988.

Turner, William H., and Edward J. Cabell, eds. *Blacks in Appalachia*. Lexington: University Press of Kentucky, 1985.

U.S. War Department (USWD). *War of the Rebellion: A Compilation of the Official Records of the Union and Confederate Armies*. 130 vols. Washington, DC: Government Printing Office, 1880–1901.

Van Noppen, Ina W. "The Significance of Stoneman's Last Raid." *North Carolina Historical Review* 38 (1961): 19–44, 500–526.

Van Noppen, Ina W., and John L. Van Noppen. *Western North Carolina Since the Civil War*. Boone, NC: Appalachian Consortium Press, 1973.

Walker, Gary C. *The War in Southwest Virginia, 1861–1865*. Roanoke, VA: A & W Enterprises, 1985.

Wallenstein, Peter. " 'Helping to Save the Union': The Social Origins, Wartime Experiences, and Military Impact of White Union Troops from East Tennessee." In Kenneth W. Noe and Shannon H. Wilson, eds., *The Civil War in Appalachia: Collected Essays*, 1–29. Knoxville: University of Tennessee Press, 1997.

Waller, Altina L. *Feud: Hatfields, McCoys, and Social Change in Appalachia, 1860–1900*. Chapel Hill: University of North Carolina Press, 1988.

———. "Feuding in Appalachia: Evolution of a Cultural Stereotype." In Mary Beth Pudup, Dwight B. Billings, and Altina L. Waller, eds., *Appalachia in the Making: The Mountain South in the Nineteenth Century*, 347–376. Chapel Hill: University of North Carolina Press, 1995.

Ward, George Gordon. *The Annals of Upper Georgia, Centered in Gilmer County*. Nashville, TN: Parthenon Press, 1965.

Warner, Ezra J. *Generals in Blue: Lives of the Union Commanders*. Baton Rouge: Louisiana State University Press, 1964.

———. *Generals in Gray: Lives of the Confederate Commanders*. Baton Rouge: Louisiana State University Press, 1959.

Washington, Booker T. "Boyhood Days." In William H. Turner and Edward J. Cabell, eds., *Blacks in Appalachia*, 43–50. Lexington: University Press of Kentucky, 1985.

Weizenecker, Lorayne B. "Kingston, Georgia: The Early Years." In Olin Jackson, ed., *A North Georgia Journal of History*, Vol. 3, 7–11. Alpharetta, GA: Legacy Communications, 1995.

Wert, Jeffry D. *Mosby's Rangers*. New York: Touchstone Books, 1990.

Williams, Cratis D. "The Southern Mountaineer in Fact and Fiction." *Appalachian Journal* 3 (1975): 8–61.

Williams, John Alexander. "Class, Section, and Culture in Nineteenth-Century West Virginia Politics." In Mary Beth Pudup, Dwight B. Billings, and Altina L. Waller, eds., *Appalachia in the Making: The Mountain South in the Nineteenth Century*, 210–232. Chapel Hill: University of North Carolina Press, 1995.

———. *West Virginia: A History*. New York: Norton, 1984.

Index

About the Author

SEAN MICHAEL O'BRIEN is a freelance writer with experience in the U.S. military and in education. A former college instructor, he calls the Southern Appalachians home. He is the author of numerous articles on the Civil War and Southern military history.